WIDER THAN HEAVEN

Eighth-century Homilies on the Mother of God

T0324443

ST VLADIMIR'S SEMINARY PRESS
Popular Patristics Series
Number 35

The Popular Patristics Series published by St Vladimir's Seminary Press provides readable and accurate translations of a wide range of early Christian literature to a wide audience—students of Christian history to lay Christians reading for spiritual benefit. Recognized scholars in their fields provide short but comprehensive and clear introductions to the material. The texts include classics of Christian literature, thematic volumes, collections of homilies, letters on spiritual counsel, and poetical works from a variety of geographical contexts and historical backgrounds. The mission of the series is to mine the riches of the early Church and to make these treasures available to all.

Series Editor
BOGDAN BUCUR

Associate Editor
IGNATIUS GREEN

* * *

Series Editor
1999–2020
JOHN BEHR

Wider Than Heaven

EIGHTH-CENTURY HOMILIES ON THE MOTHER OF GOD

Translation and Introduction by

MARY B. CUNNINGHAM

ST VLADIMIR'S SEMINARY PRESS
CRESTWOOD, NEW YORK
2008

Library of Congress Cataloging-in-Publication Data

Wider than heaven : eighth-century homilies on the Mother of God / translation
and introduction by Mary B. Cunningham.
    p. cm. — (Popular patristics series ; no. 35)
    Includes bibliographical references.
    ISBN 978–0–88141–326–7 (alk. paper)
    1. Incarnation—Sermons—Early works to 1800. 2. Mary, Blessed Virgin,
Saint—Sermons—Early works to 1800. I. Cunningham, Mary.

BT220.W86 2008
232.91—dc22

2008040089

COPYRIGHT © 2008
ST VLADIMIR'S SEMINARY PRESS
575 Scarsdale Road, Crestwood, NY 10707
1-800-204-2665
www.svspress.com

ISBN 978–088141–326–7
ISSN 1555–5755

All Rights Reserved

PRINTED IN THE UNITED STATES OF AMERICA

To Richard

Contents

Abbreviations

AASS	*Acta sanctorum quotquot toto orbe coluntur.* Antwerp, 1643–
AnBoll	Analecta Bollandiana
BHG	*Bibliotheca hagiographica Graece.* Edited by F. Halkin, S.J. 3 vols. 3d ed. Brussels, 1957
Brenton	*The Septuagint with Apocrypha: Greek and English.* Sir Lancelot C.L. Brenton
ByzZ	*Byzantinische Zeitschrift*
CCSG	Corpus Christianorum: Series graeca. Turnhout, 1977–
CCSL	Corpus Christianorum: Series latina. Turnhout, 1953–
CPG	*Clavis patrum graecorum.* Edited by M. Geerard. 5 vols. Turnhout, 1974–1987
DOP	*Dumbarton Oaks Papers*
EO	*Échos d'Orient*
KJV	King James Version
L&S	*A Greek-English Lexicon.* H.G. Liddell and R. Scott
Lampe	*A Patristic Greek Lexicon.* G.W.H. Lampe, D.D.
LCL	Loeb Classical Library
LXX	Septuagint
NPNF[1]	*Nicene and Post-Nicene Fathers*, Series 1
NPNF[2]	*Nicene and Post-Nicene Fathers*, Series 2
NRSV	New Revised Standard Version
OCP	*Orientalia christiana periodica*
ODB	*The Oxford Dictionary of Byzantium.* Edited by A. Kazhdan. 3 vols. New York, 1991

OSB	*The Orthodox Study Bible: New Testament and Psalms, New King James Version.* Edited by P.E. Gillquist et al. Nashville, 2001
PG	Patrologia graeca [= Patrologiae cursus completus: Series graeca]. Edited by J.-P. Migne. 162 vols. Paris, 1857–1886.
PO	Patrologia orientalis
Rahlfs	*Septuaginta. Id est Vetus Testamentum graece iuxta LXX interpretes.* Edited by A. Rahlfs. 2 vols.
REByz	*Revue des études byzantines*
SC	Sources chrétiennes. Paris, 1943–
Sophocles	*A Greek Lexicon of the Roman and Byzantine Periods (from BC 146 to AD 1100).* E.A. Sophocles
SVTQ	*St Vladimir's Theological Quarterly*
SynCon	*Synaxarium ecclesiae Constantinopolitanae: Propylaeum ad Acta sanctorum Novembris.* Edited by H. Delehaye. Brussels, 1902
TLG	*Thesaurus linguae graecae: Canon of Greek Authors and Works.* Edited by L. Berkowitz and K.A. Squitier. 3d ed. Oxford, 1990
Trapp	*Lexikon zur byzantinischen Gräzität: besonders des 9–12. Jahrhunderts.* E. Trapp

Foreword

This book would never have been completed without a generous grant from the Academic Higher Research Council of Great Britain, which provided me with the support and resources necessary for pursuing my study of eighth-century homilies on the Mother of God between 2003 and 2006. Professor Leslie Brubaker, of the University of Birmingham, was instrumental in obtaining this grant and I am immensely grateful for her energetic and inspired participation in this project.

I also owe a huge debt of gratitude to Dr Bob Jordan, of Queen's University in Belfast, for his help in checking the translations. He went through each text with meticulous care, identifying many errors and helping me to reach a fluent and understandable translation. Fr Andrew Louth also checked John of Damascus's homily on the Nativity of the Mother of God and offered useful corrections and comments.

I am grateful to Paul Géhin and his team of researchers at the Institut de Recherche et d'Histoire des Textes, of the Centre National de la Recherche Scientifique in Paris, who helped me in my search for manuscripts containing Germanos of Constantinople's homily on the Annunciation and allowed me to consult microfilms of manuscripts there. The Bibliothèque Byzantine of the Collège de France was also most hospitable during my two-month stay in Paris while working on this project.

Finally, I would like to thank Fr John Behr and the St Vladimir's Seminary Press Editorial Board for including this publication in their valuable and affordable Popular Patristics Series. As Associate Editor of the series, Sr Nonna Verna Harrison checked the whole draft of the book meticulously before submitting it for publication. I am very grateful to her for helping to bring this volume to fruition and for suggesting the inclusion of a glossary of rhetorical terms. While acknowledging all who have helped me in the course of this project, I accept full responsibility for any errors or inadequacies that may remain.

I would like to dedicate this book to my husband, Richard Corran, for his unfailing support and enthusiasm for my work.

Introduction

"Be glad in her, heaven! For she imitated you, who could not contain the Lord in yourself, when she contained him without constriction!"[1]

Andrew of Crete, a Byzantine preacher and archbishop who lived in the late seventh and early eighth century, expounds here the theological doctrine which lies behind both the title of this book and the exuberant praise for the Mother of God contained in the homilies translated in this volume. Mary, the blessed Virgin and Theotokos, truly mortal, was chosen by God to conceive and give birth to his only Son, Jesus Christ, at the time and place which prophets had foretold throughout the Old Testament. This exalted role justifies the praise that the Theotokos receives, not only from humankind, but also from angels and every created thing. Andrew goes on in the same homily to exclaim, "Celebrate her in dance, earth! For her pregnancy raised your condition heavenwards and made those who dwell on earth heavenly! Let even the sea applaud the miracle of the Virgin! For Christ experienced childbirth through her with his body and, having been baptized in the waters, sanctified their moist substance. So then, let all creation rejoice and clap its hands!"[2]

As Orthodox bishops eventually decided at the third ecumenical council held in Ephesus, AD 431, the Virgin Mary contained God himself in her womb. She should therefore be called "Theotokos" ("God-bearer" or "Birth-giver of God") and be praised for her essen-

---

[1]Andrew of Crete, *In Nativitatem* IV.7, PG 97, 881A; below, 138.
[2]Andrew of Crete, *In Nativitatem* IV.7, PG 97, 881A–B. See below, 138.

tial role in the mystery of the Incarnation.[3] Mary provided the physical material, or "nature," that enabled Christ to become fully human; at the same time, her virginal innocence and purity, recorded in the Gospel of Luke, but more fully in the apocryphal *Protevangelion of James*,[4] proclaimed his divinity. As Proclus of Constantinople expressed in his first homily on the Theotokos, Mary was "the workshop" (ἐργαστήριον) where the union of natures took place.[5] This theological formulation explains why, from this period onward, the Virgin Mary came to occupy such an exalted role in relation to the celestial hierarchy. It is also likely that in addition to the church's recognition of her importance in christological doctrine, popular veneration of the Theotokos began to take off from the middle of the fifth century and especially in the course of the sixth.[6] Relics,

[3]General introductions to the controversy leading up to the Council of Ephesus and the decisions reached there abound. See, for example, J. McGuckin, *St Cyril of Alexandria and the Christological Controversy* (Leiden: Brill, 1994; repr. Crestwood, NY: SVS Press, 2004); R.M. Price, "Marian Piety and the Nestorian Controversy," in *The Church and Mary* (ed. R.N. Swanson; Studies in Church History 39; Woodbridge, Suffolk and Rochester, NY: Boydell & Brewer, 2004), 31–8; N.P. Constas, "Weaving the Body of God: Proclus of Constantinople, the Theotokos and the Loom of the Flesh," *Journal of Early Christian Studies* 3 (1995): 169–94. Works which posit political influence, and especially that of the empress Pulcheria, on the proceedings at Ephesus include K. Holum, *Theodosian Empresses: Women and Imperial Dominion in Late Antiquity* (Berkeley and London: University of California Press, 1982); V. Limberis, *Divine Heiress: The Virgin Mary and the Creation of Christian Constantinople* (London: Routledge, 1994); K. Cooper, "Contesting the Nativity: Wives, Virgins, and Pulcheria's *Imitatio Mariae*," *Scottish Journal of Religious Studies* 19 (1998): 31–43; J.A. McGuckin, "The Paradox of the Virgin-Theotokos: Evangelism and Imperial Politics in the Fifth-Century Byzantine World," *Maria* 3 (Autumn 2001): 5–23.

[4]J.K. Elliott, ed., *The Apocryphal New Testament. A Collection of Apocryphal Christian Literature in an English Translation based on M.R. James* (Oxford: Clarendon Press, 1993; rev. ed. 2004), 57–67.

[5]See N. Constas, *Proclus of Constantinople and the Cult of the Virgin in Late Antiquity. Homilies 1–5, Texts and Translation* (Leiden: Brill, 2003), 136.14.

[6]This is not to say that veneration of the Mother of God, as holy figure and intercessor, did not exist before this period. The earliest known Greek prayer, called the "Sub tuum praesidium," preserved in John Rylands Papyrus 470 and dated by scholars to between the third and late fourth centuries, has been restored to read as follows: "Under your mercy we take refuge, Theotokos. Do not overlook our petitions in adversity but rescue us from danger, uniquely holy one and uniquely blessed one."

such as her robe and belt, were discovered in Palestine and brought to Constantinople, churches began to be founded in her honor, and feasts commemorating events in her life were added to the liturgical calendar.[7] This process culminated in the Virgin's special place as protector and patroness of the imperial city, Constantinople. The Akathistos Hymn is the most famous witness to this phenomenon,[8] but various other sixth- and seventh-century sources also attest to the importance of the Theotokos as a symbol of strength and mercy for Constantinopolitan Christians in this period.[9]

The twelve sermons translated in this volume were all produced in the eighth century, not only in Constantinople, but also in Jerusalem, Crete, and possibly another outlying province in mainland Greece or Syria. They are the work of five preachers, John of Damascus, Germanos of Constantinople, Andrew of Crete, John of Euboea,

This text, along with the writings of the Cappadocian fathers and other fourth-century writers suggests that devotion to the Theotokos was already increasing in the course of the fourth century. For the text, see O. Stegmüller, "*Sub tuum praesidium*: Bemerkungen zur ältesten Überlieferung," *Zeitschrift für katholische Theologie* 74 (1952): 76–82; cf. G. Giamberardini, "Il 'Sub tuum praesidium' e il titolo 'Theotokos' nella traditzione egiziana," *Marianum* 31 (1969): 324–62; R. Price, "Theotokos: The Title and Its Significance in Doctrine and Devotion," in *Mary. The Complete Resource* (ed. S.J. Boss; New York and London: Continuum, 2007), 56; S. Shoemaker, "Marian Liturgies and Devotion in Early Christianity," ibid., 130–1.

[7]A good survey of this process now exists in C. Mango, "Constantinople as Theotokoupolis," in *Mother of God. Representations of the Virgin in Byzantine Art* (ed. M. Vassilaki; Milan and Athens: Skira, 2000), 17–25. Mango argues that churches dedicated to the Theotokos in Constantinople only began to be built in the second half of the fifth century, rather than soon after the Council of Ephesus as has previously been thought.

[8]For the most recent study and translation of this important hymn, see L.M. Peltomaa, *The Image of the Virgin Mary in the Akathistos Hymn* (Leiden: Brill, 2001), who argues that it should be dated to the early fifth century, between the councils of Ephesus (431) and Chalcedon (451). Not all scholars agree with this early dating, however; see N. Constas's review of Peltomaa in *SVTQ* 49, no. 3 (2005): 355–58.

[9]For example, Romanos the Melode refers to the Virgin as "wall" and "support" of the city in his kontakion on her Nativity, 35.10. See P. Maas and C.A. Trypanis, *Sancti Romani Melodi Cantica: Cantica Genuina* (Oxford: Clarendon Press, 1963; repr. 1997), 280.1. See also Corippus's poem, *In laudem Justini*, discussed in A. Cameron, "The Theotokos in Sixth-Century Constantinople: A City Finds its Symbol," *Journal of Theological Studies* 29 (1978): 79–108.

and Kosmas Vestitor, four of whom were clergymen whereas the last was one of a small number of lay Byzantine preachers whose texts survive in liturgical manuscripts. The homilies commemorate feast-days which had been added to the fixed calendar of the Constantinopolitan Church in the course of the sixth century or, in some cases, two centuries later. It is likely that many of these homilies were preached in the course of all-night vigils for the feasts; some, such as Andrew of Crete's first three sermons on the Nativity of the Mother of God, were delivered as a trilogy, that is, in three parts in the course of the vigil, interspersed perhaps with psalms or hymns.[10] Eighth-century sermons on the feast of the Dormition, recently translated and published by Brian Daley in the same series as this volume,[11] display the same structure: Andrew of Crete, John of Damascus, and Germanos all produced homiletic trilogies for this important feast.[12] In translating the remaining Marian festal sermons dating from this period, I aim to make these texts available to readers who may not be able to read them in the original Greek.

As Daley points out in his Introduction, these sermons are written in a "high" literary style.[13] From late antiquity onwards, flowery speeches, delivered *ex tempore* but in an atticizing style, represented a popular form of public entertainment. The tropes and devices of epideictic oratory embellished speeches on both secular and religious topics; the ability to deliver such an oration represented a badge of honor for men in high positions.[14] As the Roman empire slowly became christianized in the course of the

[10]C. Chevalier, "Les trilogies homilétiques dans l'élaboration des fêtes mariales, 650–850," *Gregorianum* 18 (1937): 361–78.

[11]B.E. Daley, S.J., trans., *On the Dormition of Mary. Early Patristic Homilies* (Crestwood, NY: SVS Press, 1998).

[12]*CPG* 8010–12; 8061–63; 8181–83. Most of these homilies are translated in Daley, *On the Dormition of Mary*, 103–239.

[13]Daley, *On the Dormition of Mary*, 1.

[14]For a good introduction to late antique and early Christian rhetoric, see G. Kennedy, *Classical Rhetoric and its Christian and Secular Tradition from Ancient to Modern Times* (London: Croom Helm, 1980); S.E. Porter, ed., *Handbook of Classical Rhetoric in the Hellenistic Period, 330 BC–AD 400* (Leiden: Brill, 1997).

fourth and early fifth centuries, bishops and spiritual leaders such as the Cappadocian fathers successfully adapted the art of rhetoric to a Christian context.[15] The genre of the festal sermon, which we see in its first full flowering in the writings of Gregory Nazianzen, was particularly well suited to such treatment.[16] The point of these sermons is firstly to offer fitting praise to the subject being celebrated and secondly, but no less importantly, to inspire and instruct the congregation. The first of these functions, however, explains the close relationship between many festal sermons and hymnography. Gregory frequently employed short rhythmic phrases in his festal homilies, in which allusive language, metaphor, and other rhetorical devices such as homoioteleuton (rhyming ends of phrases) and anaphora (the use of one word at the beginning of successive lines) abound. We can only imagine the delight with which sermons such as these must have been received, especially by those in church who were sufficiently educated to recognise their literary and theological profundity.

Fifth- and sixth-century preachers continued to build on this tradition; sermons honoring the Virgin Mary especially tended to employ the rhythmic, "Asianic" style and to develop an ever-expanding tradition of typology and imagery associated with this holy fig-

[15]See G. Kennedy, *Greek Rhetoric under Christian Emperors* (Princeton: Princeton University Press, 1983); I. Ševčenko, "A Shadow Outline of Virtue: The Classical Heritage of Greek Christian Literature (Second to Seventh Century)," in *Age of Spirituality: A Symposium* (ed. K. Weitzmann; New York and Princeton: Princeton University Press and The Metropolitan Museum of Art, 1980), 53–73.

[16]For the festal sermons of Gregory Nazianzen, see the editions in PG 35–36 (*CPG* 3010); J. Bernardi, ed., *Grégoire de Nazianze: Discours 1–3* (SC 247; Paris: Éditions du Cerf, 1978); M.-A. Calvet-Sebasti, ed., *Grégoire de Nazianze: Discours 6–12* (SC 405; Paris: Éditions du Cerf, 1995). General studies include J. McGuckin, *Saint Gregory of Nazianzus. An Intellectual Biography* (Crestwood, NY: SVS Press, 2001); R.R. Ruether, *Gregory of Nazianzus: Rhetor and Philosopher* (Oxford: Clarendon Press, 1969). Good new translations of some festal sermons may be found in B.E. Daley, S.J., *Gregory of Nazianzus* (London and New York: Routledge, 2006); M. Vinson, *St Gregory of Nazianzus. Select Orations*, The Fathers of the Church (Washington, DC: The Catholic University of America Press, 2003); and N.V. Harrison, *Gregory of Nazianzus: Festal Orations* (Crestwood, NY: SVS Press, 2008).

ure. Although the corpus of texts continued to grow in the seventh
century, with such important sermons as those by Theoteknos of
Livias and John of Thessalonike on the Dormition,[17] not to mention
the homiletic works of Sophronios of Jerusalem,[18] there is evidence
that the art of preaching was not so widely understood in this period.
Kanon 19 of the Quinisext Council "in Trullo" (AD 692) enjoins the
clergy to teach every day and especially on Sundays, but rather omi-
nously forbids those who "through lack of skill may have departed
from what is fitting" to preach at all. Rather than "depart from the
tradition of the God-bearing Fathers," they should read out the
works of these earlier luminaries in order to educate the faithful.[19]
It is possible that the military and political setbacks of the seventh
century did lead to a decline in educational standards among clergy
in this period.[20] At the beginning of the eighth century, however, we
see a revival of festal preaching, much of which focuses on Marian
feasts that had not yet received homiletic treatment. The surviving
sermons, many of which are translated in this volume, display the
rhetorical skill of their authors, along with their knowledge of Scripture and of the Marian homiletic tradition. Modern readers may
find this style unfamiliar and in some respects obscure, but there is
also much material here that continues to inspire. It is also striking
how varied these sermons are and how individual preachers, while
remaining faithful to tradition, may also interpret their themes with
creativity and insight. Their methods of exegesis and praise range

[17]*CPG* 7418 and 7924. Both homilies are translated in Daley, *On the Dormition
of Mary*, 47–81.

[18]Sophronios wrote homilies on the Annunciation (*CPG* 7638) and Hypapante
(*CPG* 7641). See P. Allen, "The Greek Homiletical Tradition of the Feast of the Hypapante: The Place of Sophronius of Jerusalem," in *Mediterranea Byzantina. Festschrift
für Johannes Koder zum 65, Geburtstag* (ed. K. Bleke, H. Kislinger, A. Külzer, and M.A.
Stassinopoulou; Vienna, Cologne and Wimar: Böhlau, 2007), 1–12.

[19]See J.D. Mansi, ed., *Sacrorum Conciliorum Nova et Amplissima Collectio* 11
(Florence and Venice: A. Zatta Veneti, 1759, ff; repr. Graz: Akademische Druck, 1961),
952. Translated in *NPNF*², 14:374–75.

[20]For a good historical introduction to the "dark age" of the seventh century,
see J.F. Haldon, *Byzantium in the Seventh Century. The Transformation of a Culture*
(Cambridge: Cambridge University Press, 1990).

from acclamation, based on the "chairetismos" of the archangel Gabriel (Luke 1.28), to historical exploration of Mary's Davidic ancestry, to imaginative dialogue between Gabriel and the Theotokos, as in Germanos's homily on the Annunciation. These sermons fulfilled many functions, which included not only the expression of fitting praise towards the Mother of God, but also the inspired, and at times entertaining, instruction of the faithful.

The Development of the Marian Feast-days

Fundamental to the development of preaching on the Mother of God was the introduction of special feast-days in her honor into the liturgical calendar. This process is unfortunately difficult to reconstruct, owing to the lack of liturgical and historical sources for the period before the ninth century. Historians have mostly used homilies and hymns as evidence, although they have also been able to glean some information from other literary sources. Whereas some feasts, such as the Nativity of the Theotokos and the Presentation or Meeting of Christ with Symeon (Ὑπαπαντή), which also commemorates Mary's purification, had their origins in the Jerusalem rite, others may have originated in Constantinople. It is clear nevertheless that practices in Jerusalem influenced liturgical developments in Constantinople throughout this period, with such elements as stational liturgies and holy relics receiving an enthusiastic reception in the capital city.[21]

Sometime during the early decades of the fifth century, the first and at that time only feast, sometimes called "In Memory of the Holy Mary," in honor of the Mother of God began to be celebrated throughout the Byzantine empire. Proclus of Constantinople's first homily on the Theotokos may in fact be the earliest witness to the observance of this feast in Constantinople.[22] Scholars do not agree

---

[21]See M. van Esbroeck, "Le culte de la Vierge de Jérusalem à Constantinople aux 6e–7e siècles," *REByz* 46 (1988): 181–90 = idem, *Aux origines de la Dormition de la Vierge* (Aldershot: Ashgate Publishing, 1995), x.

on the precise day when this Marian feast was celebrated: it is possible that it fell on one of the Sundays in the weeks leading up to Christmas or, as in the Orthodox Church today, on the day after Christmas.[23] It is also likely that liturgical practices varied in different parts of the empire, with Egypt and Palestine observing a different day from that celebrated in Constantinople and Syria.[24] This feast inspired a number of early homilies and hymns in honor of the Mother of God, including many which focused on the theme of the Annunciation.[25] It is clear, however, that most of these liturgical texts, apart from those associated with the Jerusalem rite, were delivered in the context of Christ's Nativity and celebrated his Incarnation from the moment of his conception.

[22]Constas, *Proclus of Constantinople*, 57.

[23]Much has been written on this subject, and views still differ about the exact date of this celebration. See, for example, M. Jugie, "La première fête mariale en Orient et en Occident: l'Avent primitif," *EO* 22 (1922): 153–81 = idem, *Homélies mariales byzantines* II (PO 19, fasc. 3, no. 93; Paris: R. Graffin, 1925; Turnhout: Éditions Brepols, 1990), 297–309. Jugie argues for a Sunday before Christmas, as part of a full advent cycle in which St John the Baptist, the Theotokos, and events connected with her conception of Christ were all celebrated, whereas Constas believes that Proclus's first homily was preached on the day after Christmas. See Constas, *Proclus of Constantinople*, 58.

[24]M. Aubineau argues convincingly that the feast, "Of the divine maternity of Mary," was originally celebrated in Jerusalem on August 15. At the beginning of the fifth century, this date had no association with the Dormition of the Virgin, and the feast was celebrated at the site of Mary's short rest ("kathisma"), three miles from Bethlehem, before giving birth to Christ. See M. Aubineau, *Les homélies festales d'Hésychius de Jérusalem* (2 vols.; Brussels: Société des Bollandistes, 1978), 1:132–41; E. de Strycker, *La Forme la plus ancienne du Protévangile de Jacques* (Subsidia hagiographica 33; Brussels: Société des Bollandistes, 1961), 142–45; A. Renoux, *Le codex arménien Jérusalem* 121 (PO 36; Turnhout: Brepols, 1971), 2:191, 355; B. Botte, "Le lectionnaire arménien et la fête de la Théotokos à Jérusalem au 5e siècle," *Sacris Erudiri* 2 (1949): 111–22; B. Capelle, "La fête de la Vierge à Jérusalem au Ve siècle," *Le Muséon* 56 (1943): 1–33.

[25]These are ascribed to such authors as Gregory Thaumatourgus (*CPG* 1775–76), Athanasius of Alexandria (*CPG* 2268), John Chrysostom (*CPG* 4519), and Basil of Seleucia (*CPG* 6656 [39]). It is likely that many of these texts are spurious, however, and should be assigned to the fifth or even sixth centuries. For a preliminary study, see P. Allen, "Portrayals of Mary in Greek Homiletic Literature (6th–7th centuries)," in *The Cult of the Mother of God in Byzantium: Texts and Images* (ed. L. Brubaker and M. Cunningham; Aldershot: Ashgate), forthcoming.

Two more feasts, the Nativity of the Virgin (8 September)[26] and the Annunciation (25 March), may have been added to the Constantinopolitan calendar during the reign of Justinian I (AD 527–65). The evidence for the introduction of the feast of the Annunciation is more decisive than that for Mary's Nativity. Romanos the Melode composed kontakia for both feasts,[27] but that of the Annunciation is also mentioned in a homily by Abramios of Ephesus, dated to before 553, which affirms that it had been introduced recently into the calendar.[28] Even more importantly, a letter purportedly written by Justinian in 561 defends 25 March as the historical date of the Annunciation, also affirming that the feasts of Christ's Nativity (25 December) and Presentation in the temple (2 February) depend on its date.[29] The first official recognition of the feast of the Annunciation appears in Kanon 52 of the Quinisext Council (in Trullo,

[26]It appears that the feast of the Nativity of the Virgin originated in Jerusalem as a dedicatory feast associated with the church built near the Probatic Pool (John 5.2–9) by the mid-fifth century. This was believed to represent the place of Mary's birth and it is mentioned in some of our homilies. See H. Vincent and F.-M. Abel, *Jérusalem: recherches de topographie, d'archéologie et d'histoire* 2 (Paris: J. Gabalda, 1926), 669–76. Whereas some scholars accept that the feast was adopted in Constantinople during the sixth century, others are more cautious, positing instead a late sixth- or seventh-century date. See on the one hand, *ODB* 1, 291; T. Antonopoulou, *The Homilies of the Emperor Leo VI* (Leiden: Brill, 1997), 163; but on the other, J. Lafontaine-Dosogne, "Iconography of the Cycle of the Life of the Virgin," in *The Kariye Djami. Studies in the Art of the Kariye Djami and Its Intellectual Background* 4 (ed. P. Underwood; London, 1975), 164.

[27]Maas and Trypanis, *Sancti Romani Melodi Cantica*, 276–93. Romanos also wrote a kontakion on the Mother of God which may have been intended for 26 December. See E. Lash, trans., *Kontakia on the Life of Christ. St Romanos the Melodist* (San Francisco, London, and Pymble: HarperCollins, 1995), 16.

[28]*CPG* 7380; M. Jugie, ed., *Homélies mariales byzantines* (PO 16 , fasc. 3, no. 79; Paris: R. Graffin; repr., Turnhout: Brepols, 2003), 443.2. See also R. Fletcher, "Three Early Byzantine Hymns and Their Place in the Church of Constantinople," *ByzZ* 51 (1958): 58.

[29]M. van Esbroeck, "La lettre de l'empereur Justinien sur l'annonciation et la noël en 561," AnBoll 86 (1968): 355–62; 87 (1969): 442–44. According to R. Taft and A. Weyl Carr, the date of the Annunciation, which was first introduced in Antioch and slightly later into the rest of the Christian world, "was chosen not in order to coordinate with Christmas, but because the identification of John the Baptist's conception with the autumn equinox put Jesus' conception at the spring equinox six months later and his Nativity (25 December) at the winter solstice." See *ODB* 1, 106.

691–92), in which it is decreed that the Liturgy of the Presanctified Gifts should not be celebrated on this day.[30]

The feast of Christ's Presentation or Meeting with Symeon (Hypapante), already mentioned above, also became associated with praise of the Theotokos in the course of the sixth century. In fact it has been called one of the five great mariological feasts of the Eastern tradition due to the fact that it also celebrates Mary's purity and central role in the Incarnation of Christ.[31] The feast originated in Jerusalem and the pilgrim Egeria participated in the celebrations between AD 381 and 384.[32] At that time the feast fell on 14 February, forty days after the Nativity of Christ which was celebrated on 6 January. According the ninth-century chronicler Theophanes, Justinian introduced the feast into the Constantinopolitan rite in 542, to be celebrated on 2 February, following the long accepted date of 25 December for Christmas.[33] A number of homilies, written both before and after the wider acceptance of the feast, celebrate both christological and Marian themes in the story.[34] This tendency culminated in such sermons as that written by Leo VI ("the Wise") in the late ninth or early tenth century, which contains a hymn to the Theotokos,[35] and in the Marian emphasis in the hymnography devoted to this feast, some of which was written by eighth-century preachers such as Andrew of Crete and Germanos of Constantinople.[36] Unfortunately, no sermons on the subject of the Hypapante

[30]Mansi, *Sacrorum Conciliorum* 11, 968; T.T. Talley, *The Origins of the Liturgical Year* (Collegeville, MN: Liturgical Press, 1986), 153.

[31]See *ODB* 2, 961–62.

[32]J. Wilkinson, *Egeria's Travels* (Warminster: Aris & Phillips, Ltd, 1999), 147–48.

[33]C. de Boor, ed., *Theophanis Chronographia* (2 vols.; Leipzig: B.G. Teubner, 1883; repr. Hildesheim: Georg Olms, 1963), 1:222; C. Mango and R. Scott, trans., *The Chronicle of Theophanes Confessor. Byzantine and Near Eastern History, AD 284–813* (Oxford: Clarendon Press, 1997), 322.

[34]See the useful survey of the homiletic tradition in Allen, "The Greek Homiletic Tradition of the Feast of the Hypapante."

[35]PG 107, 28–41; Antonopoulou, *The Homilies of the Emperor Leo VI*, 179. For further discussion of the Marian element in homilies on the Hypapante, see ibid., 182–83.

[36]Mother Mary and Arch. K. Ware, trans., *The Festal Menaion* (London: Faber & Faber, 1969; repr. S. Canaan, PA: St Tikhon's Seminary Press, 1998), 406–34.

survive from the eighth century, so this feast is not covered in the texts translated below.

It is likely that the Dormition was the next major Marian feast to be added to the liturgical calendar. According to the later historian Nikephoros Xanthopoulos, the emperor Maurice (582–602) was responsible for this innovation.[37] Narratives concerning Mary's death and assumption into heaven had been circulating in Eastern Christendom from the end of the fourth or beginning of the fifth century.[38] About a century later, after the foundation of a basilica honoring the tomb of the Mother of God at Gethsemane, the celebration of 15 August, which originally commemorated the divine maternity of the Theotokos and was observed at the site of the Kathisma church between Bethlehem and Jerusalem, was moved to Gethsemane and associated with her Dormition.[39] It is thus likely that when the emperor Maurice introduced the feast into the Constantinopolitan church calendar, he was influenced by current practices in the patriarchate of Jerusalem. Liturgical texts in honor of this feast began to be composed in the course of the late sixth and seventh centuries,[40] continuing apace in the eighth with sermons,

[37] Xanthopoulos wrote his *Ecclesiastical History* after 1317. See PG 147, 292.

[38] Much has been written on the apocryphal narratives describing the death and assumption of the Virgin Mary, which took various forms and were quickly translated into a number of languages. See, for example, M. Jugie, *La mort et l'assomption de la sainte Vierge* (Studi e Testi 114; Vatican City: Bibliootheca Apostolica Vaticana, 1944); S.C. Mimouni, *Dormition et assomption de Marie: Histoire des traditions anciennes* (Théologie historique 98; Paris: Beauchesne, 1995); S. Shoemaker, *Ancient Traditions of the Virgin Mary's Dormition and Assumption* (Oxford: Oxford University Press, 2002); A. Wenger, AA, *L'Assomption de la T.S. Vierge dans la tradition byzantine du Vie au Xe siècle* (Archives de l'Orient Chrétien 5; Paris: Institut Français d'Études Byzantines, 1955).

[39] See M. Aubineau, *Les homélies festales d'Hésychius de Jérusalem* 2 (Brussels: Société des Bollandistes, 1978), 132–41.

[40] Homilies included those by John of Thessalonike (*CPG* 7924), Jugie, *Homélies mariales byzantines*, PO 19, 375–405; Theoteknos of Livias (*CPG* 7418), Wenger, *L'Assomption de la T.S. Vierge*, 272–91; and (ps)-Modestos of Jerusalem (*CPG* 7876), ed. PG 86, 3277–312. The last of these homilies is spurious and was probably written after the third Council of Constantinople (AD 680–681). All three are translated in Daley, *On the Dormition of Mary*, 47–102. For arguments concerning the later date of the homily attributed to Modestos, see ibid., 15.

or even trilogies of sermons, by many eighth-century preachers, including Andrew of Crete,[41] Germanos of Constantinople,[42] John of Damascus,[43] and Kosmas Vestitor.[44] It is interesting, however, that even in this period, celebration of the feast does not appear to have been universal. John of Euboea appends it to his list of ten great ecclesiastical feasts (interestingly, the feasts of the Entry, or Presentation, of the Virgin into the temple and of Palm Sunday are also omitted from this list), remarking that this important celebration was added to the calendar later than the others.[45]

The origins of the feast of the Entry of the Mother of God into the temple (21 November) are even more obscure and it is possible that the feast was introduced into the Constantinopolitan calendar as late as the early eighth century.[46] Although it has been argued that the emperor Justinian founded the Nea Church in Jerusalem on 21 November, 543 in honor of an existing commemoration of the Virgin's Entry,[47] there is no conclusive proof that the date was connected with this event at this time. It is just as possible that the date of the feast was later chosen to coincide with the foundation date of this important hagiopolitan church.[48] The first liturgical texts in

[41]*CPG* 8181–3; PG 97, 1045–1109.

[42]*CPG* 8010–2; PG 98, 340–72.

[43]*CPG* 8061–3; B. Kotter, ed., *Die Schriften des Johannes von Damaskos* 5 (Berlin and New York: Walter de Gruyter, 1988), 483–555; P. Voulet, *S. Jean Damascène, Homélies sur la nativité et la dormition* (SC 80; Paris: Éditions du Cerf, 1961), 80–196.

[44]*CPG* 8155–8; Wenger, *L'Assomption de la T.S. Vierge*, 315–33 (in Latin). Many of the eighth-century homilies are translated into English in Daley, *On the Dormition of Mary*.

[45]John of Euboea, *In Concept.* 10, PG 96, 1473, 1497D–1500A.

[46]For general orientation on this feast, see *ODB* 3, 1715; S. Vailhé, "La fête de la presentation de Marie au temple," *EO* 5 (1901–1902): 221–4; M.J. Kishpaugh, *The Feast of the Presentation of the Virgin Mary in the Temple: An Historical and Literary Study* (Washington, DC: The Catholic University of America Press, 1941).

[47]See, for example, M. Barker, "Justinian's 'New Church' and the Entry of the Mother of God into the Temple," *Sourozh* 103 (February 2006): 15–33.

[48]Significantly, there is no mention of the feast of the Entry of the Theotokos into the temple in Jerusalem lectionaries before the eighth century. These include Renoux, *Le codex arménien*, the Georgian redactions dating from the fifth–eighth centuries, M. Tarchnischvili, ed., *CSCO* 188–89, and the sixth-century Syriac lectionary of the Old Testament and Epistle lections, A.S. Lewis, ed., *A Palestinian Syriac Lectionary:*

honor of the Entry of the Virgin are in fact the two homilies attributed to Germanos I of Constantinople and translated in the present
volume. As we shall see later, there exists some doubt concerning
the authenticity even of these, especially the first oration, which
displays a rhetorical eloquence and fondness for neologisms that
seems excessive for our early eighth-century homilist, although he
did enjoy inventing some new words, as we see in other, probably
authentic, homilies. Various other unedited homilies attributed to
Andrew of Crete or Germanos, listed in *CPG* and *BHG*, and cited by
scholars as evidence for at least eighth-century origins of the feast,
have proved to be spurious.[49] Thus, even in our period, the liturgical evidence for the feast remains scanty. By the end of the eighth
and especially by the middle of the ninth centuries, preachers and
hymnographers began to produce texts honoring the feast in great
abundance. These included such distinguished writers as the patriarchs Tarasios[50] and Euthymios,[51] George of Nicomedia,[52] Joseph

Containing Lessons From the Pentateuch, Job, Proverbs, Prophets, Acts, and Epistles
(London: C.J. Clay and Sons, 1897). On the Nea Church, see also N. Avigad, "The Nea:
Justinian's church of St Mary, Mother of God, discovered in the Old City of Jerusalem,"
in *Ancient Churches Revealed* (ed. Y. Tsafrir; Jerusalem and Washington: Israel Exploration Society, 1993), 128–35; Shoemaker, *Ancient Traditions*, 133–7, 140.

[49]These include a homily attributed to Andrew of Crete (*CPG* 8201), which I have
identified as a section of George of Nicomedia's fourth homily on the Entry, PG 100,
1420–40 and another attributed to Andrew that is in fact a section of his fourth homily
on the Nativity (*CPG* 8173) with a new incipit added. Several other homilies that were
identified in Athonite manuscript catalogues as unedited, but remained unlisted in
CPG or *BHG*, have also proved to be spurious. My findings will be discussed in more
detail in a forthcoming publication. See also H. Chirat, "Les origins de la fête du 21
novembre: St Jean Chrysostome et St André de Crète: ont-ils célébré la Présentation
de la Théotokos?," in *Psomia Diaphora. Mélanges E. Podechard: Études de sciences
religieuses offertes pour son émériat au doyen honoraire de la Faculté de Théologie de
Lyon* (Lyons: Facultés Catholiques, 1945), 121–33.

[50]Patriarch of Constantinople (784–806). *In praesentationem*, BHG 1149; PG 98,
1481–1500.

[51]Hegoumenos of the Monastery of Psamathia in Constantinople; patriarch (907–
912). *In praesentationem*, BHG 1112q; unedited. See A. Ehrhard, *Überlieferung und Bestand der hagiographischen und homiletischen Literatur der griechischen Kirche* 3 (Leipzig:
J.C. Hinrichs Verlag, 1936–39), 580.

[52]George wrote the first trilogy of sermons in honor of the feast of the Entry:
BHG 1152, 1108, 1078; PG 100, 1401–56.

the Hymnographer,[53] and the emperor Leo VI.[54] Such a burst of liturgical composition reinforces the hypothesis that the feast was introduced into the churches of Constantinople in the early eighth century, but only gained wider recognition as a major Marian festival in the course of the ninth.[55]

As for the feast of the Conception of St Anna (which means in fact her conception of the Virgin Mary), celebrated on 9 December in the Byzantine Church, the earliest evidence is again located in an eighth-century homily. John of Euboea, writing in the middle of the eighth century,[56] produced the first surviving homily on the subject of the Conception.[57] John refers in this oration to ten main liturgical feasts, both Dominical and Marian, of which the Conception of St Anna is one.[58] It is possible that this list, although affirmed so forcefully by this preacher, is an eccentric one; it is also possible that it reflects the liturgical rite of a provincial, rather than Constantinopolitan, parish. In any case, this homiletic witness for the existence of the feast in this period is important, as is a kanon attributed to Andrew of Crete[59] and, somewhat later, another by Kosmas Vestitor.[60]

The days that celebrate the translation of the two most important relics of the Mother of God, her robe and belt, on 2 July and 31

[53]Joseph wrote kanons on Mary's Nativity, Entry, and belt, among other hymnographic works in her honor. See PG 105, 984–1000, 1009–17.

[54]Leo VI wrote four sermons on the Virgin Mary, as follows: *In nativitatem*, *In praesentationem*, *In annuntiationem*, and *In dormitionem*. These are published in PG 107, 1–28, 157–72; Hieromonk Akakios, Λέοντος τοῦ σοφοῦ πανυγηρικοὶ λόγοι (Athens, 1868), 110–117, 139–45, 91–101. T. Antonopoulou is currently preparing a new, critical edition of Leo's homilies.

[55]Theodora Antonopoulou in fact suggests that the feast may have been reintroduced under the patrarich Tarasios after the first phase of Iconoclasm. See Antonopoulou, *The Homilies of the Emperor Leo VI*, 165, n. 24; V. Grumel, "Le jeûne de l'Assomption dans l'Église grecque. Étude historique," *EO* 32 (1933): 163–94, esp. 188, ff.

[56]See below, 46.

[57]*CPG* 8135; PG 96, 1460–1500.

[58]PG 96, 1473.

[59]PG 97, 1305–15.

[60]PG 106, 1013–17.

August respectively, do not represent major feasts in the Orthodox calendar, but were honored from the early eighth century onward with homilies and hymns. According Byzantine tradition, the robe of the Virgin was brought to Constantinople during the reign of Leo I (457–474) and his wife Verina and placed in a church, that of the Blachernai, which they later dedicated to the blessed Theotokos.[61] Evidence concerning the origins of the Virgin's belt (ζωνή) is meager, with narratives about its discovery dating from no earlier than the ninth century.[62] Germanos of Constantinople's sermon on the belt and on Christ's swaddling clothes, translated below, in fact is the earliest witness to their presence in the Constantinopolitan church of the Chalkoprateia.[63]

Finally, it is necessary to discuss briefly the feast of the holy progenitors, SS Joachim and Anna, on 9 September. Kosmas Vestitor's homily on this subject is the earliest witness to the feast, which must have developed in association with that of the Nativity of the Mother of God. This commemoration shares many characteristics with the feast of the Conception of St Anna on 9 December.[64] Its object is to celebrate the blessed qualities of Mary's parents, as well as to emphasize the miraculous nature of her birth. As in the cases of the Conception, Nativity, and Entry of the Mother of God into the temple, the feast of SS Joachim and Anna is based on the narrative contained in the second-century *Protevangelion* of James. The

[61]Two main versions of the story are edited in Wenger, *L'Assomption de la T.S. Vierge*, 294–311. Further bibliography includes N. Baynes, "The Finding of the Virgin's Robe," in *Byzantine Studies and Other Essays* (ed. idem; London: Athlone Press, 1955), 240–7; A. Cameron, "The Virgin's Robe: An Episode in the History of Early Seventh-Century Constantinople," *Byzantion* 49 (1979): 42–56; A. Weyl Carr, "Threads of Authority: the Virgin Mary's Veil in the Middle Ages," in *Robes and Honor. The Medieval World of Investiture* (ed. S. Gordon; New York and Basingstoke: Palgrave, 2001), 59–94.

[62]These include Euthymios, *In venerationem pretiosae zonae*, ed. Jugie, *Homélies mariales byzantines*, PO 16, 511; the *Menologion* of Basil II, PG 117, 613; *SynCon, AASS, Novembris Propylaeum*, 935–9.

[63]*CPG* 8013; PG 98, 372–84; below, 247–55.

[64]On feasts, forefeasts, and "commemorations," see Mother Mary and Arch. Kallistos, *The Festal Menaion*, 42–6.

emphasis in homilies and hymns composed in its honor, however, is theological: the righteousness of Mary's parents and God's miraculous intervention in overturning their sterility prepared the way for the greatest mystery of all, the Virgin's conception of a divine and human Son.

Structure and Style

One of the interesting aspects of the twelve Marian homilies collected in the present volume is their varied nature. Usually called "logoi" or "encomia" in the manuscripts that transmit them, these festal homilies differ markedly from each other in structure, style, and content. Some of these variations reflect different levels of education on the part of the preachers; more often they seem to depend on circumstances or intent. It is clear that the genre of the panegyrical sermon allowed considerable scope for imaginative development of the feasts or theological themes being celebrated.

As far as structure is concerned, the homilies all possess a prologue, argument, and epilogue.[65] Within this general framework, however, huge variation in the choice of subject matter, style, and method of teaching exists, even in sermons dealing with the same feast. The formal structure of the encomium, according to the rules established by Menander and others,[66] is scarcely visible here. Instead we find extensive hymnic passages characterised by such devices as anaphora and apostrophe, sections of narrative or dialogue, and others of theological discourse. Unlike the encomia of saints or important figures such as emperors, the panegyrical sermons on the Mother of God tend to focus on her significance in christological terms. By the early eighth century, she is also addressed as an intercessor and holy figure in her own right, who is

[65]These are the structural terms used by M. Heath in his chapter "Invention" in S.E. Porter, ed., *Handbook of Classical Rhetoric in the Hellenistic Period, 330 BC–AD 400* (Leiden: Brill, 1997), 89–119. See also the Glossary below, 257–60.

[66]See examples in N. Wilson and D.A. Russell, eds., *Menander Rhetor* (Oxford: Clarendon Press, 1981).

physically accessible to Constantinopolitans through relics such as her robe or belt.

The prologue of a festal homily serves to set the scene and to invoke a devotional state of mind in the worshippers celebrating the feast. Frequently the preacher calls attention to himself in this section of the oration, referring to himself as the "initiator" or "host" of the celebrations.[67] In keeping with the rules of the Second Sophistic, he may also express his humility, however, concluding that in spite of his unworthiness, it is still incumbent on him, as preacher, to offer praise. The sublimity of the subject matter is traditionally contrasted with the poverty of human speech here; nevertheless, it is the preacher's role to mediate the mysteries of God's dispensation, as revealed in this feast-day, to the faithful. John of Euboea, who expresses an unusual degree of humility in the prologue to his homily on the Conception of the Theotokos, exclaims, "Shall I dare, unworthy though I am, to undertake this? What shall I say? Shall I rebuke myself?" before calling on the Virgin herself to assist him in his undertaking.[68]

Perhaps the most important function of the prologue in a festal sermon, however, is to introduce a sense of immediacy, lifting the audience out of their everyday existence and initiating them into the eternal and unchanging timeframe of the feast. Paradoxically, however, historical time is not eradicated in this process. Many feasts celebrate specific historical events whose importance is also emphasized in the sermon. Preachers call on their congregations to experience Biblical or apocryphal events as if they were happening today; at the same time, they expound the eternal significance of those events and their importance in God's saving dispensation for humankind. A frequent device, using anaphora, is to provide a sequence of rhythmic phrases introduced by the word σήμερον ("today") in this context, helping to induce a sense of immediacy,

---

[67]See, for example, Andrew of Crete's second and third homilies on the Nativity of the Virgin, PG 97, 821, 844.

[68]John of Euboea, *In Conceptionem* 2, PG 96, 1460C. Below, 173.

as we see in Germanos's first homily on the Entry of the Virgin into
the temple:

> Today she enters the temple of the law . . .
> Today an infant is offered to the priest . . .
> Today the newest and most pure, unblemished volume . . .
>   is brought as a gift of thanksgiving . . .
> Today Joachim . . . is shown again to be a spiritual teacher
>   of holiness according to the law.
> Today also Anna . . . is proclaimed to the ends [of the
>   earth] as having acquired fruit . . .[69]

Chairetismoi, or hymnic greetings to the Virgin Mary, also feature frequently in the prologues of Byzantine Marian sermons. Here
anaphora and apostrophe are used together to draw the listener
into a feeling of direct contact and prayerful devotion towards the
Mother of God. The many types and epithets employed in these
sections reflect a long tradition of praise, in both homilies and
hymns, which receives its most famous treatment in the Akathistos
Hymn.[70]

Having thus exhorted his listeners to participate fully in timeless, but also historical events, the preacher moves on to develop
his theme, or themes, in the sermon. As we have already seen, the
variety of ways in which this is undertaken is striking in our twelve
festal sermons. In his four homilies on the Nativity of the Theotokos, the first three of which were probably preached in the course of
one all-night vigil, Andrew of Crete chooses several, quite different,
approaches to the feast. In his first homily, the preacher concentrates
on expounding the theological importance of the feast, whereas
in the second and third, he explores the prophetic and historical
background for Mary's designation as the Mother of God. John of

[69]Germanos, *In praesentationem* I.2, PG 98, 293. Below, 146–7.
[70]For the most recent text and translation, see Peltomaa, *The Image of the Virgin
Mary*, 2–19.

Damascus, in his sermon on the same subject, embarks on a rich, intertextual exposition of the place of the Theotokos in the divine economy and her essential role in the mystery of the Incarnation. His namesake, John of Euboea, undertakes a rambling, and somewhat obscure, account of the reasons for the existence of ten feasts in the Orthodox calendar and exhorts his congregation on the importance of celebrating them. Germanos of Constantinople, perhaps influenced by Syriac liturgical poetry, but certainly in a unique manner for the Byzantine homiletic tradition, expounds the feast of the Annunciation by means of vivid dramatic dialogue. This sermon is nevertheless carefully structured, with a prologue and epilogue framing the dialogic middle section, or argument, of the homily.

The epilogues of festal sermons sometimes follow a homiletic convention in offering ethical injunctions or spiritual advice, but more frequently do not. The use of the epilogue for more practical or personal concerns seems to belong more to the genre of the exegetical homily, as we see in many of John Chrysostom's series of homilies or in later, occasional works, than it does to the panegyrical sermon. Instead, our preachers frequently use this section of the homily to summarize what has been said, to offer further praise, or to draw important theological conclusions. The doxology at the end of every homily reflects its liturgical context. In the case of Marian sermons, the preacher skilfully refers the listeners' attention from the subject at hand back to the Trinitarian God who is the cause of all things, including the mystery of the Incarnation by means of the all-pure Virgin.

Biblical Exegesis: Narrative, Typological, and Allegorical

The primary basis for expounding the place of the Mother of God in the mystery of the Incarnation is Scripture. Eighth-century preachers demonstrate complete familiarity with both Old and New Testaments in their festal sermons. The narrative basis for the

stories of the Annunciation and Nativity of Christ may be found in
the Gospel of Luke, with further elaboration especially about Joseph
in Matthew. In addition to the simple narrative of the archangel's
arrival in Nazareth, his greeting to the Virgin Mary, and her eventual
acceptance of his message, Luke provides insight into the young girl's
innocence and thoughtful nature in such verses as, "But she was
much perplexed by his words and pondered what sort of greeting
this might be" (Luke 1.29). Preachers who deal with the theme of
the Annunciation explore Mary's response further by inventing the
dialogue that might have occurred at this encounter, as well as in the
Virgin's subsequent conversation with Joseph (Matt 1.19–21), as we
see in Germanos's dramatic homily on this subject.

Whereas events such as the Annunciation and the Meeting of
our Lord share a firm scriptural foundation in Luke, however, the
remaining Marian feasts are based on apocryphal texts, including
the *Protevangelion* of James, probably written towards the end of
the second century,[71] and various accounts of the Dormition which
began circulating in the course of the fifth century.[72] The Conception and Nativity of the Theotokos, celebrated on 9 December and
8 September respectively, follow the *Protevangelion*'s account of the
righteous couple, Joachim and Anna, who became objects of shame
in the Jewish community because of their infertility, prayed to God
and were rewarded with the gift of the blessed Virgin Mary. The feast
of the Virgin's Entry into the temple follows this account further:
when Mary reached the age of three, her parents took her to the

[71]E. de Strycker, S.J., ed., *La forme la plus ancienne du Protévangile de Jacques*
(Subsidia Hagiographica 33; Brussels: Société des Bollandistes, 1961); trans. Elliott,
The Apocryphal New Testament, 57–67. For further study of the *Protevangelion* in
middle Byzantine sermons, see M.B. Cunningham, "The Use of the *Protevangelion*
of James in Eighth-Century Homilies on the Mother of God," in Brubaker and Cunningham, *The Cult of the Mother of God in Byzantium,* forthcoming.

[72]Some of these texts are translated in Elliott, *The Apocryphal New Testament,*
691–723. See also Shoemaker, *Ancient Traditions of the Virgin Mary's Dormition and
Assumption,* 290–407. For further bibliography, see Daley, *On the Dormition of Mary,*
7–10, with notes. I shall not treat this body of literature further here because I am not
including the Dormition homilies which have already been translated by Daley.

temple, accompanied by a group of young virgins carrying torches, and presented her to the priest Zacharias. There she remained until she had reached the age of twelve, being "nurtured like a dove" and fed by the hand of an angel.[73] It is interesting that eighth-century preachers, whose homilies represent in some cases the first surviving texts on these subjects, frequently stray from one festal theme to another in their orations.[74] This may reflect the fact that the Marian feasts were not yet uniformly celebrated, as we saw above, or it may be intended to reveal the theological connection between all of these events.

The narrative content of Marian feasts nevertheless represents only one strand of their Scriptural foundation. It is immediately evident, on reading the homilies and hymns associated with these feasts, that they are based just as much on Old Testament prophecy and typology as they are on the Gospel accounts. Preachers understood the immanence of the Theotokos in the Old Testament: she is announced in literal terms by prophets such as Isaiah (7.14) or Zechariah (9.9), but also foretold symbolically in many other passages. Types such as Jacob's ladder (Gen 28.10–17), the burning bush (Exod 3.1–8), the tabernacle and its furniture (Exod 25–27), Gideon's fleece (Judg 6.37–40), the rich and shaded mountain (Ps 67 [68].15–16; Hab 3.3), and a host of others reveal the role of the Theotokos as a link between God and creation. Such types act not only as theological symbols, but they also evoke poetically God's miraculous presence in the created world.[75]

A further important aspect of typology is its association with eternal, or "sacred" time, which lifts it out of its historical context in

---

[73]Elliott, *The Apocryphal New Testament*, 57–60.

[74]See, for example, Andrew of Crete's *In Nativitatem* I, which treats the feast of the Entry, PG 97, 816–17; below, 71–84; John of Euboea, *In Conceptionem,* PG 96, 1481–89; below, 173–95, etc.

[75]For discussions of Marian typology, see Arch. Ephrem Lash, "Mary in Eastern Church Literature," in *Mary in Doctrine and Devotion* (ed. A. Stackpoole, OSB; Dublin: Columba Press, 1990), 58–80; P. Ladouceur, "Old Testament Prefigurations of the Mother of God," *SVTQ* 50, no. 1–2 (2006): 5–57.

the Old Testament. Sebastian Brock has commented on the way in which St Ephrem the Syrian employs typology, alluding to Old Testament events, objects, or persons that symbolised for him a meeting between God and creation.[76] It is God's activity which removes the event from linear, historical time into the realm of the sacred. While this process does not negate the importance of the original, historical occurrence, it does shift the emphasis to the universal, or eternal, truth that it represents and which continues to be played out in the context of God's dispensation.[77] Andrew of Crete explains his own understanding of the meaning and function of typology in the following passage:

> For there is not, indeed there is not, anywhere throughout the whole of the God-inspired Scripture where, on passing through, one does not see signs of [the Virgin Mary] scattered about in diverse ways; [signs] which, if you should disclose them for yourself in your industrious study of the words, you will find that a more distinct meaning has encapsulated so much glory before God.'[78]

This is followed by a long list of types, including not only those associated with the tabernacle and the temple, but also natural objects such as rock, land, garden, country, field, spring, ewe-lamb, and others. Andrew's point here is that in addition to the well-known types such as the burning bush or Gideon's fleece, almost any reference in the Old Testament may be seen to foreshadow Mary's role as a mortal being who became a container of divinity. The types listed above convey her links with creation, whereas those connected with

[76] S. Brock, *The Luminous Eye. The Spiritual World Vision of St Ephrem the Syrian* (Kalamazoo: Cistercian Publications, 1992), 46–51.

[77] See F.M. Young, *Biblical Exegesis and the Formation of Christian Culture* (Cambridge, 1997; repr. Peabody, MA: Hendrickson Publishers, 2002). See also M. Cunningham, "The Meeting of the Old and the New: The Typology of Mary the Theotokos in Byzantine Homilies and Hymns," in Swanson, *The Church and Mary*, 53–4.

[78] Andrew of Crete, *In Nativitatem* IV.2, 868; below, 127.

God's chosen habitation, that is, the Jewish tabernacle or temple, express her role as either receptacle or channel for his presence in creation.[79]

Other forms of allegorical interpretation may also be found in the eighth-century Marian sermons. A more general form of allegory is sometimes used to show that even small, apparently extraneous details in the New Testament contain symbolic meaning. In his second homily on the Nativity of the Virgin, Andrew of Crete compares the "foal of the ass," which Jacob mentions in his prophecy to his sons (Gen 49.11) to Christians or the church, since they are fastened "by an unbreakable tie" to Christ.[80] Later, as we shall see, the second half of this passage, ". . . he shall wash his robe in wine and his garment in the blood of the grape," is interpreted by preachers and hymnographers as referring both to the Passion and to the Eucharist. Allusions to this prophecy of course appear later in Scripture, in Zechariah 9:9 and the Gospel accounts of Christ's entry into Jerusalem (Matt 21.2; Mark 11.2; Luke 19. 30; and John 12.15), building on the messianic overtones of the passage in Genesis. Andrew thus uses the well-established Biblical tradition of linking events with prophecy; beyond this, however, he sees in them symbolic references to the Christian church.

Another example of such allegorical teaching, this time on a simpler level, is the insistence on the importance of the number three in homilies referring to the Entry of the Virgin Mary into the temple.

---

[79] As Brock points out in his discussion of Ephrem's understanding of typology, the Syrian poet viewed both Scripture and creation as replete with God's symbols and mysteries. See Brock, *The Luminous Eye*, esp. 41–51. The natural images cited in Andrew's and other Byzantine writers' works express not only Mary's roots in creation, but also God's presence and love for the natural world. For further discussion of this concept, see Cunningham, "The Meeting of Old and New," 60.

[80] Andrew of Crete, *In Nativitatem* II.8, PG 97, col. 836; trans. below, 98–9: "And we may be his foal since we have become one in him and have been joined, by an unbreakable tie through the Incarnation, to the One who, wealthy as he was, impoverished himself on our behalf . . . 'The foal of his ass' may be comprehended in a more mystical way as the all-sacred Church through which the calling of the gentiles is typologically understood, and in which we are led upwards."

John of Euboea, who treats this event in his homily on the Conception, suggests that Anna's and Joachim's decision to introduce her
into the temple at the age of three symbolises the holy Trinity: ". . .
they did not bring her forward at two years, nor again at four years;
but at the age of three, like the undivided Trinity, they brought her
as a bride and spotless bridal chamber alike, since she was about to
be both [of these]."[81] Germanos discusses the same topic in his first
homily on the Entry into the temple, listing many other examples of
the number three in Scripture, including the three stones in David's
slingshot, the three days that Jonah passed in the belly of the whale,
the three children in the furnace, and finally, the various manifesta-
tions of the number in the life of Christ culminating in the three
days that he waited before his resurrection.[82] This form of allegorical
exegesis may seem simplistic, but it helped to teach an important
concept, namely, the unity of Scripture, including both Old and New
Testaments, and its prophetic revelation of the Trinity and Christ's
Incarnation.

Origen's three levels of Scriptural interpretation, including literal, moral, and allegorical, thus all feature in Marian festal sermons.[83] None of these preachers ignores the narrative or literal
meaning of Scripture, as he emphasizes the historical importance
of the events surrounding the Incarnation of Christ. The moral, or
spiritual, meaning of Biblical stories is more prominent in weekday
or Lenten hymns and homilies than in festal panegyrics such as
these, but it does occasionally appear in preachers' exhortations to
their congregations to imitate the Mother of God and to lead their
lives in holiness.[84] The allegorical meaning of both Old and New
Testaments, however, assumes a dominant role in most homilies. As
we have seen, this may take the form of seeking out hidden, eternal
truth in Old Testament passages, recognising the types of Christ or

[81]John of Euboea, *In Conceptionem* 14, PG 96, col. 1480; below, 185.

[82]Germanos, *In Praesentationem* I.4, PG 98, col. 296; below, 148–50.

[83]See G.W. Butterworth, trans., *Origen, On First Principles* IV.ii.4–6 (Gloucester, MA: Peter Smith, 1973), 275–81.

[84]For example, John of Damascus, *In Nativitatem* 12, Kotter, *Die Schriften* 5, 182.

of the Theotokos, and tracing the meaning of symbolic numbers. Such an approach to Scripture assumes familiarity not only with well-known texts such as the Pentateuch and the Psalms, but also a frequently erudite knowledge of both canonical and apocryphal texts.

The Authors and Their Historical Backgrounds

The biographies of our five eighth-century preachers have received treatment elsewhere, so it is necessary only to outline these briefly in this section.[85] What has perhaps not yet received sufficient scholarly treatment is their relationship, both individually and as a group, with the political and theological events that took place in their lifetimes. Did the outbreak of Iconoclasm, for example, affect their preaching on subjects such as the Mother of God, as it did their political careers, at least in the case of Germanos of Constantinople and John of Damascus?[86] The paucity of historical records and literary sources for the early eighth century means that we may never be able to answer this question completely. In the case of John of Euboea and Kosmas Vestitor, who are not mentioned in contemporary sources, we know even less. Homilies and hymns attributed to all five authors represent our best witnesses to the literary careers of these preachers; however, the genre of festal sermon does not include many topical references or personal details about the author. A further problem, which awaits detailed research, is that of the dubious attribution of some sermons. Germanos of Constantinople is one of the most

[85]See, for example, the brief introductions to Andrew of Crete, Germanos of Constantinople, and John of Damascus in Daley, *On the Dormition of Mary*, 15–25. Short surveys of each of the five preachers may also be found in *ODB*.

[86]Scholarly opinions on this subject vary. N. Tsironis has argued in various contexts that these preachers reacted to Iconoclasm by writing their Marian sermons since veneration of the Theotokos was closely related to that of icons in this period. See, for example, her article, "The Mother of God in the Iconoclastic Controversy," Vassilaki, *Mother of God*, esp. 35–38.

elusive of our preachers; some of his works are confused with those of a later namesake, Germanos II (patriarch of Constantinople based at Nicaea, 1223–40), whereas others await detailed analysis on the basis of style.[87] For the purposes of this volume, we shall confine ourselves to a short discussion of the lives and Marian sermons of each preacher, treating them roughly in chronological order.

Germanos of Constantinople

The date of Germanos's birth is unknown, but is likely to have been between AD 630 and 650, judging by accounts of his age at the time of his death in circa 742.[88] According to his *Vita*, Germanos was about thirty-seven when his patrician father was executed for treason and he himself was castrated. Elected bishop of Kyzikos in about 705, Germanos, along with Andrew of Crete, may have supported the emperor Philippikos-Bardanes in his revival of Monotheletism;[89] both bishops recanted however after the fall of this emperor in 713. Germanos was elevated to the rank of ecumenical patriarch on 11 August, 715, and initially supported the emperor Leo III, praising him for his victories over the Arabs. We know from various letters attributed to Germanos, however, that he opposed Leo III's iconoclastic policy.[90] He was eventually deposed on 17 January, 730, and forced to retire to his estate at Platanion where he probably lived on for several more years. Germanos offers a few tantalizing references to himself in his liturgical writings: in his second homily on the Entry of the Mother of God into the temple, for example, he begs

[87]See *ODB* 2, 846–7.

[88]See C. Garton and L. Westerink, eds., *Germanos on Predestined Terms of Life* (Buffalo, NY: SUNY, 1979), v; L. Lamza, *Patriarch Germanos I. von Konstantinopel* (Würzburg: Augustinus-Verlag, 1975), 57.

[89]De Boor, *Theophanis Chronographia* 1, 382; Mango and Scott, *The Chronicle of Theophanes* 532.

[90]These are published in Mansi, *Sacrorum Conciliorum* 13, 100–28, and in PG 98, 156–88. See L. Brubaker and J. Haldon, *Byzantium in the Iconoclast Era (ca. 680–850): The Sources. An Annotated Survey* (Aldershot: Ashgate Publishing, 2001), 277.

the Virgin to reunite him after death with a beloved female relative or friend.[91]

In addition to his trilogy of sermons on the Dormition of the Mother of God, Germanos has been credited with the two sermons on her Entry, or Presentation, into the temple[92] and that on the Annunciation,[93] all three of which are translated in this volume. It is not possible to enter into the problems associated with the authenticity of the Presentation homilies in this context; suffice it to say that the highly ornate style and numerous *hapax legomena*, or neologisms, in the first of these texts brings its authorship into doubt.[94] Although Germanos is a sophisticated orator, his other sermons do not display such complexity as this. He tends generally to write in an uncluttered literary style which may be described as an elevated *koine*.[95] Although he does occasionally invent new words, mostly compounds formed from familiar prefixes and roots, Germanos does not employ these to excess. It is also striking that of all our preachers, Germanos is the most likely to make topical allusions in his sermons; for example, he attacks unnamed people "who are speaking against" the Mother of God in his second homily on the Entry, suggesting that they question the veracity of the story of her early life recounted in the *Protevangelion* of James.[96] It is impossible to determine whether Germanos is referring to iconoclasts here or

[91]"Look upon and assent to my supplication, fulfil my thirsty desire, and join me together with my kinswoman and fellow maid-servant in the land of the meek, in the tabernacles of the righteous, and in the company of the saints!" PG 98, 320; below, 172–2.

[92]*CPG* 8007–8; PG 98, 292–320; below, 145–72.

[93]*CPG* 8009; below, 221–46.

[94]Since its inauthenticity has not yet been conclusively proved, I shall continue in this volume to refer to the first homily on the Presentation as the work of Germanos I.

[95]Studies of Germanos's homiletic style may be found in J. List, *Studien zur Homiletik Germanos I. von Konstantinopel und seiner Zeit* (Athens: Byzantinisch-neugriechischen Jahrbücher, 1939); A. Kazhdan with L.F. Sherry and C. Angelidi, *A History of Byzantine Literature (650–850)* (Athens: The National Hellenic Research Foundation, 1999), 55–73.

[96]Germanos, *In Praesentationem* II, PG 98, 312; below, 164.

to Christians who opposed the veneration of the Mother of God. Nevertheless, this passage stands out as a rare reference in a liturgical text of this kind to the cultural and religious climate of the period.

Germanos's sermon on the Annunciation also presents us with a puzzle. Scholars have long been intrigued by the unique structure of this sermon, which takes the form of two dialogues arranged in alphabetical acrostics, first between Mary and the archangel Gabriel and then between Joseph and Mary, both of which are framed by a laudatory prologue and epilogue.[97] The dramatic nature of this sermon raises questions about its delivery both at the time it was composed and later as a liturgical reading.[98] Although scholars have generally dismissed the idea that it represented a form of liturgical drama similar to the medieval mystery plays in the West, it is still difficult to imagine one preacher alternating between the parts of the three protagonists. The resemblance of this sermon to Syriac dialogue poems, especially the *soghyatha* written mostly in the fifth and sixth centuries, seems indisputable, especially given the addition of the alphabetic acrostic which appears frequently in that genre.[99] It is possible that this link with Syriac liturgical tradition was reinforced by Romanos the Melode in the sixth century, with his extensive use of dramatic dialogue and interest in the emotions of Biblical characters.[100] On the other hand, the dramatic presentation of this theme is already present in earlier Greek homilies including, most strikingly, (ps-) Proclus's sixth homily, which contains two long dialogues between Mary and Gabriel, then Mary and Joseph.[101] A. Kazhdan

[97]For example, G. La Piana, *La rappresentazioni sacre nella letteratura bizantina dale origini al secolo IX* (Grottaferrata: Tip. Italo-orientale "S. Nilo," 1912; repr. London: Variorum Reprints, 1971), who argues that this homily provides evidence of a form of liturgical drama in the early Byzantine Church.

[98]See M. Cunningham, "Dramatic Device or Didactic Tool? The Function of Dialogue in Byzantine Preaching," in *Rhetoric in Byzantium* (ed. E. Jeffreys; Aldershot: Ashgate, 2003), 101–13.

[99]See S. Brock, *Bride of Light* (Moran 'Eth'o 6; Kottayam, India: St Ephrem Ecumenical Research Institute, 1994), 12–13.

[100]Romanos wrote two kontakia on the Annunciation in which these literary devices play a role. See Maas and Trypanis, *Sancti Romani Melodi Cantica*, 280–93.

[101]*CPG* 5805; F.J. Leroy, ed., *L'homilétique de Proclus de Constantinople. Tradi-*

has noted Germanos's sophisticated portrayal of the characters in this homily, as Mary moves slowly from a state of incomprehension to acceptance of her exalted role, revealing this progression in the style of her speeches to the archangel.[102] The development of character through the use of dialogue represents the device of ethopoiia, or *sermocinatio*, in Greek rhetoric; Germanos employs this with consummate skill in his exploration of the characters not only of the Mother of God, but also of the archangel Gabriel and Joseph, Mary's intended husband.

Andrew of Crete

Andrew, archbishop of Gortyna in Crete, was a near contemporary of Germanos, having been born in Damascus in about 660 and dying probably in 740. He was educated in Jerusalem as a monk at the monastery of the Holy Sepulchre, but travelled to Constantinople in 685 where he served as a deacon in the Great Church and administered an orphanage and an almshouse for the poor. The date when he was ordained metropolitan of Crete is unknown, but this occurred sometime between 692 and 711.[103] He wrote a number of

tion manuscrite, inédits, etudes connexes (Studi e Testi 247; Vatican City: Bibliotheca Apostolica Vaticana, 1967), 298–324. Many scholars believe this to be a composite text, which underwent several redactions after the time of Proclus. See Constas, *Proclus of Constantinople*, 388. Other, probably fifth-, sixth-century, dialogic sermons on the theme of the Annunciation also exist. See, for example, (ps-) Gregory Thaumatourgus, *In Annunciationem* 1, PG 10, 1145–56; (ps-) Athanasius, *In Annunciationem*, PG 28, 917–40, and others. It should be emphasised again that most of these early Greek sermons were intended for the feast of the Memory of Mary, not for that of the Annunciation which, as we saw above, was only introduced into the liturgical calendar during the reign of Justinian. For a recent overview of this material, see P. Allen, "Portrayals of Mary in Greek Homiletic Literature (6th–7th Centuries)," in *The Cult of the Mother of God in Byzantium: Texts and Images* (ed. L. Brubaker and M.B. Cunningham; Aldershot: Ashgate, forthcoming).

[102]Kazhdan, *A History of Byzantine Literature*, 61–4.

[103]The best study of Andrew's life remains S. Vailhé, "S. André de Crète," *EO* 5 (1902), 278–87. See also M.-F. Auzépy, "La carrière d'André de Crète," *ByzZ* 88.1 (1995), 1–12.

homilies and encomia, including exegetical sermons on the Sunday
of the Publican and the Pharisee, Lazarus Saturday, and Palm Sunday, as well as trilogies on the Nativity and Dormition of the Mother
of God, a sermon on the Annunciation, and panegyrics of saints.[104]
Most of these texts are impossible to place, although a few contain
small indications of their provenance and date. Andrew is probably
best known in the Orthodox tradition for his composition of the
Great Kanon, the long hymn in nine odes that is read out annually
during Lent.[105] He is even credited with the invention of this new
hymnographic form, although it is more likely that this evolved
organically out of liturgical practice in the Palestinian monasteries.[106] Whether or not Andrew actively opposed iconoclastic policies
remains a matter of dispute among scholars: his liturgical sermons
and hymns reveal little about his political views, but a fragment of a
homily in defence of images, plus one or two references in his other
works, suggest that he was an iconophile.[107]

The sermons translated in this volume reveal Andrew's rhetorical and theological sophistication, as well as his creative approach
to preaching. The trilogy on the Nativity of the Mother of God, for
example, displays a variety of didactic methods. In his first sermon,
Andrew extols the Virgin as the bridge between the old and new
covenants: she "mediates between the height of divinity and the
humility of flesh."[108] Pauline language contrasting the letter and
grace, darkness and light, and extolling the renewal of all things in

[104]Many of these texts are published in PG 97, 805–1304. See *CPG* 8170–214.

[105]The Great Kanon is published in PG 97, 1329–85; P.C. Chrestou, *Theologika
Meletemata* 4: *Hymnographika* (Thessalonike: Patriarchikon hidryma paterikon
meleton, 1981), 231–74. Trans., Sisters Katherine and Thekla, *St Andrew of Crete, The
Great Canon; The Life of St Mary of Egypt* (Normanby, Whitby: The Greek Orthodox
Monastery of the Assumption, 1974), 29–64. For a new study, which includes two later
Byzantine commentaries on the kanon, see A. Giannouli, *Die beiden byzantinischen
Kommentare zum Grossen Kanon des Andreas von Kreta. Eine quellenkritische und
literarhistorische Studie* (Vienna: Verlag der Österreichischen Akademie der Wis-
senschaften, 2007).

[106]See *ODB* 2, 1102.

[107]PG 97, 1301–4.

[108]*In Nativitatem* I.2, PG 97, 808; below, 73.

Christ reinforces the importance of this day, which initiates once and for all the new dispensation. In his third homily on the same subject, however, Andrew switches to a more discursive, historical enquiry into the Virgin Mary's Davidic ancestry. His argumentation, which involves the Jewish marital laws set out in Numbers 36, seems somewhat tendentious, especially since, as he admits himself, they were no longer observed at the time that Mary was born. The three sermons, taken together, display various methods of biblical exegesis, an exercise that Andrew, in time-honoured fashion, compares to the mastication of a well-cooked meal.[109] In his fourth homily, which probably does not belong to the trilogy, the preacher reverts to eulogy of the Theotokos, employing a rich array of typological and metaphorical images.

A. Kazhdan has described Andrew of Crete's style as "abstract, motionless [and] repetitive ... freed from concrete persons and objects, and from the marks of time and place ... he tried to be as impersonal and rational as possible."[110] It is also noticeable that Andrew is deeply influenced by the writings of ps-Dionysios the Areopagite, frequently employing mystical terms used by the fifth-century writer and invoking the sense of a celestial hierarchy in which the earthly Church participates. Andrew's sermon on the Annunciation contrasts significantly with that of Germanos. Instead of focusing on the dynamic encounter between Gabriel and Mary, Andrew is interested in the timeless interaction between the divine and created worlds, the nature of the archangel and his way of approaching the Virgin, and the cosmic transformation that takes place when she give him her *fiat*. Like Germanos and John of Damascus, Andrew of Crete reveals a distinctive homiletic style that is all his own, while at the same time varying his didactic methods and rhetorical techniques.

[109]See *In Nativitatem* II.10, PG 97, 840; below, section 10, 101–2.
[110]Kazhdan, *A History of Byzantine Literature*, 53.

John of Damascus

The most famous of our preachers is John of Damascus, who wrote compendious treatises on Orthodox doctrine, against the heresies, and in defence of icons.[111] John, like Andrew of Crete, came from an eastern background: born between AD 650 and 660 in Damascus to a wealthy Christian Arab family involved in the Umayyad fiscal administration in Syria, John moved at some point to Palestine where he became a monk in a monastery near Jerusalem. It is possible that this move took place in about 706 when the civil administration under the Umayyads changed its official language from Greek to Arabic. Orthodox tradition has accepted that John was based primarily at the Monastery of St Sabas near Jerusalem, although the earliest sources do not substantiate this theory.[112] In any case, John spent the rest of his life as a monk-priest, studying and writing treatises, preaching, and also contributing to the growing body of hymnography intended for the monastic rite in this period.[113]

John of Damascus's surviving Marian sermons include a trilogy for the feast of the Dormition and the homily on the Nativity that is translated in this volume.[114] Bonifatius Kotter, who has provided us with a critical edition of all of John's literary works, has expressed doubts about the authenticity of the homily on the Nativity.[115] He argues that differences in style, christological teaching, and biblical imagery suggest that this text should in fact be attributed to another, unidentified, author. Against these arguments, we may cite the

[111]For an excellent recent study of St John of Damascus and his works, see A. Louth, *St John Damascene. Tradition and Originality in Byzantine Theology* (Oxford: Oxford University Press, 2002).

[112]The earliest source to place John in the Monastery of St Sabas is a tenth-century *vita*, composed by John, patriarch of Jerusalem. See Louth, *St John Damascene*, 6.

[113]For a list of his works, see *CPG* 8040–127.

[114]*CPG* 8060–3.

[115]Kotter, *Die Schriften* 5, 149–50. See also J.M. Hoeck, "Stand und Aufgaben der Damaskenos-Forschung," *OCP* 17 (1951): 37, n. 84. The homily is also published, with a French translation by P. Voulet, in *S. Jean Damascène, Homélies sur la nativité et la dormition* (SC 80; Paris: Éditions du Cerf, 1961), 46–78.

extraordinary quality of this sermon, with its rich use of imagery, passages of theological exposition, and biblical citations, which sets it above the rest of the eighth-century corpus. The polemical mention of heretical opponents, including "Akephaloi," or the followers of the extreme Monophysite, Peter Mongos, and "Nestorians," is unusual in a festal sermon of this type, suggesting perhaps that the author was engaged in disputing these heresies.[116] In addition, the sermon contains some interesting Trinitarian images, such as that of Christ the Word as the "arm" of God, while the Holy Spirit is his "finger."[117] This statement is questionable in doctrinal terms, to say the least, but should perhaps be understood in the context of poetic theological expression, which in the Byzantine context is never systematic. In sum, although it is tempting to assign this sermon to John of Damascus on the grounds of its rhetorical power and theological depth, we may never be able to prove this attribution conclusively.[118]

John of Euboea

This somewhat obscure figure is cited in liturgical collections of homilies and saints' lives as the author of three sermons and one hagiographical work, the *Passion* of St Paraskeve.[119] The three sermons attributed to John of Euboea are dedicated to the Conception of the Virgin Mary, the Massacre of the Innocents, and the Raising of Lazarus. Scribes frequently confuse this preacher with his contemporary namesake, John of Damascus, but more often describe him as John, presbyter (or sometimes even bishop) and monk of Euboea. The spelling of the name "Euboea" varies in manuscripts, appearing

[116]John of Damascus, *In Nativitatem* 3, Kotter, *Die Schriften* 5, 171; below, 56.

[117]John of Damascus, *In Nativitatem* 3, Kotter, *Die Schriften* 5, 171; below, 56.

[118]Andrew Louth, in assessing Kotter's arguments concerning the authenticity of this homily, agrees with me that they are "not absolutely conclusive." See Louth, *St John Damascene*, 226.

[119]For a list of his works, see *CPG* 8135–8.

most frequently as Εὐβοία, but also occasionally as Εὐοία or Εὐαρία. Scholars have argued about John of Euboea's provenance and career, suggesting either that he was a priest-monk on the island of Euboea (or Euroia, Epiros) in Greece or that he hailed from a small town called Euaria, south of Damascus in Syria.[120] He is not mentioned in any historical records, which leaves only the geographical placement of the name and the style and content of his homilies as evidence for his life. John of Euboea does provide one small clue, however, which allows us to date his homilies to the middle of the eighth century. In his homily on the Massacre of the Innocents, the preacher states that he is writing this work 742 years after the event took place in Palestine and 744 years after the birth of Christ.[121]

The style of the homilies ascribed to John of Euboea is distinctive: he writes in a lively, colloquial manner with short periods, unsophisticated syntax, and much use of dialogue, apostrophe, and colorful ekphrasis. His homily on the Conception of the Mother of God, which is the first Byzantine festal sermon on this subject, focuses especially on her righteous parents, Joachim and Anna, building on the narrative in the *Protevangelion* of James. He describes how Joachim, after being rebuked by Reuben, went off to pray on the mountain for forty days and how Anna is left to weep and pray in her house and garden. The preacher's sympathetic treatment of Anna is especially striking in this section of the homily as he portrays her talking to herself, wondering what has become of her beloved husband and whether she will soon become a widow in addition to being childless.[122] The homily also displays an interest in Old Testament history, prophecy, and typology. As we saw

---

[120]See F. Dölger, "Iohannes von Euboia," AnBoll 68 (1950): 5–26; D. Stiernon, "Jean d'Eubée," *Dictionnaire de Spiritualité* 8 (1974): 487; F. Halkin, "La passion de Ste Parascève par Jean d'Eubée," in *Polychronion. Festschrift für Franz Dölger* (ed. P. Wirth; Heidelberg: C. Winter, 1966), 231–7. There was not bishopric at this time in Euboea, but this does not rule out the possibility that he preached as a presbyter. See also Kazhdan, *A History of Byzantine Literature*, 93–4.

[121]John of Euboea, *In Sanctos Innocentes*, PG 96, 1504D–1505A.

[122]John of Euboea, *In Conceptionem* 8, PG 96, 1472.

earlier, John of Euboea provides a list of the main Dominical and Marian feasts that were celebrated in his region: oddly, this includes the feast of the Conception of St Anna, but excludes the Entry of the Theotokos into the temple, Palm Sunday, and the Dormition.[123] One other feature of John of Euboea's writing, which appears in all of his homilies and which may offend modern readers, is his fondness for anti-Judaic invective.[124] This device is of course endemic in Byzantine homiletics, especially in texts connected with Holy Week and events leading up to the Passion of Christ, but it seems especially virulent in the homilies of John of Euboea.[125] It is impossible to determine what caused him to inveigh against the Jews so forcibly and whether this reflects his historical circumstances or simply a theological obsession. John of Euboea's sermons are thus important on historical, liturgical, and literary grounds; as rare examples of a more colloquial, perhaps even "provincial," style of preaching in the mid-eighth century, they deserve more scholarly attention than they have so far received.

Kosmas Vestitor

Even more shadowy than John of Euboea is Kosmas Vestitor, who probably lived in Constantinople sometime between AD 730 and 850.[126] According to his title, he was a functionary in the Byzantine

[123]John of Euboea, *In Conceptionem* 9, PG 96, 1473.

[124]See especially *In Conceptionem* 18–19, PG 96, 1489–92.

[125]For a study of the place of anti-Judaic invective in Byzantine homilies, see M. Cunningham, "Polemic and Exegesis: Anti-Judaic Invective in Byzantine Homiletics," *Sobornost* 21:2 (1999): 46–68; and for similar conclusions with regard to Slavonic preaching, see A. Pereswetoff-Morath, *A Grin Without A Cat: "Adversus Judaeos" Texts in the Literature of Medieval Russia, 988–1504* (Lund: Slavonic Monographs, 2002). It is important to note that anti-Judaic polemic is usually included in Byzantine homilies and hymns for theological reasons and that it tends to be associated with particular liturgical events such as the Raising of Lazarus, Holy Week, etc. See E. Theokritoff, "The Orthodox Services of Holy Week: The Jews and the New Sion," *Sobornost* 25:1 (2003): 25–50; 25:2 (2003): 74–8.

[126]For a list of his homilies, see *CPG* 8142–63.

court in Constantinople, but he also produced sermons as a lay
preacher. The manuscripts containing his works call him μακάριος
("blessed"), which suggests that he possessed no special qualifica-
tions for this role apart from his rhetorical ability and personal piety.
The surviving sermons, which include four on the Dormition,[127] five
on the translation of St John Chrysostom's relics to Constantinople,[128] a number of so far unedited works on both Chrysostom and
St Zacharias,[129] and the homily on SS Joachim and Anna translated
below,[130] are not especially distinguished in their literary composition or originality. In fact, Kosmas borrowed heavily from the works
of earlier writers, including especially Germanos of Constantinople
for his sermons on the Dormition.[131] According to *CPG*, some of his
works remain unedited, but study of his life and work is currently
underway in Greece.[132]

Kosmas's homily on SS Joachim and Anna focuses, like that of
John of Euboea, on these holy figures, building on the account contained in the *Protevangelion* of James. After a short narrative section,
Kosmas turns to praising the saints in a short section of *chairetismoi*,
employing some unusual images such as the "oystershell of the
spotless pearl," "the pure emerald," and "water-jug for the thirst of
child-bearing."[133] Like Andrew of Crete, Kosmas is interested in the
genealogy of the Virgin Mary and expounds this on the basis of Luke
3: 23–38. Overall, this is a short and comprehensible festal sermon,
intended for the commemoration of Mary's parents on 9 September,
the day after her Nativity. Kosmas's homily is the first liturgical text

---

[127]These survive only in Latin and are published in Wenger, *L'Assomption de la
T.S. Vierge*, 315–33.

[128]K.I. Dyobouniotes, ed., "Κοσμᾶ Βεστίτωρος ἀνέκδοτα ἐγκώμια εἰς τὴν
ἀνακομιδὴν τοῦ λειψάνου τοῦ ἐν ἁγίοις πατρὸς ἡμῶν Ἰωάννου τοῦ Χρυσοστόμου,"
Epeteris Hetaireias Byzantinon Spoudon 2 (1925): 55–9.

[129]F. Halkin, "Zacharie, père de Jean Baptiste. Trois panégyriques par Cosmas
Vestitor," AnBoll 105 (1987): 251–63.

[130]*CPG* 8151; PG 106, 1005–12.

[131]See Wenger, *L'Assomption de la T.S. Vierge*, 152–3.

[132]This work is being carried out in the form of doctoral theses; for the time
being, the scholars involved in this research prefer to remain anonymous.

[133]Kosmas Vestitor, *In Ioachim et Annam* 7, PG 106, 1009.

in honor of this feast; by the tenth century, it is recorded in the Typikon of the Great Church of Constantinople.[134]

Texts and Translations

The translations of the twelve sermons contained in this volume are, with a few exceptions, based on seventeenth- or eighteenth-century editions reprinted in Migne's Patrologia graeca. For the most part, these editions are excellent, being based on the sound scholarship of Roman Catholic scholars working in France and Italy. It is important to bear in mind, however, that F. Combefis, A. Gallandi, P. Ballerini, and others usually based their editions on single manuscripts; in the case of Combefis, for example, these usually belonged to the royal French library which is now preserved in the Bibliothèque Nationale in Paris. This method was probably necessitated by restrictions of time and funding, but we should remember that most Byzantine homilies, especially those written by such popular writers as Andrew of Crete, Germanos I, and John of Damascus, survive in scores if not even hundreds of liturgical manuscripts.[135] The goal of editing each of their sermons critically is in most cases unobtainable; nevertheless, we should bear in mind that we are usually looking at just one strand of a complicated manuscript tradition. In the preparatory work for a new edition of Germanos's homily on the Annunciation, I have found considerable variation in the texts contained in the eight earliest manuscripts which I have so far been able to examine.[136]

Germanos's homily on the Annunciation represents in fact a special case since the text contained in Patrologia graeca 98 is

[134] J. Mateos, ed., *Le Typicon de la Grande Église: Ms. Sainte-Croix no. 40, Xe siècle* 1 (Rome: Pont. Institutum Orientalium, 1962), 126.4–2.

[135] See Ehrhard, *Überlieferung und Bestand*.

[136] According to the Greek Index Project database held at the Institut de Recherche et d'Histoire des Textes in Paris, the homily is contained in 59 manuscripts. It is unlikely that I will be able to provide a fully critical edition of the text, but I aim to examine as many of these witnesses as possible.

incomplete, being based on Codex Parisinus Graecus 773 (fifteenth century), which has folios missing, thus accounting for Combefis's lacuna in the prologue and at the end of the homily in the middle of Joseph's dialogue with the Theotokos. D. Fecioru published a complete edition of the homily, using one nineteenth-century manuscript in the national library of Bucharest, but the periodical in which it appears is difficult to access.[137] I have based my translation on this text because it is complete, while recognising regretfully that many readers may not be able to check it against the original Greek. Although Fecioru's edition represents the fullest published version of the text, it has its problems too. In the course of translating the homily, I discovered that a lengthy section in the epilogue consisting of a succession of sentences beginning with the words, "This one . . . ," according to the rhetorical device of anaphora, is identical to a passage in (ps-)Proclus's dialogic Homily 6, probably intended for the original Marian feast but dealing primarily with the Annunciation.[138] The manuscripts that I have consulted so far, in the course of preparing a new edition of the homily, do not contain this passage.

References to the Old Testament of course refer to the Septuagint version since this was the text used by the Byzantines and is accepted as inspired Scripture by the Orthodox Church.[139] It should be remembered that the numbering of psalms and titles of books such

[137] D. Fecioru, ed., "Un nou de predica in omiletica ortodoxa," *Biserica Ortodoxa Romana* 64 (1946): 65–91; 180–92; 386–96. Having searched unsuccessfully in libraries of the UK and the US, I eventually tracked down a tattered copy of the Romanian periodical in the Byzantine library of the Institut Catholique in Paris. I would like to express my gratitude to that library for allowing me to make a photocopy of the text.

[138] *CPG* 5805; *BHG^a* 1110; *BHG^n* 1126e; F.J. Leroy, ed., *L'homilétique de Proclus de Constantinople* (Studi e Testi 247; Vatican City: Bibliotheca Apostolica Vaticana, 1967), 298–324. The authenticity of this homily has been much debated; Leroy supports its attribution to Proclus, 275–9.

[139] I have used the edition by A. Rahlfs, *Septuaginta. Id est Vetus Testamentum graece iuxta LXX interpretes* (ed. A. Rahlfs; 2 vols.; Stuttgart: Privilegierte Württembergische Bibelanstalt, 1935; repr. 1982). For translations, I have consulted, but often diverged from Sir L.C.L. Brenton, *The Septuagint with Apocrypha: Greek and English* (London: Samuel Bagster & Sons, 1851; repr. Hendrickson Publishers, 1998).

as Kings and Samuel differs in the Septuagint from the Hebrew text; words and whole passages often differ in the two versions as well. My translation of the New Testament generally follows the English version of the NRSV, but I have occasionally substituted my own interpretation or chosen to follow a variant version used by the preacher. It is not clear whether our homilists are always quoting directly from a written text of the books of the Old Testament or of the New; sometimes they may quote from memory, forgetting or adding a word or two, and sometimes they may even paraphrase Scriptural texts. It is often difficult to determine, especially given the textual problems described above, where changes have crept into the text.

With regard to formatting, I have chosen to set out most of the homilies as prose compositions since they employ such a variety of literary styles, from an Asianic, rhythmic form to discursive prose. Germanos's homily on the Annunciation, however, which is composed entirely of poetic sections of praise, or occasionally *chairetismoi*, to the Mother of God and of two long dialogues, has been arranged line by line in order to demonstrate this unusual structure. It is of course impossible to bring out the rhythmic, repetitive, and sometimes rhyming nature of this sermon, but it is hoped that readers will be able to see something of its highly rhetorical and dramatic nature by this means. It is important to remember that all of the sermons translated in this volume are liturgical compositions, which would have been spoken *ex tempore*, or perhaps in some cases read aloud, in the context of a divine office or liturgy. Their transmission in liturgical collections, which continued to be used in Byzantine monasteries and parish churches throughout the Byzantine period, suggests that they continued to be used in this way. They are arranged in this volume according to their order in the liturgical year, just as they would have appeared in most of the manuscripts compiled from about the ninth century onwards in Byzantium.[140]

---

[140]For lists and examples of the contents of these liturgical manuscripts, see Ehrhard, *Überlieferung und Bestand.*

JOHN OF DAMASCUS[1]

An Oration on the Nativity of the Holy Theotokos Mary[2]

1 [169] Come, all nations, every race of men, every language, every age and every rank! Let us joyfully celebrate the nativity of joy for the whole world! For if children of pagans used to mark with every honor the birthdays of demons,[3] who deceive the mind with a false story[4] and obscure the truth, as well as of kings, each offering a gift according to his ability, and [they did] this even while [the objects of devotion] were destroying their lives—by how much more ought we to honor the nativity of the Theotokos, through whom the whole human race has been restored, [and] through whom the pain of our ancestress Eve has been transformed into joy? For whereas the latter heard the divine statement, "In pain you shall bring forth children" (Gen 3.16), the former [heard], "Rejoice, favored one!" (Luke 1.28). The latter [heard], "Your recourse shall be towards your husband!" (Gen 3.17)[5] and the former, "The Lord is with you!" (Luke 1.28).

[1]On the authenticity of this homily, see Introduction above, 44–5.

[2]*CPG* 8060; *BHG*ᵃ 1087; Kotter, *Die Schriften* 5, 169–82.

[3]By the term δαιμόνων the preacher probably refers to pagan gods (see Lampe, 328, C for this usage).

[4]It is likely that John refers here to the myths of ancient gods, using the word μῦθος.

[5]The Septuagint word here is ἀποστροφή, which is translated as "submission" by Brenton. The KJV and NRSV versions prefer "desire." Other possible translations for the word are "recourse" or even "amusement" (see L&S, 220, II and V). For consistency with most patristic interpretations of this passage, I have chosen "recourse" in order to convey the sense of refuge in Eve's relationship with her husband after the Fall. See A. Louth, ed., *Ancient Christian Commentary on Scripture, Old Testament I: Genesis 1–11* (Chicago and London: Fitzroy Dearborn Publishers, 2001), 91–4.

What then should we offer to the Mother of the Word other than an oration? Let the whole of creation make festival and sing of the most holy birth-giving of the holy Anna. For she bore for the world an inviolable treasury of blessings. Through her the Creator transformed all nature into a better state by means of humanity. For if a human being stands between mind and matter, since he is the bond between all visible and invisible creation, the creative Word of God, having become unified with the nature of humanity, was unified through it with the whole of creation. [170] Let us then celebrate the dissolution of human sterility since our incapacity[6] for blessings has been dissolved.

2   But why has the Virgin Mother been born from a sterile woman? For that which alone is new under the sun,[7] the culmination of miracles, the way had to be prepared by means of miracles, and what was greater had to advance slowly from what was more humble. And I have another more exalted and divine reason. Nature has been defeated by grace and stands trembling, no longer ready to take the lead. Therefore when the God-bearing Virgin was about to be born from Anna, nature did not dare to anticipate the offshoot of grace; instead it remained without fruit until grace sprouted its fruit. For it was necessary for her to be the first-born, she who would bear the "Firstborn of all creation" in whom "all things subsist" (Col 1.15,17).

O blessed couple, Joachim and Anna, all nature is indebted to you! For through you it has offered a gift to the Creator which is more excellent than all [other] gifts: a holy mother who alone is worthy of the Creator. O most all-blessed loins of Joachim, from which a wholly unblemished seed was sent forth! O renowned womb of Anna, in which slowly, with additions from her, an all-holy infant

[6]The word πήρωσις may mean "mutilation," "disablement," or "disability." In some contexts it also means "blindness." The implication here is that owing to the Fall, human beings were incapacitated until the Incarnation of Christ and thus incapable of receiving God's grace in full measure.

[7]Cf. Eccl 1.9; John of Damascus, *Expositio fidei* 45, Kotter, *Die Schriften* 2, 108.44–45.

grew, and once it had taken shape, was born![8] O belly that contained within itself a living heaven, vaster than the immensity of [all] the heavens![9] O threshing floor which contained the heap of life-giving grain, since Christ himself declared: "Unless a grain of wheat which falls into the earth dies, it remains just a single grain . . ." (John 12.24). O breasts that suckled her who fed the Feeder of the world! O marvel of marvels and miracle of miracles! For it was necessary that the ineffable and condescending incarnation of God should be prepared by means of miracles. But how shall I advance further? My understanding is confounded, while fear and longing have divided me. My heart quakes and my tongue has been paralysed. I cannot bear my happiness! I am overcome by miracles! I am possessed by longing! Let longing be overcome! [171] Let fear be banished! Let the harp of the Spirit sing, "Let the heavens rejoice and let the earth exult!" (Ps 95[96].11).

3 Today sterile gates are opened and a virginal, divine gate comes forth, from which and through which God (cf. Ezek 44.1–3), who is beyond all existing things, will enter "into the world" (Heb 1.6) "bodily" (Col 2.9), according to Paul who heard ineffable things (cf. 2 Cor 12.4). Today a rod was begotten from the root of Jesse (cf. Isa

[8]This sentence expresses the Byzantine view of pregnancy and childbirth, according to which the father provides the seed and therefore most of the genetic material for the child. John implies here, however, that the mother, in this case Anna, adds parts of herself to the fetus during its gestation. This is transmitted by means of her blood. The emphasis on the contribution of the mother in the formation of the child is affirmed in Christian theology by the dogma that the Virgin Mary provided the material of Christ's humanity, from the moment of his conception. See Maximos the Confessor, *Ambigua*, in A. Louth, trans., *Maximus the Confessor* (London: Routledge, 1996), 173: "And the Virgin declares this when she conceives him in a way that transcends nature and the Word who is beyond being is humanly formed without a man from her virginal blood by a strange ordinance contrary to nature." On patristic and Byzantine views of conception and childbirth, see now L. Brusson, M.-H. Congourdeau, J.-L. Solère, eds., *L'embryon: formation et animation. Antiquité grecque et latine. Traditions hébraique, chrétienne et islamique* (Histoire des doctrines de l'antiquité classique, vol. 38; Paris: Librairie Philosophique J. Vrin, 2008).

[9]Cf. (ps-) Modestos, *In dormitionem BMV*, PG 86, 3296C.

11.1), out of which a divine[10] flower will arise for the world. Today he, who once in ancient times established the firmament out of water and raised it up to the heights, has prepared heaven on earth out of earthly nature. And truly, this [heaven][11] is much more divine and miraculous than that [firmament]. For the One who at that time prepared the sun, arose from this [earthly nature] as a Sun of righteousness (Mal 4.2). There are two natures, despite the ravings of the Akephaloi![12] There is one hypostasis, despite the curses of the Nestorians![13] For the eternal light, which came into existence out of eternal light before the ages, the immaterial and bodiless One, takes a body from this [woman] and comes forth from the bridal chamber as Bridegroom although he is God; and later, having become earthborn, he will rejoice as a giant to run the course of our nature (cf. Ps 18[19].6), to journey through sufferings towards death, to bind the strong man and seize from him his goods (cf. Matt 12.29), that is, our nature, and to lead the wandering sheep back up to the heavenly land (cf. Matt 18.12).

Today the "Son of the carpenter" (Matt 13.55), the universally active[14] Word of him who fashioned all things through him,[15] the strong arm of God the Highest, with the Spirit as his own finger,[16]

[10]The word θεουπόστατος may mean simply "divine." Cf. Germanos of Constantinople, *In vivicam crucem*, PG 98, 221C.

[11]That is to say, the Mother of God.

[12]The term "akephaloi," which means literally "headless ones," refers to followers of Peter Mongos, a Monophysite patriarch of Alexandria (477–90), who rejected him after his acceptance of the Henotikon formula promoted by the emperor Zeno and patriarch Akakios in 482. In this passage, John is probably using the term to refer to all Monophysites.

[13]The verb διαρρήγνυμι means literally to "break in two." A more literal translation of this passage might be "the breaking [in two] of the Nestorians"!

[14]Ὁ παντεχνήμων: this may be a *hapax legomenon* or neologism. See Lampe, 1004; Sophocles, 838. Both dictionaries cite this passage for the meaning of the word.

[15]See John 1.3: "All things came into being through him, and without him not one thing came into being . . . "

[16]See Matt 12.28 and Luke 11.20, in which the Spirit is described as God's finger. As Fr Andrew Louth pointed out to me on reading this passage, the imagery that John is using here is nevertheless odd. With Christ as the Father's arm and the Spirit as his finger, he seems to be approaching the doctrine of the *filioque*.

after sharpening the blunted axe of [our] nature, has prepared for himself a living ladder whose base has been set on earth and whose top [reaches] to heaven itself. God has come to rest in her; the type that Jacob saw was of her (cf. Gen 28.12); God descended without change through her, [172] or in other words, having accommodated himself, he was seen on earth and lived along with humankind (cf. Bar 3.37). For these [events sum up] his descent, his gracious[17] humility, his life on earth, [and] the knowledge of him that was given to those on earth. The spiritual ladder, the Virgin, has been established on earth, for she had her origin from earth. But her head [was lifted up] to heaven—for every woman's head is her husband (Eph 5.23)—but since this woman knew no man, God the Father served as her head, having dealings with her through the Holy Spirit and sending forth his own Son and Word, that all-powerful force, as it were, a divine, spiritual seed. For with the Father's good will, it was not by a natural union but from the Holy Spirit and the Virgin Mary that the Word, without change and in a manner above the laws of nature, became flesh and dwelt among us. For the union of God with humanity comes about through the Holy Spirit. Let anyone who can admit this admit it! (Cf. Matt 19.12). Let anyone who has ears to hear, hear it! (Cf. Luke 8.8). Let us go beyond corporeal matters! Divinity is impassible, O men, and he who formerly begot [his Son] impassibly according to his nature, begets the same Son impassibly a second time in accordance with the dispensation. And David, the ancestor of God, is a witness [to this], saying, "The Lord said to me, 'You are my Son; today I have begotten you'" (Ps 2.7). But "today" has no place in the begetting [that took place] before the ages, for this was outside of time.

4   Today the gate that looks eastward, through which Christ will come in and go out (cf. Ezek 44.2–3), has been built, and the gate will be closed; inside it is Christ, "the door of the sheep" (John 10.7),

---

[17]Another possible translation for the adjective συγκαταβατικός would be "condescending," but the connotation of this word in English is perhaps unhelpful.

"his name is Orient" (Zach 6.12),[18] and through him we have gained access to the Father, who is the source of light.[19] Today breezes have begun to blow, foretelling universal joy. Let the heavens rejoice on high[20] and let the earth exult; let the sea of the world be shaken! (Ps 95[96].11). For an oyster is born in her, the one who will conceive in her womb from the heavenly lightning-flash of divinity [173] and will bear the pearl of great price, Christ.[21] From her the King of glory,[22] putting on the purple [robe] of flesh and having dwelt among them, will proclaim deliverance to the captives.[23] Let nature skip [for joy]: for the ewe-lamb, from whom the Shepherd will clothe the sheep and tear off the tunics of ancient mortality,[24] is born. Let virginity dance, since in accordance with Isaiah, the virgin has been born "who will conceive in her womb and shall bring forth a son and they will call his name Emmanuel" (cf. Isa 7.14), that is, "God is with us."

"God is with us." Learn, Nestorians, and be defeated: [learn] that God is with us. He is not a human being, not an ambassador, but he is the Lord himself who will come and save us.[25] "Blessed is he who comes"; "God is the Lord and has appeared to us" (Ps 117[118].26–27).

[18]Both Brenton (LXX) and the NRSV translate this as "Branch," which derives from the Hebrew. The Greek word ἀνατολή means "rising," "dawn," or "east." Cf. Luke 1.78.

[19]Ἀρχίφαντον may be a neologism. See Lampe, 241; Sophocles, 259.

[20]John adds ἄνωθεν here, but adhered more closely to the Septuagint text in the earlier citation of this passage (see above, section 2).

[21]The metaphor of the oyster (Mary) and the pearl (Christ) derives from Syriac liturgical poetry. Ephrem used the image in five hymns on the subject and was followed by other Syriac hymnographers. See S. Brock, *The Luminous Eye. The Spiritual World Vision of St Ephrem the Syrian* (Rome: Corso Vittorio Emmanuele, 1985; rev. ed., Kalamazoo, MI: Cistercian Publications, 1992), 106–8. We also find the metaphor in John of Euboea's homily on the Conception, below, 176. Although the image of the pearl may have numerous references, its mariological significance stems from the ancient belief that it came into existence when lightning struck the oyster in the sea. This signifies the miraculous conception of Christ, who became incarnate through the interaction of opposites, or disparate elements such as fire and water.

[22]See Ps 23(24).8.

[23]Isa 61.1; cited in Luke 4.18.

[24]See Gen 3.22.

[25]Cf. Isa 63.9.

Let us gather for a feast[26] on the nativity of the Theotokos. Rejoice, Anna, "barren one who does not bear; break forth and shout, you who have not been in labor!" (Isa 54.1). Exult, Joachim, since from your daughter "a child has been born for us and given to us," and "his name is called 'Messenger of great counsel'" (Isa 9.6), [that is to say], of universal salvation, "Mighty God."[27] Let Nestorius be put to shame and let him place a hand upon his mouth. The child is God; how could she who gave birth to him not be Theotokos? "If one does not confess the holy virgin to be Theotokos, he is separated from divinity." The oration is not mine and yet it is my oration, for I have received this most theological inheritance from the theologian Father, Gregory.[28]

5 O blessed and wholly undefiled couple, Joachim and Anna! You were known by the fruit of your womb just as the Lord says somewhere, "You will know them by their fruits" (Matt 7.16). Your conduct was pleasing to God and worthy of the one who was born from you. For having conducted yourselves discreetly and piously, you offered up the precious vessel[29] of virginity who was a virgin before giving birth, a virgin during the birth-giving, and a virgin after having given birth;[30] [174] she alone is virgin and ever-virgin; she alone forever remains a virgin in mind and soul and body. It was indeed necessary that virginity, having sprouted forth from discre-

[26]Cf. Ps 117(118).27.

[27]Cf. Dan 9.4, etc.

[28]Cf. Gregory of Nazianzus, Letter 101, PG 37, 177C. The text in Migne in fact reads, "If someone does not uphold that the holy Mary is Theotokos, he is separated from divinity." This is a classic citation of Gregory the Theologian, exemplifying his orthodox view of Mary's role in Trinitarian and christological doctrine.

[29]On the epithet κειμήλιον to describe the Theotokos, see Constas, *Proclus of Constantinople*, 149.

[30]This represents a clear statement of the doctrine of the Theotokos as "ever-Virgin," which was officially affirmed at the fifth ecumenical council of Constantinople in 553. The Church Fathers were not completely in agreement about Mary's virginity before, during, and after the birth of Christ until about the fifth century. See H. Graef, *Mary: A History of Doctrine and Devotion* (London: Sheed & Ward, 1963; repr. 1987), 38–114.

tion should produce the unique and only-begotten Light in bodily form, who begets not, but who is ever begotten, and whose only distinguishing characteristic is to be begotten, with the goodwill of the One who begot him without a body.

O, by how many marvels and by what alliances has this little daughter become a workshop![31] Offspring of sterility, virginity that bears a child, a mixture of both divinity and humanity, of suffering and impassibility, of life and death, as if [for him] the inferior had been vanquished by the greater in all things! And all these things, O Master, are for the sake of my salvation! You so loved me that you brought about this [salvation], not by means of angels,[32] nor by any creature, but, just as in the first creation, you worked with your own hand [my] regeneration. And so I dance and boast and rejoice; I return again to the source of the miracles and, filled with the stream of happiness, I again pluck the harp of the Spirit and sing a divine hymn of the nativity.

6   O most chaste pair of rational turtle-doves[33] Joachim and Anna! Having kept the law of nature, chastity, you were deemed worthy of things that surpass nature; you have given birth for the world to a Mother of God[34] who knows no husband. Having conducted yourselves piously and blessedly in human nature, you have now given birth to a daughter who surpasses angels and has dominion over the angels. O most beautiful and sweet little daughter! O lily among thorns engendered from a most noble and regal Davidic root! Through you royalty has enriched the priesthood. Through you has come about a change of law[35] and the spirit which was hidden

---

[31]For the epithet ἐργαστήριον, see Constas, *Proclus of Constantinople*, 149–50.

[32]Cf. Isa 63.9.

[33]Cf. Lev 5.7; 12.8. Cited in Luke 2.24.

[34]Note the use of the epithet μήτηρ Θεοῦ here. I. Kalavrezou argues that the use of such terms as "Mother of God" (μήτηρ Θεοῦ, θεομήτηρ or θεομήτωρ) only developed in the course of, or after, the period of Iconoclasm. See I. Kalavrezou, "When the Virgin Mary Became *Meter Theou*," *DOP* 44 (1990): 165–72.

[35]Cf. Heb 7.12.

beneath the letter has been revealed, for the dignity of the priesthood has passed from the tribe of Levi to that of David. O rose which has sprung from Judaic thorns and [175] which has filled everything with divine perfume! O daughter of Adam and Mother of God! Blessed are the loins and the womb from which you sprouted forth! Blessed are the arms that carried you and the lips which tasted your pure kisses—the lips only of your parents that you might always be a virgin in every way! Today is the beginning of salvation for the world. "Cry aloud to the Lord, all the earth, praise and exult and sing psalms!" (Ps 97[98].4). Lift up your voice, "Lift it up, fear not!" (Isa 40.9). For a Mother of God, from whom the Lamb of God who takes away the sin of the world has been pleased to be born, has been born for us in a holy sheepfold.[36]

Skip, mountains,[37] rational natures, reaching up to the height of spiritual contemplation![38] For the most manifest mountain of the Lord is born, which surpasses and transcends every hill and every mountain, [that is to say], the height of men and of angels, from which Christ the cornerstone (Eph 2.20) was pleased to be cut bodily without hands (cf. Dan 2.34,45); the one hypostasis which joins together things that were divided—both divinity and humanity, angels and men, those who came from gentiles and the corporeal Israel—[all were joined] into one spiritual Israel.[39] "Mountain of God, rich mountain, curdled mountain, rich mountain, the mountain which God has been pleased to dwell in. The chariot of God is ten-thousandfold, with the divine grace of rejoicing ones" (cf. Ps

[36]The tradition that Mary was born near the "probatic" pool by the Sheep Gate in Jerusalem (John 5.2), where her parents had a house, appeared early although it is not attested in the New Testament or the *Protevangelion* of James. In the fifth century, a church was built at this site to commemorate the Virgin's nativity. See H. Vincent and F.-M. Abel, *Jérusalem: recherches de topographie, d'archéologie et d'histoire*, vol. 2 (Paris: J. Gabalda, 1926), 2:669–76. From the sixth century onwards, the event was celebrated at this spot with a reading from the *Protoevangelion*. See G. Garitte, *Le calendrier palestino-géorgien du Sinaiticus 34 (Xe siècle)* (Brussels: Société des Bollandistes, 1958), 324, ff.

[37]Cf. Ps 113(114).4.
[38]Cf. Isa 40.4.
[39]Cf. Eph 2.14–22; 1 Cor 10.17.

67[68].16–18), I mean cherubim and seraphim! Summit more holy
than Sinai, which is covered not by smoke, nor shadow, nor tempest,
nor fearful fire, but by the shining illumination of the all-holy Spirit!
For there the Word of God wrote a law on tablets of stone, [using] the
Spirit as a finger[40]; but in this [Virgin], the Word himself has been
made flesh by [the action of] the Holy Spirit and by her blood, and
he has given himself to our nature as the most efficacious medicine
of salvation. There it was manna, [176] here the One who gave the
sweetness of manna [is contained] in her. Let the celebrated tabernacle which Moses constructed in a desert with all manner of very
precious materials, and the [tabernacle] of the patriarch Abraham
before that, give way to the living and rational tabernacle of God. For
she was the receptacle not just of the activity of God, but essentially
of the hypostasis of the Son of God. Let a tabernacle that was entirely
covered with gold recognize that it cannot compare with her, along
with a golden jar which contained manna, a lampstand, a table, and
all the other objects from long ago.[41] For they have been honored as
her types, as shadows of a true archetype.

7   Today the Word of God, who makes all things [and] whom the
Father emitted[42] from his heart, has fashioned a new book which will
be written on by the tongue of God (cf. Ps 44[45].2), as if by a pen[43]
which is the Spirit. This [book] was given to a man who knew letters, but who did not read it (cf. Ps 44[45].2; Isa 29.11–12). For Joseph
did not know Mary or the power of the mystery itself. O most holy
little daughter of Joachim and Anna: you escaped the notice of the
powers and principalities and "the flaming arrows of the evil one"

[40]See above, note 6.

[41]These are the objects contained in the tabernacle, which God commanded
Moses to build. They represent classic types for the Mother of God, conveying both
her sanctity and her role as a container or vessel for the divine presence. See Exod
25–27.

[42]The verb ἐξερεύγομαι, which usually means "vomit forth" or "belch," is used in
connection with the emission of the Logos from the Father by Theophilus of Antioch,
Ad Autolycum 2.10 and a few other patristic writers. Cf. Lampe, 495.

[43]The word κάλαμος here refers to a pen made of reed.

(Eph 6.16); you dwelt in the bridal chamber of the Spirit and were preserved intact to become the bride of God and Mother of Son of God by nature! O most holy little daughter: while still carried in your mother's arms you were a source of fear to all the rebellious powers! O most holy little daughter: you were nourished on breast-milk and surrounded by angels! O little daughter beloved of God, the glory of those who bore you: generation after generation blesses you, as you most truthfully stated! (Cf. Luke 1.48). O little daughter who is worthy of God! The beauty of human nature! The restoration of Eve our first mother—for through your child-bearing, she who fell has been restored! The adornment of women! For if the first Eve fell into transgression and "death entered in" (cf. Rom 5.12; Wis 2.24) through her when she acted with the snake against our first father, yet Mary, obedient to the divine will, deceived the deceitful snake and introduced immortality into the world.

[177] O ever-virginal little daughter who needed no man to conceive! He who has an eternal Father was borne in the womb by you! O earth-born little daughter who carried the Creator in your God-bearing[44] arms! The ages competed as to which one would be exalted by your birth, but God's will, which had been determined beforehand, defeated the competition of the ages—God having created the ages [in any case]—and the last became first[45] and were in happy possession of your nativity. Truly you became more precious than the whole of creation. For from you alone the Maker received a share, [that is], the first-fruit of our dough. For his flesh is from your flesh, and his blood is from your blood, and God suckled milk from your breasts, and your lips were united with the lips of God. O incomprehensible and ineffable matters! The God of all things, having known in advance your worth, loved you; and because of this love, he predestined you,[46] and "at the end of times" (1 Pet 1.20) he brought you into being and revealed you as Theotokos, Mother, and Nurse of his own Son and Word.

[44]This word, θεογενικαῖς, may be a neologism. See Lampe, 624.
[45]Cf. Heb 1.2.
[46]Cf. Rom 8.12.

8 They say therefore that opposites are cures for opposites, but opposites do not come out of opposites. Even if each thing has sprung up as a tissue of opposites, it has sprung from a superfluity [of these] in its source. For just as sin, by bringing about death for me through that which is good, [reveals itself] as sinful to an extreme degree, so does the Cause of good things bring about for us by means of opposites that which has sprung up. "For where sin increased, grace abounded all the more" (Rom 5.20). For if we had preserved our first fellowship with God, we would not have been deemed worthy of the greater and more miraculous one.[47] And now, when we were deemed unworthy of the former fellowship since we had not preserved what we had received, we have both found mercy in God's sympathy and been received yet again, with the result that the fellowship became secure. For he who has received us again is able to preserve undivided unity.

For then the whole world, having fornicated, continued to fornicate (cf. Hos 1.2), and the people of the Lord were led astray "by the spirit of fornication" from the Lord their God (Hos 4.12), who had taken possession of them [178] "with a mighty hand and with a high arm" and led them by means of signs and miracles out of the Pharaoh's "house of slavery" (cf. Exod 13.14; Deut 4.34; Ps 135[136].12; Jer 39.21), and led them through the Red Sea, and "guided them with a cloud by day and all the night with a light of fire" (Ps 77[78].14). And their heart turned towards Egypt and the people of the Lord became not his people, while he who was merciful became unmerciful, and he who was beloved was no longer loved.[48] It is for this reason that a Virgin is now born as an adversary of the ancestral

---

[47]The theology of atonement in this passage is subtle and the preacher expresses it in a complex way. The underlying idea is that by experiencing sin and corruption, humanity has arrived at a higher state, with a better understanding of true goodness, than it would have done without experiencing the Fall. For further reflections on this subject, see John of Damascus, *Expositio fidei* 25, Kotter, *Die Schriften* 2, 71–4; Louth, *St John Damascene*, 131–2. I am grateful to Father Andrew Louth for providing me with these references.

[48]Cf. Hos 2.25; Rom 9.25; 1 Pet 2.10.

fornication, and she is given as bride to God and bears the mercy of God. And the people of God, who formerly were not his people, are re-established; he who was merciful became merciful, and he who was beloved came to be loved.[49] For indeed the beloved Son of God, in whom he was well pleased,[50] is born from her!

9 "A luxuriant vine" (Hos 10.1)[51] has sprouted from Anna and bloomed with a cluster of grapes of sweetness,[52] a drink of nectar for those who dwell on earth which wells up into eternal life. Joachim and Anna have sown in themselves [a source] leading to righteousness and harvested a fruit of life.[53] They have illumined in themselves a light of knowledge and have sought out their Lord; and an offspring of righteousness has come to them. Let the earth and children of Zion take courage! "Rejoice in the Lord your God" since "a wilderness has budded"; a barren woman has born her fruit![54] Joachim and Anna, like spiritual mountains, "have dropped sweetness" (Joel 3.18). Be glad, most blessed Anna, for you have born a female [child]. This female [child] will be Mother of God, gateway of light and source[55] of life, and she will do away with the accusation against the female sex. "The rich of the people shall supplicate the person" (cf. Ps 44[45].13) of this female. Kings of nations will venerate this female, offering gifts. You will lead this female to God, the Universal King, as if "robed in golden-tasselled garments" (Ps 44[45].14), which are the well-ordered comeliness of her virtues, and adorned in the grace of the Spirit whose glory is within. For whereas the husband who comes from outside represents the glory of every

---

[49]See above; cf. Hos 2.25; Rom 9.25; 1 Pet 2.10.

[50]Cf. Matt 3.17; Mark 1.11; Luke 3.22.

[51]Cf. also Ps 127(128).3.

[52]Cf. Isa 65.8; Num 13.23.

[53]Cf. Hos 10.12; Isa 61.11.

[54]Cf. Joel 2.21– 23.

[55]I prefer the reading πηγή (source) here, found in two manuscripts and in Voulet's edition, since it varies the vocabulary; Kotter, however, suggests the reading πύλη ("gate").

woman, the glory of the Theotokos is from within, [since it is] the fruit of her womb.

[179] O desired and thrice-blessed female! "Blessed are you among woman and blessed is the fruit of your womb!" (Luke 1.42). O female, daughter and mother of the King, daughter of King David and Mother of God, the Universal King. O divine, living image in whom God the Creator has rejoiced, possessing a mind which is governed by God and which is devoted to God alone, whose whole aspiration has been directed towards that which alone is desirable and worthy of love and whose anger is directed only against sin and against him who engendered it, [offering] a life that is better than [human] nature! For you did not live for yourself, just as you were not born for your own sake. Hence you lived for God, on whose account you have come into life, in order that you may assist in the salvation of the whole world, [and] in order that the ancient plan of God for the incarnation of the Word and for our deification may be fulfilled through you. [Your] appetite is to feed on the divine words and to be fattened on them, like "a fruitful olive in the house of God" (Ps 51[52].10), like a "tree planted by the streams of waters" (Ps 1.3; cf. Rev 22.2) of the Spirit, like a tree of life, which gave its fruit at the time predetermined by God, [fruit which is] the incarnate God, the eternal life of all things. You draw on every thought that is nourishing and useful for the soul, but you reject every one that is superfluous and harmful for the soul before even tasting it. Your eyes are "continually before the Lord" (Ps 24[25].15), seeing eternal and unapproachable light (cf. 1 Tim 6.16). Your ears hear the divine words and delight in the harp of the Spirit; through them the Word entered that he might become flesh. Your nostrils are charmed with the scent of the Bridegroom's ointments, who is himself a divine ointment which is willingly poured out to anoint his own humanity, for "Your name is ointment poured out," says Scripture (Song 1.2). Your lips praise the Lord and are attached to his lips. Your tongue and throat discern the words of God and are filled with divine sweetness (cf. Ps 118[119].103). Your heart is pure and unblemished, seeing and desiring the unseen God.

A womb in which the Uncontained dwelt and [180] breasts of milk from which God, the little child Jesus, was nourished! Ever-virginal gateway of God! Hands which carried God and knees, a throne that is higher than the cherubim, through which "weak hands and feeble knees" (Isa 35.3) were strengthened! Feet which were guided by the law of God as by a lamp of light,[56] and which run behind him without turning back until they have drawn the beloved One back to the one who loves him. Her whole being is the bridal chamber of the Spirit; her whole being is a city of the living God which "the flowings of the river gladden" (Ps 45[46].5); [that is] floods of the gifts of the Holy Spirit. She is "all fair," entirely the "companion" of God (cf. Song 4.7; 5.16). For she who was raised above the cherubim and the seraphim, as a transcendent being, was called "companion of God."

10 O marvel above all marvels! A woman has become higher than the seraphim since God has been seen "made a little less than angels"! (Cf. Ps 8.6). Let the most wise Solomon be silent and let him not say, "There is nothing new under the sun" (cf. Eccl 1.9).[57] O Virgin full of divine grace, holy temple of God which the Spiritual Solomon, Prince of Peace, constructed and inhabited; you are not adorned with gold and lifeless stones, but in place of gold you shine with the Spirit. Instead of precious stones you have Christ, "the pearl above price" (Matt 13.46), the coal of divinity (cf. Isa 6.6–7). Beg that it may touch our lips so that purified, we may praise him together with the Father and the Spirit, crying, "Holy, holy, holy, Lord God of Hosts!" (Isa 6.3), one divine nature in three hypostases.[58]

Holy God: who is Father, well pleased in you[59] and in the accomplishment from you of the mystery which he had determined before

---

[56]Cf. Ps 118(119).105.

[57]Note that this wording represents a variation from the Septuagint.

[58]This passage evokes the allusion to Isa 6:3 which is made in the Anaphora of the Divine Liturgy of St John Chrysostom. See *The Orthodox Liturgy* (Oxford: Oxford University Press, 1982), 121.

[59]Cf. Matt 3.17; Mark 1.11; Luke 3.22.

the ages.[60] Holy, Strong: the Son of God and Only-begotten God, who has brought you forth today as first-born from a barren mother in order that, since he himself is Only-begotten from the Father and "First-born of all creation" (Col 1.15), he might be born from you a virgin mother as only son, "first-born among many brethren" (Rom 8.29), like us since he partook of flesh and blood from you (cf. Heb 2.14). But he did not bring you forth from a father or from a mother alone, in order that to the Only-begotten alone should be reserved [the title] of Only-begotten in every way: for he alone is [181] Only-begotten from the Father alone and alone [born] from a mother alone. Holy Immortal: the all-holy Spirit, who with his own divine dew kept you unharmed from the divine fire. For this is what the bush of Moses hinted at in advance.

11   Hail, sheep-pool,[61] most holy precinct of the Mother of God! Hail, sheep-pool, ancestral abode of the queen! Hail, sheep-pool, which once was the enclosure for Joachim's sheep but now is the heaven-imitating[62] Church for Christ's rational flock! Once a year you received a visit by the angel of God, who troubled the water, strengthening and healing one man from the illness that paralysed him (cf. John 5.4), whereas now you contain a multitude of heavenly powers who sing hymns with us to the Mother of God, the source of miracles [and] spring of universal healing. [No longer] do you accept a "ministering angel" (cf. Heb 1.14), but rather "the Angel of Great Counsel" (Isa 9.6), dropping noiselessly onto a fleece as a rain of beneficence (cf. Ps 71[72].6), and upon all nature which was sick and inclined towards corruption, as he restored [it] to health which is free of illness and to life without age. Through him the paralytic [who lay] in you has "leaped like a hart!" (Isa 35.6). Hail, honored sheep-pool, may your grace be multiplied!

<hr />

[60]Cf. 1 Cor 2.7.

[61]See n. 6.

[62]The Greek word οὐρανομίμητος may be a neologism. Lampe cites this passage for the meaning of the word, 978.

Hail, Mary, sweetest little daughter of Anna! For my desire draws me towards you again. How shall I portray your most pious bearing, your robe, your gracious countenance? [You possessed] mature judgement in a youthful body. Your modest dress escaped all softness and delicacy. Your gait was pious and undisturbed, free from foolish ostentation. Your manner was austere,[63] but mixed with gaiety; you were unapproachable by men—a witness to this is the fear that came over you at the unaccustomed address of the angel. [You were] docile and obedient towards your parents, while your humble mind was engaged in the highest contemplation. Your cheerful speech came forth from a soul that was free of anger.[64] And what other dwelling-place could be worthy of God? All the generations bless you deservedly as chosen glory of the human race. You are the boast of priests, support of emperors, hope of Christians, fertile plant of virginity! For through you [182] the beauty of virginity has been spread abroad. "Blessed are you among women and blessed is the fruit of your womb" (Luke 1.42). Those who confess you as Theotokos have been blessed and those who deny you have been cursed!

12 O holy couple, Joachim and Anna, accept from me this birthday oration! O daughter of Joachim and Anna and lady, accept an oration from one who is a sinful servant but who is on fire with love and reverence, and who has clung to you alone as hope of joy, supporter of life, mediator towards your Son, and firm pledge of

---

[63]The participle ἐστυμμένον from the verb στύφω is unusual: according to L&S it refers to something drawn in tight: hence "astringent," "austere," or even "harsh."

[64]It is unusual to find a passage such as this, praising the personal qualities and asceticism of the Mother of God, in middle and later Byzantine homilies and hymns. Such discussions appear occasionally in fourth-century writings on the Theotokos, but were not emphasized in liturgical praise from about the fifth-century onwards. Texts of other genres, such as the ninth-century *Life of the Virgin Mary*, written by Epiphanios, monk of the Monastery of Kallistraton, do, on the other hand, deal with her holy way of life. See Graef, *Mary. A History of Doctrine and Devotion*, 48–55; Epiphanios, *De vita b. Virginis*, PG 120, 186–216.

salvation! May you disperse the burden of my sins and the cloud that overshadows my mind and dissolve my material insensibility! And may you put a stop to my temptations, govern my life in holiness,[65] and lead me by the hand to the blessed state above! May you grant peace to the world and perfect joy and eternal salvation to all the orthodox inhabitants of this city through the prayers of your parents and of the whole body of the Church! Let it be, let it be! "Hail, favoured one, the Lord is with you; blessed are you among women and blessed is the fruit of your womb" (Luke 1.28,42), Jesus Christ, the Son of God. To him be glory with the Father and the Holy Spirit to the infinity of the ages of ages. Amen.

---

[65]The meaning of the adverb αἰσίως is "fittingly" or "auspiciously" (Lampe, 54), but if we follow the meaning of the hymn, "Joyful Light," which speaks of "holy voices" (αἰσίαις φωναῖς), we may arrive at the suggested translation.

On the Nativity I

On the Nativity of the Supremely Holy Theotokos[1]

1 [805] The present festival is for us the beginning of feasts. It represents the first [boundary] of the [feasts] against the Law and the shadows,[2] yet also the entrance of those [that lead] to grace and truth. It is this [first entrance], but also the middle and the last. It has as its beginning the accomplishment of the law; as its middle, the conjunction with high things; and as its end, the manifestation of the truth. "For Christ is the end of the Law" (Rom 10.4), who does not so much lead us away from the letter as lead us into the Spirit. For this is the completion, even as he, the Giver of the Law, having concluded all things, transferred the letter to the Spirit after having recapitulated everything in himself and reconciled the law with grace.[3] And having subjugated the one, he joined the other onto it harmoniously.

---

[1] *CPG* 8170; *BHG^a* 1082, *BHG^n* 1082a; A. Gallandi, ed., PG 97, 805–20.

[2] The word σκιά may also mean "type" or "foreshadowing." In this context it would appear to have a negative connotation with regard to the law of the old covenant.

[3] On the doctrine of recapitulation, see J. Behr, *The Way to Nicaea, Formation of Christian Theology* (Crestwood, NY: SVS Press, 2001), 1:123–4, 126–30. Irenaeus of Lyon first developed this concept, using the Pauline understanding of the term ἀνακεφαλαίωσις (cf. Eph 1.10), as well as the rhetorical meaning of the word, as "a summing up" or "recapitulation," with reference to the renewal of humankind and creation through Christ's Incarnation, which "recapitulated" the events in Genesis. See also A. Rousseau and L. Doutreleau, eds. and trans., *Irénée de Lyon: Contre les heresies*, esp. III. 22–23 (SC 211; Paris: Éditions du Cerf, 1974), 431–69; J. Behr, trans., *St Irenaeus on the Apostolic Preaching* (Crestwood, NY: SVS Press, 1997), esp. 60–62; D. Minns, *Irenaeus* (London: Georgetown University Press, 1994), 92–94.

He did not mix the individual qualities of one with the other, but in a manner entirely fitting for God, he transferred what had been burdensome, slavish, and subordinate into lightness and freedom, that we might no longer be enslaved under the elements of the universe (cf. Gal 4.3; Col 2.8, 20), as the Apostle says, or be fastened in a yoke of servitude to the letter of the Law. For this is the culmination of Christ's good works on our behalf. This is the manifestation of the mystery; [808] this is the nature which has been renewed,[4] [to become both] God and man, and the deification of the acquisition [of human nature]. But for such a bright and most splendid sojourn of God with humankind [to take place], it was entirely necessary for there to be a joyful introduction through which the great gift of our salvation advances. The present festival is the prologue that contains the nativity of the Theotokos. But it [also contains] the conclusion, [that is], the renunciation [which consists] in the union of the Word with flesh, according to which the newest expression of all things is proclaimed continually in miracles, even as it remains difficult to grasp and to understand how much that which is being revealed, is hidden, and that which is being hidden, is revealed.[5]

2   Henceforth, then, this first day of the feasts, which is graced by God, bearing the light of virginity above its head and gathering as its crown as much as possible from the untouched flowers of Scripture's spiritual meadows, offers creation a new joy. Have courage, it says, this festival is a birthday and a remodeling of the race. For a Virgin now is born and nursed and molded; and a Mother is prepared for God, the All-Ruler of the ages. And this has summoned the spiritual spectacle for us out of David [and] with David. For she, as divine

---

[4]The text has κενωθεῖσα, but I have adopted the reading καινωθεῖσα suggested by Gallandi.

[5]The syntax of this rather involved sentence is difficult and I have paraphrased it somewhat in order to render it understandable in English. The final clause reveals Andrew's love of rhetorical tropes: here he employs antithesis, chiasm, and homoioteleuton in order to express the paradox: ὅσῳ κρύπτεται φανερούμενον, καὶ ὅσῳ φανεροῦται κρυπτόμενον.

Mother, has set forth[6] her own God-given birth, while he indicated the good inheritance of the race and the utterly new relationship of God with humankind. O, what a miracle! She mediates between the height of divinity and the humility of flesh, and becomes Mother of the Creator, while [David] prophesies what is to come as if it were already present and with an oath receives from God the glorious continuance and preservation of the race from [his] loins. The mystery of the day must therefore be suitably celebrated and speeches themselves must be bestowed on the Mother of the Word since nothing is so pleasing to her as speech and the honor of speeches.[7] Thus there will be a double advantage for us in composing [an oration], [809] [first] that it will lead us to the truth and [second] that it will lead [us] away from the legal slavery and way of life [that resides] in the letter.

How and in what way? When the shadow clearly withdraws at the arrival of the light and grace substitutes freedom from the letter, the present festival stands in the middle, joining together[8] the truth of typological symbols and substituting new things for the old.[9] And in this connection, Paul, the divine trumpet of the Spirit, cried aloud, saying, "If anyone is in Christ, there is a new creation," [and] you are renewed. "The old things have passed away; behold, all things have become new!" (cf. 2 Cor 5.17).[10] For since "the law made nothing perfect [and] there is the introduction of a better hope, through which we approach God" (Heb 7.19), the truth of grace has clearly shone forth. The Giver of the Law, having ineffably brought

[6]The verb προτίθημι is frequently used in liturgical contexts to mean a "setting forth" in offertory. For patristic references, see Lampe, 1190. Here the participle is active, so the Mother of God has "set forth" her own nativity as an offering.

[7]It is impossible to render in English the wordplay involving the Greek word λόγος in this sentence. Andrew uses it to indicate the Word (Christ) and his own speech or homily.

[8]ἀντιπαραζεύγνυσα may be a neologism. See Lampe, 156; Sophocles, 186.

[9]Note this very interesting statement on the importance and meaning of typology.

[10]The interjection of the imperative ἀνακαινίζεσθε here may represent a faulty recollection of the biblical text, a variant reading, or a gloss by the preacher.

himself into emptiness, has providentially come forth as a man that
he may fill up what was lacking and replace what was worse with
better and more perfect things. This indeed is what the lofty John,
the theologian of the Word [named] Thunder would like to indicate most clearly, saying, "From his fullness we have all received,
grace upon grace" (John 1.16). For when he was emptied, and then
miraculously took our form from us, we received completion and
were enriched with the deification that was bestowed in place of
the dough which had been received. Therefore let all things rejoice
together today and let nature skip: "Let heaven rejoice above and
let the clouds rain righteousness!" (Isa 45.8); let the mountains drop
sweetness and the hills exultation![11] For the Lord had mercy on his
people, "having raised the horn of our salvation in the house of his
servant David" (Luke 1.69), [namely] that supremely unblemished
and unwedded Virgin, from whom [came] Christ, the salvation and
the expectation of the nations. Let every right-judging soul therefore now dance, and let nature invite creation to its own renewal
and remaking! Let barren women quickly come running, for the
childless and barren woman has brought to birth the child of God
who is a Virgin! Let mothers skip, for the mother without offspring
has born the incorruptible mother and virgin! Let virgins rejoice,
for the earth without seed has ineffably born the One [who came]
changelessly from the Father! Let women applaud,[12] for a woman,
who once rashly brought about the origin of sin, has now ushered
in the beginning of salvation![13] And she who once was condemned,
has now been shown forth as God's chosen one,[14] [she, the] unwed-

[11]Cf. Amos 9.13; Joel 3.14. Andrew appears to have used these texts for inspiration, but to have changed the wording slightly.

[12]I have followed the Latin translation in emending κρατείτωσαν to κροτείτωσαν
("let them applaud").

[13]While this passage might represent a genuine reference to Andrew's audience,
it is more likely a rhetorical topos since such calls to various groups of worshippers
commonly appears in festal homilies. See, for example, Proclus, Homily I.i.13–14 in
Constas, *Proclus of Constantinople*, 137.

[14]The Greek provides here a rhythmic, antithetical balance in the phrases: ". . .
καὶ ἡ πάλαι κατάκριτος, ἐδείχθη θεόκριτος."

ded mother and restoration of the race, who has been singled out for the Creator.[15]

3   Let all creation therefore sing and dance and let it introduce with this something of those things worthy of the day! Let there be one common festival today of heavenly and earthly things and let every compound structure that exists both on earth and in a heavenly manner join in the feasting![16] For today the created precinct of the Creator of all things has been established, and the creature is newly prepared as divine abode for the Creator.[17] Today the nature that was formerly turned to earth takes on the beginning of deification, and the dust that has been exalted is urged to return to the glory that is on high. Today [812] Adam, presenting [her] out of us and on our behalf as first-fruit to God, dedicates Mary, she indeed who was not mixed with the whole dough; through her is bread made for the remodeling of the race. Today the great bosom of virginity is revealed and the

[15]This call to women of various categories to rejoice at the birth of the Virgin Mary recalls innumerable other festal homilies which use this rhetorical device. In most examples, all ranks of men and women are called to the festival and exhorted to rejoice. See, for example, Proclus's fourth homily on the Theotokos in Constas, *Proclus of Constantinople*, 229, II.31–231, II.56. On the concept that Mary redeemed all women from the sin conferred on them by Eve, see Proclus's fifth homily in Constas, *Proclus of Constantinople*, 261, III.87–263, III.108.

[16]It is likely that Andrew means humanity here. The idea that human beings are compound entities, composed of a material body and a spiritual soul, goes back to Platonic philosophy and was accepted by the early Christian fathers. In opposition to Gnosticism, both parts of human nature were seen as God's creation and as capable of deification and salvation. See, for example, Gregory of Nyssa, *De hominis opificio* 27.5, ff, PG 44, 228A, C; 229A; idem, *Oratio catechetica* 16, PG 45, 52B. Andrew of Crete explores the concept more thoroughly in his homily, *De humana vita et de defunctis*, PG 97, 1268–1301 (*CPG* 8192). He writes, "Man, that most versatile and all-resourceful instrument, the easily consumed dough, the boundary of life and death, the intellectual compound (σύγκριμα) and agreement (σύνθημα) in matter . . . ," PG 97, 1269A. For the philosophical background of this homily, see T. Nissen, "Diatribe und Consolatio in einter christlicher Predigt des achten Jahrhunderts," *Philologus* 92 (1937): 177–98, 382–85.

[17]Andrew's use of Classical vocabulary, e.g. τέμενος, ἐναύλισμα, etc., associated with pagan religion to express the preparation of the Virgin as God's dwelling-place, is striking here.

church in bridal fashion puts on the inviolate pearl of true incorruption. Today the pure nobility of humankind takes back the gift of the first divine creation and restores it to itself; and nature, offering to the mother of the One who is fair, who has just been born, the splendor of beauty which evil's ignoble nature made dull, receives a formation which is best and most pleasing to God.[18] And the formation authoritatively becomes a summons, and the summons [becomes] deification, and this [is] the likeness in the beginning. Today the barren woman is found to be a mother [in a manner] beyond her hopes, and the mother of a fatherless child, springing forth from a sterile womb, sanctifies the offspring of nature. Today the attractive dye of the divine purple has been colored and the impoverished nature of men is clothed with regal dignity. Today the Davidic shoot has sprung forth according to prophecy, since it was the evergreen rod of Aaron, and it has flowered into a rod of power for us, namely Christ. Today a virgin maiden comes forth out of Judah and David, affirming the aspect of kingship and priesthood in the One who appointed Aaron as priest[19] according to the rank of Melchizedek.[20] Today grace has made white the mystical ephod of divine priesthood that, as a type, it wove in advance with Levitical seed,[21] along with the regal purple robe which God made purple with Davidic blood. And in a word, today the reshaping of our nature begins, and the world, which had grown old, takes up a most God-like composition, receiving the beginnings of a second divine modeling.

4 For after the first formation of humankind had been fashioned from pure and undefiled earth, [813] nature concealed [our] intrinsic

---

[18]The syntax and vocabulary of this sentence are very involved: the imagery plays on the nobility of the Godly inheritance.

[19]The verb ἱεροτεύω does not appear in dictionaries and thus may be a neologism.

[20]Cf. Ps 109[110].4.

[21]The type of the "ephod" is somewhat unusual, although it appears occasionally in Marian homilies and hymns. See Exod 28.6–14. Cf. Proclus, Homily 6, 17.3; F.J. Leroy, ed., *L'homilétique de Proclus de Constantinople* (Studi e Testi 247; Vatican City: Bibliotheca Apostolica Vaticana, 1967), 322; Germanos, *In Annuntiationem*, Fecioru, "Un nou de predica," 392.19; below, 242.

honor, having been robbed of grace by the lapse of disobedience as
a result of which we were cast out of the life-giving place, and nature
exchanged the joy in paradise for perishable life, so that this became,
as it were, our ancestral heritage, [and] from it came death and hence
the corruption of our race. And then when everyone chose the land
below instead of that above, all hope of salvation was taken away;
nevertheless, nature still needed the help which is on high. There
was no law that could heal the illness, neither natural, nor written,
nor the inspired[22] and conciliating speech of the prophets. Nor did
this [law] know how to correct human nature, and by what means it
might be restored quickly and easily to its former noble state. Now
the Sovereign Artificer[23] of all things, God, has been well pleased to
make manifest one who is like another all-harmonious and newly
created universe and at the same time to hold back for awhile the
misfortune of sin which formerly fell upon [us], through which
[came] death. And so [he has been pleased] to point the way towards
a free and truly passionless new life for those of us who have, as it
were, been reborn by the baptism of divine generation.

5 And so, how would this benevolence, which is great, most
miraculous, and in keeping with divine laws, be introduced on our
behalf, unless God appeared to us in the flesh, and came in accordance with the laws of nature, and assented in a new way to dwell,
as he knew how, in accordance with our understanding of things?
In what manner might this be brought to a conclusion, unless a
pure and untouched Virgin first attended to the mystery, bearing
in her womb the One who is above being, according to a law which
transcended the laws of nature? Who could be thought of as this one
except she alone, who was chosen before all generations for the One
who engendered all nature? She is the Theotokos Mary, the name
called by God, from whose womb the Supremely Divine One came

---

[22]I have substituted "inspired" for the more literal "fire-breathing." Cf. 3 Macc
6.34.
  [23]Cf. Ps-Caesarius, *Quaestiones et responsiones* 154, PG 38, 1108 (*CPG* 7482).

forth with flesh, in which, having made [it] into a temple for himself
in a transcendent way, he dwelt as in a tent,[24] since she who bore
him did not carry corruption in her womb, nor had the One whom
she conceived needed seed. For he was God even though he chose to
be born according to the flesh, without travail and without pain, so
that the mother might escape the [pangs] of mothers, miraculously
nourishing with milk the One whom she had produced without
a husband.[25] And the Virgin, bearing an offspring without seed,
remained in purity as a virgin, bearing even after the birth the secure
signs of virginity. In such a way she is fittingly proclaimed "Theotokos," and virginity is magnified, and nativity is venerated, and God
is made one with men, since he appears in the flesh, and the honor
of his own glory is freely bestowed. For in place of the curse of that
first [woman], female nature at once receives correction; just as
[that one] initiated sin, [this one] has brought about the beginning
of salvation.[26]

6 Our discourse has indeed come to its culmination. Hence I
have come forth to you today as celebrator and shining host of this
holy banquet, setting before you the common delight. When the
Redeemer of the race, as I said, decided to show a new [816] birth
and formation [of a female] in place of the former one, just as he

[24]The idea that Christ inhabited Mary's womb only temporarily is conveyed
well by the verb πήγνυμι. The passage also evokes John 1.14: "And the Word became
flesh and lived among us . . . " where the verb is ἐσκήνωσεν, also meaning literally
"he pitched his tent."

[25]The idea that the Virgin's suckling of the Christ child was in some way miraculous is traced in E. Bolman's recent article on images of Mary as Galaktotrophousa in
Coptic art. Bolman cites Clement of Alexandria who wrote in the second century that
the milk in Mary's breasts had its origin in God and not in her own body, since virgins
are incapable of producing milk. The point was taken up by Cyril of Alexandria several centuries later; both sources may well have influenced later Byzantine thought on
the subject. For references, see E. Bolman, "The Enigmatic Coptic Galaktotrophousa,"
in *Images of the Mother of God. Perceptions of the Theotokos in Byzantium* (ed. M. Vassilaki; Aldershot: Ashgate Publishing, 2005), esp. 17–18.

[26]It is impossible to convey in English the play on the Greek words ἐνήρξατο
and ἀπαρξαμένη here.

formerly took mud from virgin, untouched earth and fashioned the first Adam, so now, acting himself on her own flesh instead of another [piece of] earth, as we might say, he selected this pure and supremely unblemished virgin from the whole of nature and made new in her, out of our [substance], that which is ours; so the Fashioner of Adam was called a New Adam in order that the One who is recent and who transcends time might rescue the old [Adam]. But who is she and what parents bore her? Come, let us speak briefly [of this], running through her history as far as we are able.

Well then, she, the boast of all people, was born a daughter of David, and seed of Joachim. [She was] a descendant of Eve, and an offspring of Anna. For Joachim was a gentle, mild man, trained in the laws of God, living in moderation, and faithful to God. But although fulfilling this way of life, he grew old without having a child, for when [his] nature was in its prime he did not possess the reward of offspring. Anna was also a lover of God, and although she was prudent, she remained sterile. She loved her husband, but remained childless, and she concerned herself with nothing else, except that she should honor the law of the Lord. She was pricked daily by the goads of sterility and like all those who suffer sterility, she was distressed, she grieved, [and] she mourned, unable to bear her childlessness. And so Joachim and his wife were consumed with pain since they had no child to uphold the race, while meanwhile the wick of their hope was not finally extinguished, but a prayer was made by each of them that a child might be granted to them for the restoration of their seed. And indeed, emulating the [earlier] Anna who had been heard [by God],[27] they each devoted themselves to the temple. They sought to soften God with supplications, that he might grant an end to childlessness and fruit to sterility; and they did not give up until they might gain that for which they longed. And indeed, they did gain it. For the Giver of the gift did not undo the gift of hope. So the power that never lingers came quite soon to those

[27] Cf. 1 Kgdms 1.10.

who implored and entreated the Divine Being. It stimulated him into fruitfulness and her into producing a child; and having meanwhile sprinkled the withered passages of the reproductive organs with the juices of sperm production, it brought them from infertility into productivity.[28] And then, out of unfruitfulness and sterility, like a splendid fruit from watered trees, this wholly unblemished Virgin blossomed forth for us. And the bonds of sterility were released, and prayer was revealed as productive beyond our hopes; the sterile one became the bearer of a child and the barren one was blessed with a fair child.

7   When the one who had germinated the ear of corn[29] of immortality in her womb came forth from her sterile mother, her parents brought her, at the first flowering of her age, and dedicated her to the temple.[30] Then the priest, carrying out the service[31] for her sanctification,[32] as he saw the company of virgins both preceding her and following behind, was utterly delighted and rejoiced, since they were already witnessing the divine, manifest results of the things which

[28]This description of the reproductive process involved in conceiving the Virgin Mary is striking in its graphic realism. The Byzantines, like the Romans, believed that in providing the sperm or seed, the father of a child supplies most of its genetic material. The mother, who nourishes the embryo during its gestation in her womb, adds some elements of herself, mainly through the exchange of blood. See also John of Damascus, *In Nativitatem*, section 2, in Kotter, *Die Schriften* 5, 170; above, 55, n. 8.

[29]This epithet is used frequently by the Fathers to refer to Christ, with reference especially to his immortality. See Lampe, 1255.

[30]The preacher's focus on the Virgin's entrance into the temple in this section of the homily is interesting, as is the fact that no authentic homilies on this subject survive from his pen. It seems possible that the feast of the Entry into the temple (21 November) was not consistently celebrated in churches in the early eighth century, the evidence of Germanos's two homilies notwithstanding. This may also represent evidence this trilogy of sermons was preached in Crete, where the feast was less established, rather than in Constantinople. See above, 24-6, and Chirat, "Les origines de la fête du 21 novembre," for discussion of this question.

[31]The word ἐφημερία is used in the Septuagint for the daily service of the temple. See LXX, 1 Chronicles 9.33, 23: 6. 25: 8; Luke 1. 5, etc.

[32]The word ἱερατεία normally means "priesthood" or "priestly function" (see Lampe, 669); here, however, it seems to refer to the Virgin Mary at her entrance into the temple.

[had existed] only in hope. And he consecrated, like a sacred, acceptable sacrifice, the divine offering to God, [817] having set the great treasure of salvation in the inaccessible reaches of the holy places.[33] In the midst of these, [he caused] the child, who was entering into these, so to speak, like bridal chambers, to be fed on ambrosia as food until the time of the betrothal arrived, [a time] which had been designated before every age by the One who was ineffably produced from her on account of [his] compassion, and by the One who also divinely produced him before all creation and time and temporality, and by his Spirit, who shares his nature and dominion and veneration. For of these [persons] there exists one divinity and nature and kingdom which is not divided or separated or alienated from anything pertaining to itself, except for the distinctive quality of the principal hypostases. It is on this account that, celebrating, I commemorate the feast and pour out libations! And I offer the feast as a gift to the Mother of the Word, since her birth made me aware of the culmination of faith in the Trinity. For whilst the Word which is without beginning and Son brought about his own Incarnation, the Father who begot [him] appeared in agreement, and the Holy Spirit assented in advance, and, as That which is beyond comprehension, sanctified the womb of the one who conceived.

8   But now it is time to question David about what the God of all things, on making this pledge, said to him. Come then, hymn-writer; go, prophet; strike up your lyre;[34] sound the melodies![35] Tell

---

[33] Andrew is referring to the "holy of holies" in the Jewish temple here.

[34] κιννύρα is the word for a Jewish-stringed instrument (kinnor), which was a lyre. Fragments of these instruments have been discovered at Ur and various other sites in Palestine. The kinnor was used to express joy, even at solemn occasions (1 Kgdms 10.5; 2 Kgdms 6.5; Isa 5.12), but never in times of mourning. David is often depicted playing a kinnor, as in a mosaic found in a sixth-century synagogue in Gaza. See Z.M. Szweykowski, "Jewish Music," *The New Grove Dictionary of Music and Musicians*, 9:620.

[35] κροῦμα (κροῦσμα) may also mean "blow," "knock," or the sounding of the simantron in a monastery. However, the meaning "musical note" or "melody" is also given in Lampe, 780.

us clearly, what did the Lord swear to you? What did the Lord swear to me? "Of the fruit of my loins he will place on my throne" (cf. Ps 131[132].11).[36] He swore this to me and he did not deny it. He swore, and he sealed his words with actions. "Have I once sworn," he said, "in my holiness that I will not lie to David? His seed shall endure forever, and his throne as the sun before me, and as the moon that is established forever, and as the faithful witness in heaven." (Ps 88[89].36–38). Having sworn these things, he carried them out, since it is impossible for God to tell a falsehood (Heb 6.18). Behold, then, and see that Christ, my Son, is being proclaimed in the flesh, and my Lord and Son, being venerated, is being hymned, and all the nations venerate him.[37] For they see him enthroned on virginal thrones. Behold, this Virgin has also now been born from our thighs,[38] from whose womb the One who [existed] before the ages, having been made flesh, came forth at the end of the ages, and renewed the composition of the ages.[39] And these things are so.[40]

9 But as for us, the people of God, a saintly company, a holy community,[41] let us celebrate our lineage, let us honor the power of the mystery. Let each, according to the blessing that was given to him, bring to the festival a worthy gift. [Let] fathers [bring] the good inheritance of the race; mothers, the blessing of children. [Let] infertile women [bring] the non-bearing of sin; virgins, double incor-

---

[36]Note how Andrew adapts the quotation so that David, rather than God, is the speaker.

[37]Cf. Ps 71[72].11.

[38]The word used here is μηρός, ὁ, meaning "thigh" or "thigh-bone," rather than the more usual ὀσφῦς, ἡ ("loin" or "loins").

[39]By this Andrew means that the old and the new covenants, encompassing all of the ages, have been brought together into the unified composition that was originally intended.

[40]Andrew's emphasis on the lineage of the Virgin Mary and his eagerness to prove her descent from David also appears in his third homily on the Nativity. The fact that the genealogies in Matthew and Luke demonstrate the descent of Christ from David through the male line, ending with Joseph, caused him concern. See also his third sermon on the Nativity of the Theotokos, below.

[41]This passage echoes 1 Pet 2.9–10, but the wording is slightly different.

ruption, I mean both of soul and body. [Let] those who are married [bring] praiseworthy moderation. If one among you is a father, let him imitate the father of the Virgin. Even if he should be childless, let him gather prayer as his harvest, bearing this as the fruit of his God-loving way of life. If one is a nursing mother, let her rejoice with [820] Anna as she suckles her child with prayers after her sterility. If one is a sterile and childless woman who does not possess fruit of a blessing, let her faithfully approach the God-given shoot of Anna, and let her be shorn of her sterility. If one is a pure virgin, let her become a mother of the Word, adorning the condition of her soul in speech. If one is married, let him bring forward spiritual fruit from those [harvests] with which he has been well supplied through prayer. In this way, let rich and poor, "young men and virgins, old men with youths" (Ps 148[149].12), priests and Levites, queens and ruling ladies, all men and women together bring illumination[42] to the maiden and Mother of God and prophetess out of whom came the One of whom the prophet Moses wrote, Christ God, the Truth.

10 Let us advance with the virgins who are running in front; let us enter with them into the holy of holies. For there the swaddling clothes,[43] after birth, after suckling, after infancy, reach puberty at the time of flowering. God prepared her nursery as if it were a bridal chamber, having guarded for himself her sanctity. On this account virgins celebrate, as those around her journey in advance towards the things to come. Next, the daughters of Sion run ahead as if she were a queen, as they lead the way into the fragrance of her perfumes. And all at once, this temple spread wide and did away with[44] its holy gates in order that it might receive the regal glory from

[42]Lampe suggests the meanings "wear bright robes" and "be resplendent" for λαμπροφορέω. I would suggest that a more general meaning of bringing brightness or illumination could be implied here.

[43]The word σπάργανα here, which normally means "swaddling clothes," must refer to the child herself here.

[44]The form ἀνήρπις is unusual, but the nearest possible reading is ἀνήρπισε from ἀναρπάζω. The literal meaning is "to snatch away" or "carry off"; I have surmised

every side. Then, indeed, then, the holy of holies was opened, having enfolded within the inaccessible sanctuaries the all holy Mother of the Holy One. As a new form[45] of nourishment for her, he who after a short time would be fed by her milk, meanwhile nourished the one who would nourish [him], without himself being present.[46] And the Holy Spirit [thus] became the nurse of the Virgin until her manifestation in Israel.[47] When the time of her betrothal arrived and Joseph, the descendent of David, was betrothed to the one who also [was descended] from David, she received the voice of Gabriel instead of seed. She then became pregnant without having experienced intercourse and bore a Son whom no father fertilized. While she remained pure and untouched in her womb, the One who had been born kept safe in her the signs of virginity even after the birth. This is Christ Jesus of Nazareth, who came into the world. He is the true God and Eternal Life. To him be glory and honor and worship, with the Father and the Holy Spirit, now and always, and to the ages of ages. Amen.

---

that Andrew here means that the temple set aside its gates in its eagerness to receive the Virgin Mary.

[45]The Greek word here is πρόσφατος, which according to Lampe, means "recent" or "new," e.g. with respect to creation vis à vis the Son.

[46]The rhetorical device of metaclisis, or the repeated use of the same word in different inflections, is used in this sentence, playing on words that share the same root and meaning, e.g. τρέφω and τροφή. Note also the rather involved antithetical treatment of the Nourisher (Christ) and nourished (Theotokos) who would nevertheless later give birth to and nourish him. The adverb ἀχειροδότως does not appear in the L&S or Lampe, but must literally mean "without using his hands." I have glossed this in the context to the sense "without himself being present" since, according to the Protevangelion of James, the Virgin Mary was fed by the hand of an angel. See Elliott, The Apocryphal New Testament, 60.8.

[47]For ease of understanding, I have kept the past tense throughout this section even though the Greek shifts from past to present in order to emphasize the liturgical immediacy of these events.

ANDREW OF CRETE

On the Nativity II

On the Nativity of Our Supremely Holy Lady, the Theotokos, with proof that she descends from the seed of David[1]

1 [820] Let others provide other explanations of feasts for those who wish them. But as for us, let this [feast] now be set forth that we may praise it: the festival which is now upon us and which has as its subject the pre-eminent Mother of the Word, [the Word] by means of whom the Spirit visits all [human beings] and speeches [821] acquire freedom[2] to speak. Hence, taking up the reins of the speech at the starting-post, I pass beyond the things that have already been stated, being on the one hand held back by fear at talking unworthily on this goal which has been set out, but on the other, impelled by the desire to make it as powerful as it deserves. Yet whatever way I turn, I shall bravely embark upon the speech, bringing the day, which is beautiful, as a defence against my cowardice or impudence.[3] We have

---

[1] *CPG* 8171; *BHG* 1080; ed. A. Gallandi, PG 97, 820–44.

[2] The adjective ἄφετος may mean "loose" or in this context "a letting loose." This could refer already to the metaphor of horse-racing which appears in the next sentence.

[3] The syntax of this clause is somewhat involved and I have emended the punctuation used in Gallandi's edition. The fact that παρρησία, which may also have the positive meaning of "openness" or "freedom of speech" in some contexts, is in the genitive links it with δειλία (cowardice).

in any case already joined in celebrating appropriately the Nativity of
the Theotokos in the speech which came before [this one];[4] myself,
as initiator of the feast, and you, along with the entire transcendent
offering up of praise.[5] We were expectant with Joachim, we ran with
the virgins, we were illumined with David, I mean the patriarch
and king, who was also the ancestor of God with respect to both
[Joachim and Anna][6], and we were brought into the temple with
Mary, the Mother of God; and having visited the inaccessible parts
of the holy places, we partook of the mysteries themselves.[7] And
[let there be] grace to [God] who has glorified his own [people] in
order that he may lead those who were once at a distance back to
himself. For now I consider it not at all discordant or superfluous to
take my speech in a different direction, so that it becomes to some
extent a digression on the good inheritance itself of the race from
which the Virgin comes, and to recount fully those matters which it
is appropriate to describe and in which the present festival delights.
It delights in the things through which the Virgin, out of whom the
supremely divine One supra-essentially came into temporal existence, is revealed as being from the seed of David; [these are matters]
which are as many and of such kinds as God told us about her by
means of law and prophets, and [which he] distinctly announced in
advance throughout the whole of Scripture.

[4]This refers to the previous sermon on the Nativity of the Theotokos which
Andrew probably just preached. It was customary to deliver three sermons in succession on important feast-days. See Chevalier, "Les trilogies homilétiques."

[5]It is likely that Andrew wishes to imply the participation in liturgy of the
entire heavenly host, as well as of human beings, as expressed in ps-Dionysius the
Areopagite's *Celestial Hierarchy* as well as in other liturgical works.

[6]Andrew is eager here is to establish the Davidic ancestry of both Joachim and
Anna. This proves that Mary, as well as Joseph, is descended from this line.

[7]This mystical language is very typical of Andrew of Crete when he describes
the Christian response to the sacraments or to the apprehension of God by means of
liturgical celebration. In this passage he is describing the encounter with the divine
that Jews would experience on entering the most sacred inner sanctuary of the temple,
an area usually barred to all but the high priest himself. See M. Barker, *The Great High
Priest* (London and New York: T&T Clark, 2003), 146–87.

2 So forthwith, after as much consideration as possible, let us advance to the contests themselves and, using the languages which have developed among the Jews who both formerly and at the present time blaspheme against Christ, let us adduce the section [of Scripture] from its foundations so that a root of bitterness may no longer sprout forth to disturb the flock of the Church.[8] Would it not be very much easier for this to be corrected if there were a precise investigation or enquiry? For it is necessary first, I think, to show forth Christ as Son of God and himself God, [using] the books of Moses, [and to show] that he arose from the [house of] Judah, according to the apostle, and that he appeared as Son of the Virgin, according to the Gospel; so then [it is also necessary] for the One who has brought the prophetic voices into our midst to touch on the highest and most important matters. In this way the Word will have irrefutable and solid [grounding] from everywhere through our accuracy and indeed, the character of our legal antiquity would be preserved unharmed. So then let Jacob of the high ladder, a clear-sighted visionary, come into our midst; and before him, Abraham the patriarch, upon whom and for whom [God enacted his] promises. For Matthew also placed him at the beginning of his evangelical narrative, having first mentioned David in the composition (cf. Matt 1.1). [824] And tracing the genealogy to [David], as each is from his birth, he acknowledged [them] in succession, taking it on again harmoniously to Joseph, the descendent of David. Thus [Matthew] showed that the one who arose out of David was duly prepared in advance by God and betrothed to Joseph, [who belonged to] the house of David, as his kinswoman,[9] in order that according to

[8] It is interesting that Andrew acknowledges here the fact that Jews and Christians share the same Scriptures, and that this can lead to differences of interpretation. The meaning of some of the words in this sentence is obscure; I have paraphrased it somewhat in order to arrive at its sense. The word θρέμμα may mean "creature" or "sheep" (metaphorically used by the Fathers for the Christian flock).

[9] The evangelist Matthew in fact nowhere states that Mary was also descended from David. The information comes from the *Protevangelion* of James, chap. 10, but it is noticeable that Andrew does not refer directly to this source here. It is possible

ancient custom, race might not be mixed with race, or a sceptre despoiled[10] for another sceptre.

3 And so indeed the great wanderer among patriarchs, on being called by God from the land of Haran, was led to gain his promises, the signs of which were not yet even to a small degree anticipated— for things fulfilled in the past are signs of what is to come. And just as he was not deceived in the hope of the covenant, neither did he chance to go astray from his inheritance of land. "For I shall give this land to you and to your seed, said the God of all things to him, for in your seed shall all the races of the earth be blessed" (cf. Gen 15.7; 22.18). For to him, as also to the divine Paul, it seemed that "when God made a promise to Abraham, because he could swear by no one greater, he swore by himself, saying, 'Surely blessing, I will bless you, and multiplying, I will multiply you.' And so," it says, "after he had patiently endured, he obtained the promise" (Heb 6.13–15). But how and in what manner the promises to him led to completion, you may learn from within, considering this with the help of truth. For when God, who had formerly called on Abraham, said to him, "In Isaac shall be called your seed" (cf. Gen 17.16–18), [Abraham], when fully assured, was able to fulfil that which had been promised. And [Abraham] "considered his own body already to be dead, for he was about one hundred years old, and [he also considered] Sarah's womb to be dead" (Rom 4.19). He was not disqualified from God's promise, but instead he was empowered and gave glory in faith to God.

And naturally, he obtained the promise and came into possession of the promised child, the one who had received what was promised;[11] and yet, since he had two sons, he blessed the inheritor of the covenants who had stolen away the promise by a trick with

that he is deliberately vague on account of its apocryphal nature. See Elliott, *The Apocryphal New Testament*, 61.10.

[10]The verb ἐπιφυλλίζω means "to glean grapes in a vineyard" or simply "to gather." See Lam 1.22; 2.20. The sense of "to despoil," which seems to be implied here, also emerges in the biblical use of this word.

[11]The repetition of different forms of ἐπαγγέλλω is deliberate here.

the agreement of the mother; [this was the inheritor] from whom the twelve tribes sprouted vigorously out of different shoots. And from these, God clearly honored and chose the two sceptres, I mean of Levi and of Judah. And while to one had been entrusted, from a long time earlier, the robe of the priesthood, the divine ephod, both the headdress and the ritual gold-plate, as well as the breast-plate engraved with oracles [which represented] a prefiguration of a better priesthood,[12] to the other [was entrusted] the kingly throne, the beautiful diadem, and the surveillance of all the tribes. In addition, the leadership of the people was marked out with chrism. Among these [people], the eternal Child of God [825] and Creator of all eternal things, having appeared in the world in a new fashion by means of flesh, "but not according to the law of the will of the flesh" (Heb 7.16), as the apostle says, came to live. And he gained the rank of both [states of being], not in the human manner, as one would say, by which I mean the visible [signs], since he was acknowledged as priest and king. Rather, "according to a power of everlasting life" (Heb 7.16), he was witnessed by his nature to have the rank that belongs to each, I mean [the rank] of priesthood and of kingship. "For remaining a high priest perpetually, he holds, as a priest, the priestly rank continuously because he remains in [this rank] eternally. Consequently he is able for all time to save those who draw near to God through him, since he always lives to make intercession for them" (Heb 7.24–25).[13] Whereas as King and Ruler of peace, who is also leader in Israel, he is shown not to have sat visibly on the throne of David his father, but in accordance with what is apprehended by the intellect, he ruled eternally over the house of Jacob and never reached the end of kingship. Who would not be surprised, these events being so, that whereas some have written in this way about

[12] By this, Andrew of course means the priesthood of Christ himself. The robe, the ephod, and the other articles mentioned here are all types, but quite unusual ones, which are not often cited in homilies or hymns.

[13] It is interesting to note the way the preacher expounds this passage from Heb 7, separating different sections of the same chapter and incorporating them into his argument.

him, others among them have testified the opposite? For they do not treat him as a successor of David's kingship, nor do they recount that he was seated on David's throne, nor is he even raised to a power of rule equal to Herod or Pontius Pilate. Instead one might attempt to understand these things in the most mystical sense of allegory, as in [the passage], "My kingdom is not of this world" (John 18.36).

4   And now let the great patriarch Jacob come into my presence, recounting matters concerning Christ in a timely fashion. Among them, he set down in advance the things that would befall his sons, beginning with Judah and in a way delineating in him beforehand, as in some very mystical manner of painting, the icon of Christ, with the result that Judah is seen like some body apprehended by the senses, whereas David, like some color, is understood in contemplation.[14] From this it will be possible in all likelihood for us to follow the meaning, discovering that whereas David sprang from the tribe of Judah, Christ came forth from that of David. Since this is clearly shown, we shall find that the Virgin is also from the family of David, who in turn sprang from that of Judah; and if she was in fact produced as an offspring of the same race and the same tribe, then indeed, O best of patriarchs and producer of the most children, come then and tell us, what is the blessed inheritance that you left to your children? What is the portion of each of these [children]? What are the [blessings] that you bestowed on them when you died, and of what kind are they? Yes, says the patriarch, the Spirit distributed appropriately to each of them the things that they deserved, according to the nature and rank possessed by each; and not [deviating] from the aim of providence which directs all things, not one thing has, in my view, been interpreted allegorically. But just as things have been predetermined by [providence], I have with foresight foretold

[14]Andrew emphasises here the parallel that exists between Old Testament types of Christ and painted icons. The passage is interesting because it reveals not only his iconophile leanings, but also his interest in the role of both conceptual and material images in leading the soul to mystical contemplation.

each of them. Therefore let there be [828] Mosaic books for everyone who wishes to take them up into his hands and learn, from the
beginning of the universe itself, about the inheritances of each of the
tribes, which I have depicted in the blessings individually to [Jacob's]
children, as God spoke [about these] in me.[15]

But now we shall be concerned with one tribe through which it is
easy to demonstrate that Christ, who was born in flesh from a Virgin,
was descended from the tribe of Judah in order that every foolish
mouth which does not confess that Christ has come from the seed
of David may be stopped. What then does the one who sees [this]
say? For in that way Scripture knows to call those who are endowed
with intellectual insight. "Judah, your brothers will praise you. Your
hands shall be on the neck of your enemies. The sons of your father
will venerate you. You are a lion's cub, Judah; you have arisen from
a shoot, my son. On falling down you slept like a lion and like a
cub. Who will raise him? A ruler from Judah and a leader from his
thighs will not fail [to appear] until the One who is waiting[16] arrives,
and he is the expectation of the gentiles. Binding his foal to the vine
and his ass's foal to its tendril, he will wash his robe in wine and his
cloak in the blood of grapes. His eyes are joyful from wine and his
teeth are as white as milk" (cf. Gen 49.8–12). Like a navigator, one
must look to whom and when the things [foretold] by prophecy
have been fulfilled.[17] Clearly, I am looking at him, who came forth as
Christ the Savior of us all, through both law and prophets, when as

---

[15]The meaning of this whole paragraph is somewhat obscure. Andrew seems
to be saying that whereas Scripture need not be interpreted allegorically, since proof
of Christ's inheritance may be found by literal understanding, typology provides a
further, deeper layer for its interpretation. The syntax is involved and at times ambigu-
ous, so that this English version should be regarded as an attempt at interpretation
rather than a literal translation.

[16]Literally "stored up."

[17]It is difficult to interpret the place of ναύτης in this sentence, although in
patristic writings it is frequently used metaphorically to indicate the church, or
leaders of the church. If it is acting as the agent of the gerundive σκοπητέον, then
the noun should be in the dative or accusative. It seems likely that the text has been
slightly corrupted here.

supreme God he came in flesh among us who are of dust at the end
of [those] times, wishing to bring to its conclusion the plan that had
been determined for him beforehand [and] eternally, in accordance
with the ineffable good will of the Begetter and of the Spirit who
is akin to him, and arose out of Judah and came forth corporeally
from a Virgin who was of [the house of] David.[18] Indeed, whereas
at that time all his brothers praised him, [now] as many people as
are in affinity with him have partaken of communion with him.
The multitudes who have believed in Christ are boundless, even
surpassing the power of computation; the lofty John intimated this
when he said, "As many as received him, to them he gave power to
become children of God . . . who were born not of blood nor of the
will of flesh, but from God" (John 1.12–13), since he is not ashamed
reasonably to call them even his brothers, nearly sharing their blood
and flesh; [and] Paul, along with David, cries as follows, [as it were]
playing on spiritual reeds.[19] For whereas [the latter] sings, "I shall
report your name to my brothers, I shall praise you in the midst of
the assembly" (Ps 21[22].23), [Paul] cries loudly, "Wherefore in all
things it behoved him to be made like his brethren, that he might
become a merciful and faithful high priest in all things pertaining
to God" (Heb 2.17).[20]

5 [829] Whose hands were once so mightily stretched out on the
back of the enemies unless they were those of Christ? This is how the
great David sings, once again inspired by the Spirit, saying, "And he
smote his enemies in the hinder parts" (Ps 77[78].66), meaning by
"hinder parts" their backs. And elsewhere he made this clear, saying,

---

[18]This sentence demonstrates Andrew's love of long, periodic passages. It is difficult to convey in English the well constructed syntax of the Greek, which allows no
confusion in the theology that it conveys.

[19]The Greek word δόναξ means literally a "reed," but also a reed instrument
such as a flute. The word is used metaphorically here, referring to their vocal chords
or voices.

[20]I have emended the punctuation in this passage since the syntax follows on
from the word ἄπειρα (boundless).

"Let your right hand find all those that hate you" (cf. Ps 20[21].9), "for you will make them turn their back" (Ps 20[21].13). And again, on being identified among them as from the Father, after the gift of God's grace and his ascent as a human being to the kingdom and his acclamation,[21] he said, "My hand will support him and my arm will strengthen him. The enemy will have no advantage over him and the son of lawlessness shall not hurt him again" (Ps 88[89].22–23). And further, "I shall cut down his enemies from before his face and I shall put to flight those who hate him" (Ps 88[89].24). And again, "Ethiopians shall fall down before him and his enemies shall lick the dust" (Ps 71[72].9). And if "you gave me the back of my enemies and you destroyed those who hate me" (Ps 17[18].41), to whom would this have reference in all likelihood, unless it was Christ? He said to the One who is in heaven, "I shall pursue my enemies and I shall overtake them; and they will be unable to stand. For they will fall under my feet" (cf. Ps 17[18].38), and the rest.

Whom did the sons of his Father venerate unless it was Christ alone who came forth from a woman? This, according to Joseph, was in all likelihood the final goal, when his dreams came to pass. But that which referred to Christ was a prefiguration of the Church of the gentiles in which all of us, as many as were made children of God through her, eternally venerate him, towards whom union through mystical regeneration came about. We are reckoned as his brothers both through deification in grace and through the wealth of his benevolence towards us, to such an extent that, on taking him on entirely, we have entirely dwelt within him, unless perchance we have transgressed his most righteous commandments. And indeed, in accordance with the manner in which he took on our [nature], he has appeared in the same nature as us, having assumed in the same manner as we did, our entire human state and all the marks of our human nature; and [yet] he manifestly escaped the taint of sin and the condemnation of the first Fall. Since all the gentiles have

---

[21] All of this seems to refer to David's kingship, but there are also christological overtones.

venerated and still do venerate Christ, who would be so rash as to contradict, on seeing the whole [earth] which is beneath the sun, all the extremities of the inhabited world which venerate and reverence him, and which are exalted in a manner befitting Christ, by the appellation of the One who is venerated, that they are Christians, and are given that name? What could he say in opposition to the prophetic voices which clearly proclaim, [saying] on the one hand, "All the gentiles will serve him," and "let all the kings of the earth venerate him" (Ps 71[72].11),[22] and on another, "Let the whole earth venerate you and sing psalms to you" (Ps 65[66].4), and "As many gentiles as [832] you have made will come and worship before you, Lord" (Ps 85[86].9), and the rest. And again, "Rejoice, gentiles, with his people" (Rom 15.10), and "Let all the sons of God worship him" (cf. Gen 49.8). Do you see how the sons of his Father have worshipped Christ, since they clearly have been enriched with the grace of his adoption as son?

6   But let us go on to the rest of the prophecy. "Judah is a lion's cub," it says, "from a shoot,[23] my son, you have risen up. Falling down, you slept like a lion and like a cub. Who will awaken him?" (Gen 49.9). Well said, prophecy! It speaks of a lion's cub. Who could this be, except Christ, who clearly issued from a kingly seed, I mean that of David? And it is in no way unreasonable to think of David as a lion, since this is the most characteristic [sign] of kingly rank, whereas a lion's cub [must be] Christ, who descended from him according to the flesh, as the rest of the prophecy makes clear. For it says, "From a shoot, my son, you have risen up." By "shoot," what would you properly understand from what followed, beloved, except clearly the holy one herself, who is even more holy than all the saints, who appeared entirely pure to the One who dwelt entire in both [her]

---

[22] Andrew diverges from the normal text of the Septuagint in the second phrase by substituting an aorist subjunctive for the future. Most LXX versions read: ". . . καὶ προσκυνήσουσιν αὐτῷ πάντες οἱ βασιλεῖς."

[23] The Greek word used in the Septuagint is βλαστοῦ. The NRSV, on the other hand, translates this as "prey."

body and [her] spirit? I mean Mary, the great and truly venerable subject and name, the Davidic descendant, the rod of Jesse, the ever-flourishing shoot of Judah, out of whom the Child of God, who is above the world, before the worlds, and co-eternal with the Begetter, issued forth in flesh.

Perhaps one might marvel at the accuracy of the prediction. For when the close kinship of the race was clearly pronounced by the naming of the lion and its cub, it added the phrase, "from a shoot, my son, you have risen up," so that it would refer clearly to what is beautifully stated by Isaiah, who says, "And there shall come forth a rod from the root of Jesse and a flower shall arise from his root" (Isa 11.1), which distinctly leads up to Christ and the Virgin. For David was certainly a shoot, she was manifestly a rod, while Christ is understood as a flower, just as he symbolically refers to himself as a sweet scent of spices in the book of Songs. "For I am a flower of the field," he says, "and a lily of the valleys" (Song 2.1). Not even the one prophesying himself was unaware that Christ is King and the most powerful of all kings. For "falling down," it says, "you slept like a lion and like a cub. Who will awaken him?" (Gen 49.9), making clear in these [words] the kingly, the terrible, and the unapproach-able [qualities], as well as the infinitely powerful nature of divine authority. And he himself shows this in the Gospels when he cries, "I have authority to lay down my life and I have authority to take it up again" (John 10.18). For in reality, everything that has been chosen and set apart for his sojourn in this world has been made subject to the authority of the Savior. [833] For this reason he says, "Destroy this temple and in three days I will raise it up" (John 10.18). For if he had not willed this and exhorted the Hebrews in this way, they would not have been able to destroy it. In speaking of a temple he meant his supremely unblemished flesh that he built around himself without human craftsmanship[24] out of the womb of her who is undefiled, even the pure, ever-Virgin Mary. Offering in it his life-giving falling

---

[24]Note the elaborate image of craftsmanship used here to describe Christ's human Incarnation.

asleep, when he willingly accepted the sleep of death on our behalf, he speaks as a human being through David, saying, "I fell asleep and slumbered; I awoke, for the Lord will assist me" (Ps 3.6). As for [the question], "Who will awake him?" (Gen 49.9), it clearly means the Father, who, with the help of his Son, raised up the temple of his body and rose together with [him],[25] in accordance with what is said in the Psalms directly from the Son to the Father: "You will not abandon my soul in hell, nor will you allow your holy one to see corruption" (Ps 15[16].10). And again, "Lord, you have brought up my soul out of hell, you have saved me from those who fall down into the pit" (Ps 29[30].4). For it was necessary, while the Son was bringing about the resurrection of his own body, for the Father to be revealed as his partner, since [the Father] has shown himself to be of the same nature and will as him, in order that whatever shares [Christ's] nature may be saved everywhere by this uniquely powerful cooperation in activity.[26]

7   But we must go on to what follows. "A ruler will not fail from Judah nor a prince from his thighs until there comes the thing stored up; and he [is] the expectation of gentiles" (Gen 49.10).[27] Good heavens, the foreknowledge! There was no deception in what was said. For it has been shown earlier [in this oration] how the Virgin was certainly produced from the Davidic loins. Her offspring is Christ, who is at once both Ruler and Prince, and who takes away spirits of

[25] Andrew is suggesting here that the Father not only raised his Son from the dead, but arose with him, because of the unity of their shared substance.

[26] This rather convoluted sentence emphasises the link that exists between the Father and Son, and between Son and humanity, showing that just as the Son was raised with the help of the Father, so will humanity be saved. It is worth noting Andrew's emphasis on the shared "nature and will" of Father and Son. This presumably does not preclude the Son encompassing two wills in one person; if not, the passage may reflect Andrew's brief phase as a Monothelite, ca. AD 711.

[27] The Brenton version puts the subject of the second phrase, "ἕως ἂν ἔλθῃ ὃ ἀπόκειται" in the plural, thus translating, "until there come the things stored up for him . . .": Brenton, *Septuagint*, 67. The Greek word ἐθνῶν may also be translated "gentiles."

rulers. It would be he who rules in the house of Jacob eternally and who allows no limit to his dominion. For the kingdom of the Jews was destroyed in former times, well before the coming of Christ; yes, it was clearly circumscribed until the times of Jechonia and until the most bitter exile into Babylon. Nevertheless, the race did not decline until Christ, being honored, adorned, and preserved the impressions[28] of kingly nobility. It remains then to understand [that the passage], ". . . until there comes the thing stored up; and he [is] the expectation of gentiles," refers to Christ, [the Son] of God, who is both himself God and himself Lord. This all-holy Virgin, the Davidic tree-trunk,[29] virginally gave birth to him with virginal labor pains.[30] For from the time when the rule of the Jews disappeared completely, no longer did another king according to the flesh sit on the visible throne of David when, at the end of the destruction, his kingdom was closed down according to the prophecy of Jeremiah which is as follows: "Jechonias was dishonored as a vessel for which he had no need. Why then was he cast out and exiled to a land which he did not know? Land, land, hear [836] the word of the Lord. The Lord says this: 'Write this man an outcast. For no man [born] of his seed will grow up to sit on the throne of David, nor will there be a ruler in Judah'" (cf. Jer 22.28–30). What [meaning for the phrase], "expectation of gentiles" (Gen 49.10), could be understood from these words of the prophet, but Christ alone, concerning whom the prophet and receiver of God,[31] the elder Symeon, had received a prophecy that he would not see death before he saw the One who was to come in the flesh.[32] And indeed, the prophetic utterance was accomplished

[28]ἀπόμοργμα, τό: "reflection" or "impression." Cf. (ps-)Dionysius the Areopagite, *De divinis nominibus* 2.6; PG 3, 644B.

[29]στέλεχος refers to the trunk or stump of a tree.

[30]By this Andrew must mean that she did not experience the normal pains of childbirth.

[31]The epithet θεοδόχος is sometimes applied to the Virgin Mary, but with controversial overtones since Nestorius preferred it. With reference to Simeon, see also Cyril of Jerusalem, *In occursum domini*, PG 33, 1187; (ps-) Methodios, *Sermo de Symeone et Anna*, PG 18, 348.

[32]See Luke 2.26.

through the actions that followed the prophecies. [Symeon] beheld
him as an infant and received in his elderly arms from maternal
hands[33] the Eternal One who was begotten before his mother; and
he at once sprang up with aged leaps (for even an old person jumps
when stimulated by extreme joy), and sang with triumphant voice
of the Lord who had become a baby. He both called him Master
and confessed him as Savior, proclaimed him a light of gentiles
and heralded him as glory of Israel, truly the Lord who had come
to dwell in the expectation of the revelation to the gentiles. For the
Father revealed the Son to them, as it is also possible to learn from
another prophet speaking very clearly: "Behold, I have given him as
a witness to gentiles, a ruler and commander among gentiles" (Isa
55.4). And again, "Behold, gentiles who do not know you will call on
you; and people who do not recognize you will flee to you" (cf. Isa
55.5). And speaking from another [chapter], "I have placed you as a
light for gentiles" (Isa 49.6). And from another [book], "I will give
you gentiles as your inheritance" (Ps 2.8), and, "all the gentiles will
be blessed in him" (cf. Ps 71[72].17).

8   "Binding the foal of his ass to a vine" (Gen 49.11), it says. Who is
the vine? It is for this reason that he cries in the Gospels, "I am the
true vine [and] the Father is the vine-grower" (John 15.1). And we
would be his foal, since we have become one in him and have been
joined, as it were, by an unbreakable tie through the Incarnation,[34]
in which he, the wealthy One, impoverished himself on our behalf
and bestowed his own [property] on us who were complete paupers.
And indeed, in this manner we have become gods on account of
him,[35] while he has been called a human being on our account. "The

---

[33]The noun ὠλένη literally means "forearm."

[34]Πρόσλημμα, which actually means "addition," can also mean Christ's acquisition of human nature. See Lampe, 1178–79.

[35]This is an explicit statement concerning the theological concept of "deification." According to patristic theology, it is possible for human beings to attain their potential status as beings created "in the image and likeness of God," (cf. Gen 1.26), with the help of God's grace and through ascetic endeavor. Christ's Incarnation is

foal of his ass" might be conceived in a more mystical way as the all-sacred Church through which the calling of the gentiles is typologically understood, in which [interpretation] we are led upwards.[36] For we were truly like beasts, held down by brutishness until the Word himself came to dwell among us and Wisdom removed [837] the veil[37] of our brutishness and, having beneficially clothed our nakedness, wrapped us in the rational robe of divine wisdom [that surrounded] him, [a robe] which "was woven in one piece from the top" (cf. John 19.23),[38] and ineffably bound us, just as he would have [bound] a foal to the tendril[39] of his salvation, and joined earthly things to heaven. For this reason, children who had been raised together in innocence, when they saw him making the journey into Jerusalem and towards that life-giving and blessed passion, and willingly granting salvation for the whole world, and riding on a foal in kingly fashion as if on a throne, cried out with one voice, "Hosanna to the Son of David; blessed is he who comes as the king of Israel!" (Matt 21.9). And indeed, Zechariah earlier declared, saying, "Rejoice greatly, daughter of Zion! Behold, your king is coming to you, gentle and saving, seated on a foal, the colt of a beast of burden" (cf. Zech 9.9; John 12.15). And what would anyone find from anywhere that is clearer [than this] for demonstrating the truth than what has been said? And so, [let us proceed] to what remains.

the key event that made deification possible, since in putting on human nature, he allowed human beings once more to participate in divine existence. See V. Lossky, *The Mystical Theology of the Eastern Church* (Crestwood, NY: SVS Press, 1998), 114–34; D. Staniloae, *The World: Creation and Deification* (vol. 2 of *The Experience of God. Orthodox Dogmatic Theology*; trans. I. Ionita and R. Barringer; Brookline, MA: Holy Cross Orthodox Press, 2000). Andrew of Crete frequently expresses in his homilies the idea that *all* Christians in fact achieve this exalted state, by means of baptism and participation in the Eucharist.

[36]Lampe lists a number of meanings for ἀνάγω. It may simply mean "reared" or "nourished" in the passive, or it may have more metaphorical meanings, including the introduction of an anagogical interpretation of Scripture.

[37]Cf. Exod 34.32–35.

[38]This reference to Christ's seamless tunic, for which the soldiers cast lots at his crucifixion, introduces an interesting juxtaposition of biblical images.

[39]Or "branch." Cf. Gen 49.11.

9 "He will wash his robe in wine," it says; "his eyes [will be] more gladdening than wine and his teeth whiter than milk" (Gen 49.11–12). With what sort of wine then will he who purifies the world of sin, the true and mature bunch of grapes of the Church, wash his robe, unless he manifestly purifies us with the blood of his wholly unblemished flesh and, as it were, cleanses a filthy garment? For he truly put on [that which belonged] to us, on whose account he became a human being, clothing himself naturally in our entire nature. But with the blood of what sort of grape will he, the undefiled One, wash his clothing? [Will he do this] by means of the living and wholly unblemished stream from the spring of his divine side?[40] For this was the most mystical bunch of grapes from the true vine, which was squeezed out in the wine-vat of the pure Church, since it had been drunkenly abused[41] by the scaffold of the cross, in order that it might purify our filth. And the flesh in which he robed himself, from us and on our behalf, was truly a divinely woven garment, which he royally dyed purple in spirit, since it was dipped in the undefiled and virginal blood, and, having donned it in the manner of imperial purple, he put on our material.[42] And this was dipped in blood like a tunic, when the stream of blood that flowed from his life-giving side dripped onto it. Isaiah is a witness, introducing the powers around him who asked questions concerning the passion itself and who spoke in the following way, "Who is this who comes from Edom, with garments dyed red from Bozrah?" (Isa 63.1), and again, "Why are your clothes red like those of a man who treads in the wine-vat?" (Isa 63.2). Revealing [the answer], I think, in the Song [of Songs], [Solomon] says, "I took off my tunic; how shall I put it

[40]This phrase refers to the piercing of Christ's side at the Crucifixion (John 19.34). The word θεόπλευρος also appears in Epiphanios, *Homilia II in Sabbato magno,* PG 43, 456A; Andrew of Crete, *Triodia,* PG 97, 1417C.

[41]The verb παροινέω has to do with drinking to excess. The various meanings all express the behavior associated with drunkenness.

[42]The Greek word φύραμα is often translated "dough" or "mixture" in a christological context. In order not to mix metaphors here, however, I have used a less specific English equivalent.

on? I washed my feet; how shall I defile them?" (Song 5.3), revealing the whole [meaning] in just a section. [840] Whose eyes are more gladdening than wine, unless they are Christ's? It is again about him when the soul wedded to God in the Songs [says], "Lead me into the house of wine" (Song 2.4), as if it were saying, "Lead me into the house of the Church in which the cup of happiness which is mixed in the blood of the lamb for our salvation is set forth." And when she has come inside, she says, "Show me your countenance and let me hear your voice, for your voice is sweet and your countenance is comely" (Song 2.14). And again, when she has seen him, she says, "Behold, my brother is white and ruddy, and also comely. His head is the most fine gold, his locks are curly and [black as those] of a raven" (Song 5.10–11). The great David also sings about him: "Then the Lord who was sleeping awoke, like a mighty man who has been inebriated with wine" (Ps 77[78].65). He it is who, after his resurrection from the dead, then addressed the myrrh-bearing women [with the word] "Hail!" (Matt 28.9), offering them a gladdening salutation and dissipating the gloom[43] of the first sorrow. And indeed he sends forth an utterance of joy to the elect of his disciples, saying, "Have courage, I have conquered the world." And again, "Peace be to you. It is I. Do not be afraid!" (Cf. Mark 6.50; Luke 24.36; John 6.20, 20.19, 21, 26).

10   But whose teeth are whiter than milk? [They are those of] the same One who said, "All the authority in heaven and on earth has been given to me" (Matt 28.18). In this [saying], the words of Christ are whiter than milk and brighter than any snow. Unless, I suppose, one would wish to understand Christ's teeth as the sayings about him that are sprinkled throughout the Holy Scriptures, both in the law and in the prophets, as well as in the Psalms, with which the Church of God chews up the interpretation of the more mystical concepts [so as to produce] the meaning of unerring teaching, like a firm, well-cooked meal, and it brings [this] to full digestion by continuing

---

[43]For the word σκυθρωπότης, see Gregory of Nyssa, *Hom. 5 in Cant.*, PG 44, 865A.

to ruminate[44] on it bit by bit.[45] For how would the speech of piety, which is digested with precision as a pleasing and sufficient [meal], preserve its nourishment without such preparation,[46] and what speech would be weakened, useless, and productive of a dangerous result? The Book of Songs, of course, as if on the part of the Church of the gentiles and of the soul that has been united to God, singing something like a wedding song, says to the Bridegroom, "What did your cheeks resemble?" (cf. Song 1.10).[47] "Your teeth are like a flock [of sheep] that have been shorn, which have come up from the bath, [and] all of which have born twins" (Song 4.2). And again, "My kinsman is mine, and I am his . . ." (cf. Song 6.2). "His cheeks are like bowls of spices . . ." (Song 5.13), showing his teeth, I think, by [the mention of] his cheeks.

That, in brief, is our unfolding of the prophecy and it takes this form. When you, beloved, hear that the Lord was prophesied as coming forth from Judah and from David—[the Lord] whom that great one among patriarchs, as though sketching it out on a tablet, addressed continuously as the Son of David who blossomed out of Judah, and was joined unanimously in this by all the prophets—you will not be in doubt, but rather will be unwavering in your opinion. Say then that [841] Christ is from the family of David. For it will become clear to you from this that the Mother herself who bore him in flesh by an ineffable pregnancy was herself a member of the family of David. Added to this is the sense of the phrase, "A tree is known by its fruit" (Matt 12.33).

[44]The noun μηρυκισμός literally means a "chewing of the cud." See Lev 11. 26.

[45]In this vivid metaphor, comparing Scriptural exegesis and teaching with cooking, eating, and digesting food, Andrew suggests that the Scriptures, including both Old and New Testaments, require constant reading and meditation. The passage also suggests the church's role in helping Christians to discern the hidden truth contained in Scripture.

[46]The Greek word ἀδιάπνευστον literally means "not blown through," "unventilated," or "unescaped" (Lampe). I have not translated the double negative in English for stylistic reasons.

[47]Rahlfs and Brenton have, "Τί ὡραιώθησαν σιαγόνες σου ὡς τρυγόνες . . ." ("How are thy cheeks beautiful as those of a dove . . ."), whereas Andrew uses the verb ὡμοιώθησαν ("resemble").

11   But let us hasten again to the nativity feast and let us strike up a short song, like a bridal ode, to Anna who now is bearing in her womb a God-given child, the pledge of a promise; and now she gives birth [in response to] her fruitful prayer, following [her] sterility, for the most visible sojourn, which is beyond reason, of God among men. It is right that she should be praised and truly thought worthy of divine acclamation for giving birth to such a shoot. Thus then, Anna's bedroom is set forth as a bridal chamber, presenting an appearance of child-bearing and of virginity, on the one hand of the one who bore, and on the other, of the one who was born. For of these [two], whereas one has now received a remission from sterility, the other, a short time later, will supernaturally consent to the birth of Jesus, who was divinely formed to be like us. It is likely, therefore, that Anna, who was chosen by God, having been made happy at the condition of her soul, cries out brightly and thrillingly, saying, "Rejoice with me, since I have born a shoot of glad tidings from my unfruitful womb and am nursing with my breast a fruit of blessing, in response to my prayers. I have slipped off [the cloak] of sterility and wrapped myself in the bright cloak of successful child-bearing. Today let the renowned Anna, who stood as rival to Peninnah, (cf. 1 Kgdms 1.2),[48] rejoice with me, and let her applaud the paradoxical miracle which has been worked in me according to her example. Also let Sarah, who skipped as an old woman,[49] dance, confirming my conception after being sterile. Let all sterile and barren women sing together in response to the wonderful visitation that has come to me from heaven. Indeed, let every mother, and fruitful one,[50]

[48]Peninnah or Phennana was the second wife of Elkanah. The adjective ἀντίθετος could also mean "in opposition to." That there is friction between the two women seems to be implied in the Hebrew Old Testament, whereas the Septuagint does not mention this. Cf. Andrew of Crete, *In Annuntiationem* 11, below, 214.

[49]This must be a reference to Sarah's laughing on hearing that she would conceive a son at the age of ninety (Gen 18.12). The Septuagint does not mention that she "skipped," however.

[50]The word γόνιμος means "productive" or "fruitful" one. It could refer to the father since the male was believed to produce the seed that would develop into a child,

say, "Blessed is he who grants the prayer of those who pray to him, and who, on opening the passages of a childless womb, bestowed his most wonderful Mother according to flesh as a shoot from an unfruitful family. Her belly is a heaven in which the One who is nowhere bounded has dwelt."

Let us also offer praise in harmony with these [words] to the one who was once called sterile, but who has now become mother of the virginal bridal chamber! Let us say to her, along with Scripture, let us say, how blessed is the house of David from which you have come forth! And also the belly in which God fashioned an ark of holiness which conceived him without seed! Thus you are blessed and thrice-blessed, who conceived in your womb a most divinely sanctified infant, whose most honored name was Mary, from whom Christ emerged as the flower of life and to whom belonged the esteemed pregnancy[51] and the transcendent childbirth. Let us also rejoice[52] with you, O wholly blessed one, for you have given birth to the God-given offspring of glad tidings, the hope of us all. You are truly blessed, and blessed is the fruit of your womb (cf. Luke 1.42). [844] Women are blessed through you, having thrown off childless-ness and become fruitful, after being sterile. The tongues of the faithful magnify your shoot, and every happy speech praises your birth-giving. For indeed it is right and especially proper, as a result of divine thoughtfulness, for the one who has been deemed worthy of an oracular [utterance][53] to be praised, having given birth to such a great fruit for us, from which sweet Jesus has come forth—Jesus who is himself entire sweetness and total desire, as well as the final object of all longings. Let us say of him that we shall live under his

but in fact such an interpretation seems to jar in this passage which is concerned predominantly with mothers.

[51] The word πρόοδος literally means "procession" or "advance." In this context it seems to refer to the process of gestation which preceded the act of childbirth itself (ὠδίν).

[52] Read συγχαίρωμεν for συγχαίρομεν.

[53] By "oracular utterance," the preacher must mean the prophetic utterance of Scripture, which foretold Anna's miraculous birth of the Virgin Mary.

shadow and take rest under his wings.[54] He is truly the One who is proclaimed through law and prophets, Jesus Christ our God, who is both grace and truth. He has come to save us sinners and to recall everyone to their ancient nobility. To him due glory, honor and veneration are offered up by all of us, along with his Father who is without beginning and his life-giving Spirit, both now and to the ages of ages. Amen.

[54]Cf. Ps 16[17].8; Ps 35[36].7; Ps 56[57].1; etc.

On the Nativity III

On the birthday of our wholly unblemished Lady, the Theotokos and ever-Virgin Mary, and a demonstration from ancient history and from diverse testimonies that she is descended from the seed of David[1]

1 [844] It is again a feast, and again a celebration, and again I am acting as a courteous host, celebrating my own salvation and summoning everyone to the spiritual feast over which the Theotokos presides, entertaining her own banqueters with a torrent of delight. Meanwhile you, the apiary of Christ, piously buzzing about, are distilling sweetness, just as if you were taking home the honeycombs that you had collected from some beehives. And who would choose to be left out of such delight, especially among those who have already tasted its benefits? For if some people have not earlier avoided the table which is extravagantly laden with delicacies[2] (unless [perchance] they enjoyed its delight beyond their fill), does it not seem entirely ridiculous if they jump up from the royal

---

[1] *CPG* 8172; *BHG*ᵃ 1127; PG 97, 861–81; edited by J. Billius, who ascribed it to John of Damascus.

[2] I have emended ὄψοις to ὄψοις here. Here the word means cooked or otherwise prepared food, eaten with bread and wine, or "delicacies." See L&S, 1283.

table before they have tasted the mysteries there?[3] For the feast is
majestic, [belonging to] a queen who is descended from royal seed.
Come then once again,[4] beloved, and accept our oration which
leads you on to that goal which I set it out very well in the preceding
[sermons] and clearly suggested is Christ's descent from the Davidic
root. As this is demonstrated, it will also be revealed in all likelihood
that the one who bore him according to the flesh was an offspring
of the same root. To introduce a second conclusion seems to me to
be entirely complimentary, since what has been said [thus becomes]
even more vivid in demonstrating the truth, having been extended
more carefully and expansively for us. But that we may direct argu-
mentative opposition, on the part of the raving Jews, to the truth,
[845] beyond the winds of falsehood, come, and let us reveal as far
as possible that the Virgin herself descends from the root of David
itself, using the evangelists as witnesses and [employing] the unique
[accounts] of Scripture. I think therefore that it is necessary to deal
with the generations after David, according to the genealogies of
both Luke and Matthew—whereas the former looks backwards,[5]
the latter goes through it in chronological order—and to extend our
understanding towards the outermost points [of each genealogy],[6]
so then to set out in sequence the mixture according to which the
kinship of those who bore Joseph was brought together, and also
to demonstrate the manner in which the Virgin manifestly issued
forth from the house of David. And may none of these things remain

[3]The meaning of this sentence is somewhat difficult to grasp, but it appears that
the preacher is chiding members of the congregation who leave church early, perhaps in order to celebrate at home, instead of remaining to partake of the eucharistic
offering.

[4]With the word "again," Andrew refers to the fact that he has already delivered
two sermons in the course of the vigil. He is recalling the attention of his congregation
to listen to a third oration.

[5]See Luke 3.23–38.

[6]See Matt 1.1–17. Christ is the culmination of this genealogy; all of the generations
were leading up to this climax in both Gospels. The phrase τῶν ἄκρων here seems to
indicate the two ends of the genealogies of each evangelist; Andrew is concerned to
harmonize their expositions if he possibly can.

unproven with regard to her. For I know that this represents the most splendid praise for her in every encomium, [namely] to arm oneself against God-fighting tongues and to stop every mouth that slanders her. And so, henceforth I shall begin [my oration].

2   And let everyone who is present here, as well as each person who has been nourished on words, be aware that I am both inexperienced in secular learning and indeed vexed because of this, seeing that I am not discovering a shortcut suited to what is needed.[7] Nevertheless, having been emboldened by the Spirit who teaches knowledge to every human being, I am preparing myself[8] for what is set before me. So, then, a law held sway in ancient times that each woman from an alien tribe might not be brought to marriage, thus not sharing [the inheritance] of the man's tribe. [To prove] that this is true, listen to the words themselves of the law, which have the following wording: "And Moses charged the sons of Israel by the commandment of the Lord, saying, '. . . So there will be no wandering about by the sons of Israel, from tribe to tribe, for the sons shall each steadfastly cleave to the inheritance of his family's tribe. And every daughter that is heiress to a property from the tribes of the sons of Israel, shall each be married to one of the people belonging to her father's tribe, that the sons of Israel may each inherit the property of his father's [tribe]'" (cf. Num 36.5–8), in the manner in which the Lord enjoined Moses. And this [law] was preserved until the present time. For as long as the affairs of the Jews flourished and the Mosaic commandments remained vigorous, there was no aspect of their customs which did not hold sway in the established manner. But from the time that they began to disappear and everything went over to the opposite, diminishing by degrees, the reason for hereditary well-being was no longer considered by them since they were tending towards a way

[7]Andrew is referring to the secular, classical education which was available only to a few in Byzantium. The assertion that he did not receive such training is manifestly untrue and represents a conventional *topos* of modesty in this context.

[8]Literally, "stripping off," as in preparation for athletic games or contests.

of life [which had more in common with] the gentiles and regarded property, however great, as of no importance, even though their law was decreeing [this], the prophets were proclaiming [it], and through almost the whole of Scripture, God himself was affirming [it], namely, that customs should not be dissipated or corrupted.[9]

3 So when the Jews paid no ordinary penalty for their insulting behavior towards God and for their frequent provocations, both by distancing themselves from their hereditary piety [848], and resorting to extreme superstition;[10] and indeed, when God punished them in many ways—on the one hand, with the besieging of their city and pillaging of their temples, with holy places trampled by profane and impure feet, and on the other, by the ravaging and plundering of the nation and by the destruction of the ancestral soil, as a result of which, driven out, they departed to a foreign land—this was a piteous sight for those who saw it and [piteous] sound for those who heard it, and, as they became hemmed in all around by disasters, the family was no longer able to be distinguished precisely when weighed down by the burden of daily calamities and by the multitude of misfortunes that assailed them. For this reason then, each of the tribes was mixed together, thus robbing their nobility of its uniqueness. But this renowned dignity of the family has not been entirely eliminated. For some remnant of the succession was still holding sway over what was important with regard to this inheritance until [the time of] the praised Virgin, I mean that one who alone among women was bride of God, Mother, and ever-Virgin, whom I am eager now to demonstrate as being [herself] of the

[9]The weakness of Andrew's argument is worth noting here: although he wants to prove that Mary had to be of the same tribe as Joseph, the practice of marrying only within families had begun to disappear by the time she was betrothed. This section of the homily reveals the preacher's pedantic tendency to state what he knows to be the historical truth, even when this does not support his underlying thesis. The long periodic sentence is consistent with the techniques of discursive oratory.

[10]The word δυσειδαιμονία does not appear in any of the dictionaries. It is probably a neologism. The Latin translation suggests "superstition" as its meaning.

Davidic tribe. Having directed the purpose of my oration towards the aim of Scripture, I burst into utterance, especially if God provides me with things to say that are worthy.[11] But come, tell me now, O blessed Matthew, what is the cause of the divergence between your genealogy and that of the teacher of sacred things, [I mean] Luke? "No," says Matthew, that mind which is most divinely skilled in writing, who was formerly a tax-collector and now a teacher of ineffable things, "There is nothing between us; there is no expression of discordance. For whereas [Luke], making his argument work backwards, left out [Jesus'] ancestors as though according to nature, recalling sometimes only those according to the law, I have clearly called to mind the natural ancestors, [acting] not unreasonably or in a manner unworthy of the Spirit." For each [of the evangelists] is inspired by one and the same Spirit and each glorifies, diminishing in no way the work of the other. And it is necessary, beloved, to investigate accurately the genealogies set out by them both and then to hunt for the discovery of what is being sought.

4   Indeed, then, according to the voice of the teacher of sacred things, the precision of the genealogy is shown to us [by recourse to] each of two [concepts] of family, I mean that according to nature and that according to law. Matthew therefore begins his compilation, saying, "A book of the birth of Jesus Christ, son of David, son of Abraham" (Matt 1.1). And this, which represents his prologue, was sufficient for [his readers] to grasp what was being investigated. [849] But he did not stop at this. For his exposition continued as far as the intended husband of the Virgin. Luke, on the other hand, after his description of the Savior's baptism [and], diverting the flow of his narrative for a short time, writes as follows, saying, "At that time Jesus himself was about thirty years old, beginning, as it was thought, as the son of Joseph, son of Heli, son of Matthat, son of Levi, son of

---

[11] It seems that Andrew is not only defending the logic of his position here, but he also seeks to explain why his sermon has diverged somewhat from the normal course of most festal sermons on this subject.

Melchi," and the rest in order until "Seth, son of Adam, son of God" (Luke 3.23–38). This conscientious mind was thus not ignorant of the matters under examination, since it is customary for Scripture to name, on the one hand, those "ancestors according to the law," who, although they died early [and] childless, were nevertheless presented with children after their deaths by means of offspring from their brothers' seed, and, on the other hand, those [ancestors] according to nature who, in accordance with nature, produced children by themselves for the succession of the family by means of their own seed. Also, if from time to time their brothers had died without issue, they contributed to their brothers' prosperity by substituting offspring. Turning back then to the two evangelists, [we see that] whereas one skipped ancestors [who were only ancestors] with respect to the law, recalling only those who represented ancestors in accordance with nature, the other dashed past the natural ones, having remembered individually those who were [ancestors] in accordance with the law—and yet neither evangelist has been mistaken in what is likely. I think that it is beneficial to remember an ancient testimony to this, [testimony] that we have received from a very learned man and which contains word for word what will follow.[12] Since they are indeed contained in the genealogy of the evangelists, some offspring succeed their own fathers whereas others, when they have been begotten by other [men], bear the names of those others; nevertheless, both are remembered, [including] those who have been begotten and those who are as if begotten, counting them according to nature and to law; thus neither one of the Gospels is in error. For the families were interwoven with each other from early times, from [the period] of Solomon and that of Nathan, by

---

[12]It is likely that Andrew refers here to a certain Africanus who, according to Eusebius, wrote a letter to Aristides on how to harmonize the Gospel genealogies. He also discusses the issue of families in Israel being grouped either by nature or by law. See Eusebius, *History of the Church*, I.7; E. Schwartz, ed., *Eusebius of Caesarea, The Ecclesiastical History* (trans. K. Lake; Loeb Classical Library 153; London: Heinemann and Cambridge, MA: Harvard University Press, 1926; repr. 2001), 54–61. In fact much of Andrew's exposition appears to be taken directly from this passage.

the substitution of children and by second marriages. And in order that what is being discussed may be clear, I shall describe the inter-weaving of the families.

5   For those reckoning the generations from David through [the line of] Solomon, Matthan is found to be third from the end. He begat Jacob who was the father of Joseph.[13] According to Luke, [who reckons from] Nathan, the son of David, the corresponding third from the end is Melchi.[14] Since Joseph is in fact the object of our study, we must make clear how each man is recorded as his father, with Jacob from Solomon and Heli from Nathan, as we derive each family. And so both Matthan and Melchi, who took in turn the same wife, fathered half-brothers, for the law did not prevent one who was widowed or divorced to be married to another [man]. So then, it has been handed down that a first Matthan, who derived his ancestry from Solomon, begat Jacob, and when Matthan died [852], Melchi, who traced his family to Nathan, took the widow, since he was from the same tribe though of another family, as I said earlier, and had a son named Heli.[15] And so we shall find that both Jacob and Heli, [who were descended] from two different families, were half-broth-ers; of these, Jacob evidently took over his wife, after his brother Heli had died without issue, and begat for himself from her a third Joseph according to both nature and text.[16] On account of this, it has been written that "Jacob begat Joseph" (Matt 1.16), although according to the law he was Heli's son. For Jacob, being his brother, raised up seed for him.[17] For this reason the genealogy according to [Luke] will not be invalidated when the evangelist Matthew enumerates

[13]See Matt 1.15–16.

[14]See Luke 3.24. This is not strictly true: Melchi is actually fifth from the end, i.e. from Jesus, son of Joseph. Andrew follows his source Africanus in making this mistake.

[15]Cf. Matt 1.15.

[16]The word used here is λόγος, which could also mean "reason" or "speech." The juxtaposition with "nature" suggests that Andrew is contrasting the natural course of events and the way in which this is recorded.

[17]Cf. Gen 38.8; Deut 25.5; Matt 22.24; Mark 12.19; Luke 20.28.

[his], saying, "Jacob begat Joseph." Luke, on the other hand, [states], "[Jesus] was the son, as was thought (for he adds this qualification), of Joseph, son of Heli, son of Melchi" (Luke 3.23–24).[18] To speak of the birth in accordance with law was not in itself too remarkable. He also omits [the words] "he begat" with regard to such a manner of procreation until the end as he traces the succession in reverse direction right to "Adam, son of God." And omitting a short [section, he goes on:][19] therefore both Heli and Jacob were half-brothers. For when Heli died without issue, Jacob, who raised up seed for him, begat Joseph as his own natural son, but as the legal son of Heli. Thus, Joseph was [in effect] the son of both men.

6 So much, then, for him. And indeed, when Joseph's genealogy has been calculated in this way, it is implicitly demonstrated that this Virgin and Theotokos, Mary, belongs to the same tribe as him if, according to Mosaic law, one tribe could not intermarry with another. For [the law] decrees that she should enter into a marriage union only with someone from her own township and native land, in case the family's inheritance should possibly be transferred from tribe to tribe. Yet if someone presumptuously demanded that the genealogy of the supremely holy and unwedded Virgin herself should be reckoned up, he would not in my opinion be acting correctly since the law nowhere allows this, nor does it permit [such an investigation] in any way. Where, in ancient times, is a woman ever shown to have a genealogy since her the more honored gender is preferred for the composition of a genealogy?[20] For it is the paternal rather than the maternal line of the family that is considered to be

[18]It is striking that Andrew leaves out two generations in the genealogy, Matthat and Levi, again following his source, Africanus. There does not appear to be an explanation for this omission.

[19]Andrew skips a long passage in Africanus's text here, jumping to the end of the quotation which appears in Eusebius, *History of the Church*, I.7.16. Andrew's extensive quotation of this text cannot really be called plagiarism since he is obviously signalling to his audience the use of the text in his sermon.

[20]In other words, genealogies are reckoned according to the male line.

more honorable [in contributing to] her good inheritance. There will be absolutely no concern for us in this [approach], [that is], never to falsify the ancient boundaries in our name and or to introduce vain [new] laws. For there exists an eternal ordinance not to change boundaries which our fathers established.

7   However, let us not digress from the brief [introduction] that was set out earlier. If Moses speaks the truth in declaring these things which have been written (and he absolutely will speak the truth since he alone spoke face to face[21] with God, who is the Truth), she who is divinely named the Mother of God[22] in accordance with the ineffable dispensation will be shown [to have come] from the same tribe as [853] the man who was betrothed to her, I mean Joseph, who issued from David. And if we were to allow that he proceeded from the seed of David, it will be necessary to state also that she who was betrothed to him was from the same tribe. For the angel who appeared to him in a dream addressed him [with the words], "Joseph, son of David, do not be afraid to take Mary as your wife" (Matt 1.20), since he was anxious concerning the miracle of the inexpressible pregnancy. Therefore Moses did not deceive [us], nor did David bear false witness; for the former decreed that families should not allow any mingling [of blood] in themselves, while the latter received a prophesy, by means of a binding promise,[23] that Christ would arise from his loins. So then, the argument,[24] running on like a stream, has clearly established for us that Christ [was descended] from Judah and David. I shall attempt also in other ways to set out for our benefit the reason for this on the basis of ancient documents,

[21]Literally "mouth to mouth."

[22]The epithet μητρόθεος is unusual. Lampe cites this passage, as well as an anonymous hymn. See J.B. Pitra, *Analecta sacra spicilegio solesmensi parata* I (Paris: A. Jouby & Roger, 1876), 532.

[23]ὁρκομοσία should be emended to ὁρκωμοσία ("binding promise" or "oath"). The word is commonly used in the Septuagint.

[24]The word used here is λόγος, which could also refer to the Scriptural source or to the oration itself.

[at least] for as many as you as have clearly drunk the unadulterated milk of the Church.[25] With regard to the others, there is no passage of prophecy, in my opinion, which so touches on their obtuseness [as the following], when it says,[26] "They will grope for a wall like blind men and will grope for it as if they had no eyes" (Isa 59.10). The divine apostle will assist us by saying, "We speak of wisdom among the perfect ones, but it is not a wisdom of this age, nor of the rulers of this age who are coming to nothing; rather [do] we speak of the wisdom of God which has been hidden in mystery, which a natural man[27] is indeed unable to understand. For it represents foolishness to him and he cannot understand it since [only] the spiritual man can discern it" (cf. 1 Cor 2.6–7, 14).[28]

8   Indeed, of the events concerning Christ, there are some which escaped the notice of many people, including all the ones which were, so to speak, usefully kept quiet for the sake of people then, [such as the events] which occurred before his baptism, and [those concerning] how he lived his life for the whole thirty years, since no Scripture recorded it. Among the events that were kept quiet, there was one [event] especially, namely the miracle of his birth, which escaped almost everyone's notice during the time until he became a man, apart from a little bit [of the story]; as a holy man by the name of Ignatios says somewhere, "And the virginity of Mary and her birth-giving were hidden from the prince of this world, as was also the death of Christ. Three mysteries of a cry were accomplished in the stillness of God."[29] It is likely, therefore, that the nativity of

[25]See 1 Pet 2.2.

[26]It is not clear to whom Andrew refers here, but the context suggests that he means, in general terms, all unbelievers.

[27]"Natural" is the meaning traditionally given to this appearance of the word ψυχικός (cf. Lampe, 1552). In this sentence (1 Cor 2.14) it is opposed to the πνευματικός man.

[28]Andrew conflates two passages here, but he also paraphrases 1 Cor 2.14.

[29]Ignatius of Antioch, *Epistle to the Ephesians*, XIX.1 (Lake, LCL). As Billius (n. 24) and Lake note, some manuscripts omit Θεοῦ in the final clause of this quotation.

Christ by means of the Holy Spirit was kept quiet among the people. Instead, Joseph was accepted in the land as the father. And so, as is reasonable, he was reckoned in the genealogy as father of the child. If [856] this had not happened, the child would have been considered fatherless, without a genealogy through his father's line.

9 The wonderful evangelists then had to reckon Joseph's genealogy since everyone had hailed him as the father of the Son. For if they reckoned [Jesus'] genealogy by the maternal line, overlooking this man, this would be both improper and also alien to the tradition of the divine Scriptures, since no one had previously had his genealogy calculated through the female line. For this reason, then, the evangelists usefully reckoned Joseph's genealogy from David and at the same time they established that the Virgin Mary was also descended from David through the family of her betrothed husband, adding in the case of his wife [the arguments] in accordance with Moses' law-giving which have been brought to our attention somewhat earlier: "You will not go about from tribe to tribe," [these laws] said to the sons of Israel, "for each of the sons of Israel will steadfastly adhere to the inheritance of his family's tribe" (cf. Num 36.7), and the rest. These things being so, it was manifest beforehand that Joseph was a just man and that he lived according to the law. And, since he was conducting his way of life lawfully, he did not court a woman who was from anywhere else other than from the tribe from which he came. She was [a descendant of] Judah, and came from both his township and his lineage, which was that of David. For such were the precepts of the law. So then, if Joseph was indeed [a descendant] of Judah and [shared] both the inheritance and lineage of David, how could it not be right that Mary also sprang from the same [sources], especially since she belonged to the same tribe of Judah and the township of David from which Joseph originated, since the law was clearly known beforehand, excluding mixture with other tribes and prescribing the opposite, thus enforcing close association with [members] of one's lineage and township who belonged to [one's]

own tribe? "You will not go about from tribe to tribe," he said to the
sons of Israel, "for each of the sons of Israel will steadfastly adhere
to the inheritance of his family's tribe" (cf. Num 36.7). In accordance
with these [words], therefore, this renowned Virgin also came from
the seed of David whence also her betrothed husband received his
genealogy. For if the man is the woman's head, according to the great
apostle (cf. 1 Cor 11.3), and the two [of them] should become one
flesh in accordance with the law of Moses (cf. Gen 2.24), and the
bride who transgresses against her husband suffers the punishment
of adultery according to the law because she has already become the
body of her bridegroom and registered her husband as her head,
how then does it not follow, since it is the genealogy of "the head"
that is calculated, that the body should be included along with the
head? And so, then, it was necessary that the Virgin joined to Joseph
should reasonably be included in the genealogy since she was united
with him; and this is especially so since she has been proved to have
descended not only from his tribe, but also from the township and
family of David. When Gabriel was uttering divine truths in his message to her, he said, along with other things, "And the Lord God will
give to him the throne of his ancestor David" (Luke 1.32). What is he
teaching here? [He is stating] that David was the progenitor of the
One who would be born from her. For how was it possible that the
angel was saying these things to the Virgin unless he was clearly con-
fessing [857] that she was [descended] from David? For he would not
have said, "God will give to him the throne of his ancestor David,"
if she had not happened to be [descended] from David. For would
the Virgin not have asked reasonably, "Of which ancestor?" as she
confessed that she did not know a man but learned that she would
conceive from the Holy Spirit, if the speech was not clearly directed
to a daughter of David? Thereupon Luke says reasonably, "Joseph
also went from the city of Nazareth in Galilee to be registered in
Judea, in the city of David, which is called Bethlehem, because he
was descended from the house and family of David, along with
Mary, who was betrothed to him and who was expecting a child"

(Luke 2.4–5). We shall no longer read the text at hand with any doubt since the registration was not simply of a Mary who accompanied him, but rather of one who, along with Joseph, [was descended] from the house and family of David; we possess the reasons for such an interpretation from what has been conveyed [earlier]. Therefore, I consider it to have been clearly demonstrated that Joseph's genealogy is not reckoned in vain by the divine evangelists, as a result of which the Virgin is consequently also recognised as a descendent of David, and also Christ Jesus, who was born of her by a supreme miracle, the pre-eternal Child of God.

And may he who is attempting to contradict these things, or rather, who is trying to sharpen the sword of his own tongue, be ejected from the holy doors of our atrium! Let it not be possible for us, to whom the Word of God, who is grace and truth, was sent, to examine anything more than what has been said, since the divine Scripture blocks the search for deeper things.[30] For it says, "What is commanded you, think on this, and do not seek out matters that are above you" (cf. Sir 3.22).

10 You then, O Jew, understand the power of what has been said and do not struggle[31] with the truth. Abandon your doubting opinion and, without any disagreement, be instructed with grace, by means of which you may be released from the bonds of the yoke that is enslaved to[32] the letter. Cast off the veil! Receive the pure light of what has been written! Run past the shadows and leave behind

[30]This is an interesting statement concerning the limits that should be observed by students of Scripture. Andrew suggests here, as well as elsewhere in the homily, that Scripture remains silent about some aspects of divine revelation, or indeed about the life of Christ, for good reasons.

[31]The word ζυγομαχέω, with its prefix ζυγο- ("yoke"), in fact suggests struggling, or quarrelling, with one's yoke-fellow. This evokes the relationship between Judaism and Christianity, both of which share the Old Testament as Scripture, but which have diverged in their interpretations of this since the coming of Christ.

[32]The word γραμματόκυφος ("of slavery to the letter") is also found in (ps-) Methodios, *In Symeonem et Annam*, PG 18, 368C (according to Lampe, xxxiv, this is actually a ninth-century work).

the types! Accept grace in its naked state! Advance unhesitatingly
to the truth! Glorify, praise the One who decreed these things in
such a way! Say, in the manner of Moses, "This is my God and I will
glorify him; my father's God and I will exalt him" (Exod 15.2). It is
always possible for you and for everyone who has the will both to
understand these things and likewise to teach them! But for us, for
whom the light of truth has been firmly indicated, there is no time
to investigate further matters and to drag out the oration endlessly,
since the favorable gist of the truth has been demonstrated in an
entirely orderly manner. Indeed, it is likely that those who do not
wish to celebrate, extend their orations into investigations—for
it is inappropriate. So let the oration proceed to its winning-post
and let the mysteries of the day go forth, especially since [this day]
is standing inside the doors [860] and calling on us with a refrain
productive of much joy. Rejoice and skip! For what was expected
is here! Restoration is before the gates, redemption is at the doors,
salvation is in our hands! How, and in what way? Let us listen to
David, who says, "God will come manifestly" (Ps 49[50].2). Whence
will he come, and how? Both from heaven and in our form. [He will
come] bodilessly from heaven and in our form, [he will assume] our
shape and nature and appearance. But how would this come about
when God has not [as yet] become corporeal? For it is not possible
to see God in his naked divinity unless he has been mixed in with
our dough, becoming like us in a union with our [nature], yet without any sin. Indeed it is clear that the Master of human nature is
united with human nature on behalf of the whole of human nature,
in order that he may save human nature.[33] Where and when? In the
virginal space and at the end of [these] times, when David foretold
that he would come. And this is what we are celebrating today, the
birthday of the Virgin, the prelude of the feasts, and the prologue of

---

[33]There is no good (one word) translation of πλάσμα. For patristic usages, see
Lampe, 1089. It clearly refers to *humanity* in this context. In the Greek, the orator
repeats the word four times, in different grammatical forms, for rhetorical effect; this
is the device of metaclisis.

the mystery concerning Christ. For it was necessary for the palace to be prepared for the King since the King would [soon] be present there. It was necessary for the regal swaddling clothes to be seen first since the regal infant would be born in such a way. And finally, it was necessary for the clay to be kneaded in advance, even as the Potter made his appearance. It is reasonable then that the marvellous Joachim and his wife Anna, who were divinely called by God's providence, provided the fruit of their prayer, I mean this queen of nature, the first-fruit of our dough, whose birthday we are approaching, whose swaddling clothes we honor,[34] and whose restoration of our race from that time onwards we venerate. For now our kindred take on the beginnings of deification. Now the bonds of the former sterile disability are loosened, the barren one becomes a mother, the childless [woman] is found blessed with a fair child, and Anna, while suckling the virginal infant, rejoices. Now the narrow passages of sterility are unblocked,[35] the veins of the reproductive organs are swollen,[36] and the fetus of the barren woman is anticipating [its birth];[37] [this is] the miracle of the Virgin! For if it is great that a sterile woman should give birth, is it not even greater that she should bear the Virgin? And whereas the former, being made known as a mother, no longer remained sterile, the other, in giving birth without

[34]Andrew may be alluding here to the swaddling clothes of Christ, which were kept as a relic at the church of the Chalkoprateia in Constantinople. It is possible that people believed that these were used for the Virgin before being wrapped around Christ. See Germanos, *In s. Mariae zonam*, PG 98, 372–84.

[35]This verb ἀντιφράσσω actually means "to block up," but the opposite seems to be implied here.

[36]The word ἀνασειράζω literally means "to draw away." Billius's Latin translation provides "swell" ("tument"), with which the sense agrees. It is likely that our author visualises the mother's veins opening up to allow the blood to flow to the fetus; it was believed in antiquity that whereas the father provides the seed of the child, the mother adds elements to its composition by means of her blood. See above, 55, n. 8.

[37]This passage represents another quite graphic description of the Virgin's conception in Anna's womb, as we saw above in John of Damascus's sermon on the Nativity. It is possible that both preachers wished to emphasise the entirely natural manner of the conception, perhaps in opposition to heretical views that she was born miraculously in some way.

a man, remained still a virgin, without any corruption to her womb and escaping the [pangs] of maternity. But that was later, while this is earlier. For the first [event] was the indicator of the second. And it was fitting for the One through whom everything is and in whom everything is, since he is the Master of nature, to make anew the miracle in his ancestress and to reveal a barren woman as a mother; and then, in the case of [another] mother, to redirect the ordinances of nature and to reveal a virgin as a mother, and to set a seal on the signs of virginity.[38]

Of such [importance], then, is the birth of the Virgin! This is the subject of the feast: the remembrance of the covenants of God towards humanity, the proof of what was prophesied, [861] the appearance and culmination of the hidden mystery, the visitation of the whole race in which we, who were formerly residing in darkness and in the shadow of death, were visited, and through which we were illumined by the inaccessible light of the One who rose from on high for us; Christ Jesus, Master of us all, and God the Savior, makes us arise. For to him [are due] glory and honor and power, along with the eternal Father and his life-giving Spirit, now and always, and to the ages of ages. Amen.

[38]This represents a clear affirmation of the dogma of Mary's virginity *in partu* and *post partum*. Andrew emphasises here God's role both in bringing about the Virgin's birth from Anna, and in causing her to become pregnant and give birth to Christ while remaining a virgin.

ANDREW OF CRETE

On the Nativity IV

On the Holy Nativity of Our Supremely Holy Lady, the Theotokos and Ever-Virgin Mary[1]

1 [861] If the earth is measured by a span and the sea is circum-scribed by a rope; if heaven is portrayed by cubits and the host of stars enumerated; if drops of rain and clods of earth and a mass of winds and quantity of sand are [all] invoked, perhaps an apprehension of the subject will be at hand for us. The festival of a Mother of God and nativity of a marvellous[2] child is being fulfilled: an ever-virgin child, a child without experience of marriage, a queen, a prophetess, whose royal swaddling-clothes David, who was great among prophets and kings, portrayed[3] with a royal glance, exclaiming, "All the glory of the daughter of the King is from within, although she is robed and adorned with golden tasselled [garments]!" (Cf. Ps 44[45].14).[4] He was signalling from afar, I think, the splendor of beauty which was

[1]*CPG* 8173; *BHG*[a] 1092, 1092b; F. Combefis, ed., PG 97, 861–81.

[2]Cf. Gregory of Nazianzus, *Oratio* 29.16, PG 36, 93C.

[3]The Greek word ἐξεικονίζω also means "to portray," "to image forth," or simply "to express," but the root εἰκών forms and important part of it. Andrew is fond of using this word and its derivatives in ways that express mystical relationships or spiritual insights. It is difficult to determine whether this was in any way connected with cur-rent controversies concerning the nature of holy, material icons.

[4]L. Brenton translates this passage: "All her glory is that of the daughter of the king of Esebon, robed as she is in golden fringed garments, in embroidered cloth-ing."

placed upon her [864] from infancy by God, by means of the diverse gifts of the Holy Spirit; for these [are represented], according to my understanding, by the garment woven with gold and the golden tassels. And, I think, the royal swaddling clothes are understood by right-minded people who are without passion; of these, [David], foreseeing the inner splendor and the comeliness which shines in the Virgin [reflecting] the external beauty, exclaimed to her with a confident[5] voice, saying, "Hear, O daughter, and see, and incline your ear, and forget your people and your father's house, and the King will desire your beauty" (cf. Ps 44[45].11–12),[6] which clearly refers to the Church of the gentiles, yet it is also without difficulty understood to refer to her since she, in her entirety, was made into a temple for the entire[7] Bridegroom of the Church by the miracle of the Incarnation. Come then, and joining with David, let us applaud with suitable encomia the Mother of God who is [descended] from David! Let us honor the brightness of the feast! Let us offer the Virgin the honorable titles of virginity! Let us bestow as gifts to the Queen of the race, as very precious unguents, the oracular sayings[8] of the prophets! Let us greet her with Gabriel's greeting! Let us say to the Mother of joy, "Hail, favored one!" (Luke 1.28). Hail, illumined one, through whom the darkness has been driven away and the light put in its place! Hail, favored one, through whom the law has acquiesced and grace has shone forth! Hail, prelude of joy and conclusion of the curse! "Hail, one who is truly favored, the Lord is with you!" (Cf. Luke 1.28). He, who later came forth from you, was formerly with you: formerly in power, and secondly in activity; now, preparing your womb as his own dwelling-place, and then, building corporeally from you the

---

[5]The verb παρρησιάζομαι is frequently used to indicate the speaker's openness or boldness before God. See Lampe, 1045–6.

[6]Rahlf's version of this psalm has, ". . . for the King *desired* your beauty," (aorist) in verse 12. The future, as Andrew uses it here, does however exist in various manuscripts; see Rahlfs, 2:47.

[7]The word ὅλῳ is awkward here, but it is added in order to emphasise the complete relationship between Christ and the Virgin Mary (τῆς ὅλης).

[8]The Classical origin of the word χρησμῳδήματα is clear. The word is also used by Cyril of Alexandria. See Lampe, 1528.

great mystery of the dispensation. Hail, one who alone contained the blessing of the Lord in order that our ancestress [Eve] might be released from the original curse! Hail, God-receiving[9] treasure of virginity from whom an incorruptible birth-giving came forth, and the wealth of virginity remained undefiled! Hail, pure mother and nursing virgin! Hail, diadem of beauty and queen of the race, made beautiful on all sides with regal privileges! Hail, sacred precinct of Christ, who alone acted singly as a priest with respect to the holy things of heaven, according to the rank of Melchisedek. [865] Hail, rod of Aaron, root of Jesse, sceptre of David, regal garment, crown of graces, unwritten type of virginity, leaf of holiness, utterance of revelations! Hail, mediator of law and grace, seal of old and new covenants, manifest fulfillment of all prophecy, acrostic of the God-inspired truth of the Scriptures, the living and also most pure volume of God and the Word in which, wordlessly and without writing, the Writer himself, God and the Word, is read each day![10] Hail, the first-fruit of our refashioning and completion of God's promises to us and predictions, sanctuary of divine glory which was heralded in advance, well-expected salvation of the gentiles! Hail, you who are truly Jacob's ladder, the smoking mountain (Exod 19.18), the ark of the sanctuary, covered entirely in gold as with the Spirit shining through (Exod 25.9, etc.), jar of beaten gold bearing Christ the heavenly manna, the undefiled nourishment for everyone! Hail, one for whom the [saying], "In pain you will bear children" (Gen 3.16), no longer has a place, since it has been transformed into birth-giving in joy! "Blessed are you among women" (Luke 1.42), through whom the believing nations call out in understanding, "Blessed is he who

[9]The adjective θεοδόχος is used not infrequently by Andrew of Crete, along with other fathers, to describe the Virgin's receiving of God in her womb. Nestorius preferred the word to the epithet θεοτόκος, but this does not seem to have affected its popularity in mariological writings thereafter. See Lampe, 625, for references.

[10]This metaphor is very interesting. It is not unusual for preachers to compare the Theotokos to a book on which the Word is written, but Andrew here combines the image with that of an acrostic whose purpose is to bind together different parts of Scripture. In other words, Mary represents the mediator between the Old and New Testaments and of law and grace.

comes in the name of the Lord; the Lord is God and has appeared
to us" (Ps 117[118].26–27).[11] "Blessed are you among women," the
mystical vine planted by God,[12] which grows luxuriantly among the
elect of the Church and blooms for us from the womb with the ripe
bunch of grapes of incorruption.[13] "Blessed are you among women,"
the field tilled by God, who bore in your womb the unsown and
unwatered Ear of Corn of our life, as it lies in a heap.[14] "Blessed are
you among women," truly the desirable earth, from which the potter of our clay took mud and remade [868] the pot which had been
broken by sin. "Blessed are you among women," the new Selon[15]
in whom the rational ark of the Incarnation of God and the Word
reposed, and further, "the whole fullness of divinity dwelt bodily"
(Col 2.9). "Blessed are you among women," truly the divine Dabir[16]
in which the God-bearing spiritual teachers of the holy Church had
their sanctuary[17] and prophesied the things to come, from divine
revelations. "Blessed are you among women," the spiritual Bethlehem, who both by disposition and by nature became and were
called the most rational house for the Bread of Life. For he dwelt in
you in a way known only by him and, having been mixed together
without confusion with our dough, he provided leaven from himself
to the entire Adam in order [that the latter] might become living
and heavenly bread. "Blessed are you among women," the grace that

[11]Many translations, including the NRSV, translate the passage, Θεὸς Κύριος καὶ
ἐπέφανεν ἡμῖν, as "God is the Lord and he has shone upon us/ given us light."

[12]Θεοφύτευτος: cf. Athanasius, PG 28, 995C.

[13]See Sir 24: 13, ff.

[14]See Job 5: 26.

[15]It is not clear what Old Testament figure is meant by Σηλών. Combefis speculates that this may be either Shillem or the family of the Shillemites (Num 26.49) or
Selon/ Silo, mentioned in 1 Kgdms, etc. Other possibilities include Sela ("Send ye
the lamb to the ruler of the land from Sela to the wilderness, unto the mount of the
daughter of Sion"), Is 16.1. See PG 97, 867, n. 37.

[16]Δαβὶρ represents another word for the ark in the Septuagint. See 3 Kgdms 6.5:
"Καὶ ἔδωκεν ἐπὶ τὸν τοῖχον τοῦ οἴκου μέλαθρα κυκλόθεν τῷ ναῷ καὶ τῷ δαβὶρ" ("And
against the wall of the house he set chambers 'round about the temple and the ark").

[17]Cf. 1 Esd 3.15. Here it means "seat of judgement," but with reference to the holy
of holies in Solomon's temple, the meaning is "sanctuary" or "oracle." L&S, 2005.

overlies[18] the legal and shadowy tabernacle, from whom Christ God, as a great Bezaleel,[19] constructed for himself a temple not made by hands, [that is] his living flesh with the architecture of the Spirit.[20] But we shall not fulfill our hymn worthily, beloved, even if we were to address a marriage oration to her, unless, having mystically gathered flowers from scriptural meadows for her, we [now] plait a crown of praises.

2　For there is not, indeed there is not, any place in the whole of the God-inspired Scripture where, on going about, one would not see signs of her scattered about in diverse ways. If you were to lay these bare, as best you could, by painstaking effort from the words, you would even find more distinctly how great was the glory that she embraced from God.[21] Indeed, see how she is adorned with names of many meanings and revealed very clearly in many places in Scripture, as, for example, whenever [Scripture] calls her a virgin, a young maiden, a prophetess, then bridal chamber, house of God, holy temple, second tabernacle, holy table, sanctuary, mercy-seat, golden censer,[22] holy of holies, cherubim of glory, golden jar, tablets of the covenant, priestly staff, sceptre of the kingdom, diadem of beauty, horn in which [is contained] the myrrh of unction, alabaster jar,[23]

[18]I have accepted Combefis's suggested emendation of ὑπερκειμένη (nominative) for ὑπερκειμένης (genitive) here.

[19]Cf. Exod 31.2; 35.30, 36–38. Bezaleel constructed the tabernacle of Moses in accordance with God's instructions.

[20]This passage is interesting because it compares or links the Theotokos with grace and Jesus Christ with a temple. It is more usual to find the Virgin herself described as a temple in Marian homilies of this period.

[21]This sentence (which I have divided into two halves) reveals once again Andrew's commitment to typological exegesis of Scripture. Like most other Fathers, he believed that the Old Testament refers constantly to the Theotokos, not only through prophecy, but also through typology and metaphor.

[22]On the depiction of the censer, as a type for the Virgin, in later Byzantine iconography, see M. Evangelatou, "The Symbolism of the Censer in Byzantine Representations of the Dormition of the Virgin," in Vassilaki, *Images of the Mother of God*, 117–31.

[23]Cf. Exod 30.34–38; Mark 14.3.

candlestick, breath,[24] lampstand, wick, chariot, shrub, rock, land, garden, country, field, spring, ewe-lamb, [869] drop, and as many other [types] as the renowned interpreters of the Spirit foreseeingly call her in accordance with the mystical insight that [reveals itself] in symbols. So, for example, [she is revealed as] a bramble bush whenever Moses says, "Having approached, I shall see this great sight. Why is it that the bramble bush burns and is not consumed?" (Exod 3.3).[25] As a rod, whenever Isaiah says, "A rod shall come out of the root of Jesse and a flower will come up from the root" (Isa 11.1). She is called a root: "And there will be a root of Jesse and he that arises to rule over the gentiles, in him will the gentiles trust" (Isa 11.10). Holy ground: "Moses, Moses, loose the sandals from your feet, for the ground on which you are standing is holy ground" (cf. Exod 3.5). Desirable land: "And they set at nought a desirable land" (Ps 105[106].24).[26] Land causing truth to arise: for "truth arose from the land" (Ps 84[85].12). Thaeman: "God will come from Thaeman" (Hab 3.3). Mountain: "The Holy One [will come] from the dark, shady mountain" (Hab 3.3). "A rock was cut from the mountain without hands" (Dan 2.45). "A mountain in which God was well pleased to dwell" (Ps 67[68].17). Olive tree: "I am like a fruitful olive tree in the house of the Lord" (Ps 51[52].10). Ark: "Arise, O Lord, into your repose; you and the ark of your holiness" (Ps 131[132].8). Throne: "I saw the Lord sitting on a high and exalted throne, and the house was full of his glory" (Isa 6.1). Gate: "And the Lord said to me, 'This gate shall be shut; it shall not be opened. And no one will pass through it, for the Lord God of Israel will enter and go out through it. And the gate will be shut'" (Ezek 44.2). Sion: "The Deliverer will come out

---

[24]Cf. Wis 7.25: "For she is a breath of the power of God . . ."

[25]On the type of the burning bush, see Arch. Ephrem, "Mary in Eastern Church Literature," 68. He argues that the word for bush used in Hebrew, Syriac, and Greek means strictly a "briar" or "bramble," thus emphasising the thorny quality of human nature which is shared by the Theotokos.

[26]The same word, γῆ, is used here as in the previous passage; however, I think that the meaning is slightly different in this quotation, so have chosen "land" in this context.

of Sion; he will turn away impiety from Jacob" (Isa 59.20). "The Lord elected Sion; he chose her as a habitation for himself " (Ps 131[132].13). She is called mother: "A man will say, 'Sion is my mother,' and a man was begotten in her and the Highest himself laid her foundations" (Ps 86[87].5), and "Why has this happened to me, that the Mother of my Lord comes to me?" (Luke 1.43). Litter: "King Solomon made himself a litter out of trees of Lebanon" (Song 3.9). Couch: "Behold, Solomon's couch; sixty powerful men of the powerful ones of Israel are around it" (Song 3.7).[27] Scroll: "And I looked, and behold, a hand stretched out to me and in it was a scroll of a book; and he unrolled it before me and things were written on it both in front and behind; and he said to me, 'Son of Man, eat this scroll'" (Ezek 2.9–3.1).[28] Book: "And all these sayings, says God, shall be for you as the words of the sealed book which, if they give [it] to a man who understands letters, saying to him, 'Read this,' he will say, 'I cannot read it, for it is sealed'" (Isa 29.11). Volume: "And the Lord said to me, 'Take for yourself a volume of a great, new [book], and write in it with a man's pen concerning the making of a rapid plunder of spoils, for it is near at hand'" (Isa 8.3–4). Tongs: "And there was sent to me one of the seraphim, and in his hand he held a coal, [872] which he had taken with the tongs from the altar, and he touched my mouth and said, 'Behold, this has touched your lips and it will purify your sins'" (Isa 6.6–7). Virgin: "Behold, the virgin shall conceive in her womb and will bear a son and they will call his name Emmanuel" (Isa 7.14). Prophetess: "And I went to the prophetess and she conceived and bore a son; and the Lord said to me, 'Call his name, "Despoil quickly" [and] "Plunder speedily." For before the child knows how to call his father or mother, he will take the power of Damascus and the spoils of Samaria'" (Isa 8.3–4). Queen: "The queen stood by on your right

[27]Song 3.7. On the depiction of this type in illustrations of the twelfth-century preacher James Kokkinobaphos's homilies, see K. Linardou, "The Couch of Solomon, A Monk, A Byzantine Lady, and the Song of Songs," in Swanson, *The Church and Mary*, 73–85, esp. 76, n. 17.

[28]Although Brenton translates κεφαλίς as "volume," it is clear that it is a scroll that is meant here, inscribed on both sides.

hand, clothed in a garment woven with gold and of many colors" (Ps 44[45].10). Companion: "You are entirely fair, my companion; entirely fair and there is no blemish in you" (Song 4:7). "Arise, come, my companion and bride; come from Lebanon. You will come and come from the beginning of faith" (Song 4.8). "Your lips drop honeycomb, my bride; honey and milk are under your tongue, and the scent of your garments is like the scent of Lebanon" (Song 4.11). Sister: "Why have your eyes been made beautiful, my sister, my bride?" (Song 4.10).[29] Garden: "[You are] an enclosed garden, a sealed spring" (Song 4.10). Daughter: "Hear, O daughter, and see, and incline your ear; forget your people and your father's house, and the King will desire your beauty" (Ps 44[45].11–12).[30] "Many daughters have obtained wealth; many have assumed power. But you have exceeded and surpassed them all" (Prov 31.29). Betrothed one: "An angel Gabriel was sent by God to a city in Galilee called Nazareth, to a virgin betrothed to a man whose name was Joseph, of the house and lineage of David. The Virgin's name was Mary" (Luke 1.26–27). Cloud: "Behold, the Lord sits on a swift cloud, and he will come to Egypt; and the hand-made things[31] of Egypt will be shaken" (Isa 19.1). Appearance: "I saw an appearance of fire, and its brightness around it, like the appearance of a [rain]bow when it is in the cloud on a rainy day; so was the position of the brightness all around: this was the appearance of the likeness of the glory of the Lord" (Ezek 1.28–2.1). Amber: "And I saw, as it were, a vision of amber; an appearance of fire from within surrounded it, from an appearance of the loins and downwards" (cf. Ezek 1.27).[32] Day, night: "Day to day

[29]The Greek, according to the Rahlfs text, has μαστοί ("breasts") for ὀφθαλμοί ("eyes") here. Brenton translates the verse: "How beautiful are they breasts, my sister, my spouse!" Cf. Rahlfs, 2:265.

[30]Andrew again substitutes the future for the aorist here ("the King will desire your beauty"), which suggests that he was using a variant version of the Septuagint. See above, n. 6.

[31]Τὰ χειροποίητα is often translated "idols."

[32]The homilist appears to have used a variant form of the text or to have quoted it incorrectly. As it stands, it does not make a great deal of sense.

utters[33] speech and night to night proclaims knowledge" (Ps 18[19].3). Heaven: "The Lord looked out of heaven; he saw all the sons of men" (Ps 32[33].13). "The heaven of heavens belongs to the Lord" (Ps 113[114].24). East: "Sing to God, O kingdoms of the earth; sing psalms to the Lord who has mounted on the heaven of heaven eastwards" (Ps 67[68].33–34). West: "Make a way for the Lord who has mounted on the West; the Lord is his name" (Ps 67[68].5). Sun: "In the sun he has set his tabernacle and he comes forth as a Bridegroom from his chamber" (Ps 18[19].5–6). City: "Glorious things were said of you, O city of God" (Ps 86[87].3). "The streams of the river gladden the city of God . . . " (Ps 45[46].5). "God is in her midst and she will not be moved" (Ps 45[46].6). Brick: "And you, Son of man, take a brick for yourself. And you will put it before your face [873] and write a city on it, Jerusalem, and you will give it fortification" (Ezek 4.1–2).[34] Place: "How fearful is this place; this is none other than the house of God and this is the gate of heaven" (Gen 28.17). "And a Spirit took me up and I heard behind me a voice [as of] a great earthquake, [saying], 'Blessed is the glory of the Lord from his place'" (Ezek 3.12). "I shall not give sleep to my eyes and drowsiness to my eyelids and repose to my temples until I find a place for the Lord, a tabernacle for the God of Jacob" (Ps 131[132].4–5). Fleece: "He will come as rain upon a fleece and as a drop dripping upon the earth" (Ps 71[72].6). Woman: "Blessed are you among women and blessed is the fruit of your womb" (Luke 1.42). "God sent out his Son, born of a woman, born under the law" (Gal 4.4). Blessed: "Blessed is she who believed that there would be a fulfilment of what was spoken to her by the Lord" (Luke 1.45). And "Blessed is the womb that bore you and the breasts that you suckled" (Luke 11.27). Mary: "Do not be afraid, Mariam, for you have found favor with God" (Luke 1.30), and, "Behold, you will conceive in your womb and bear a Son, and you will call his name Jesus" (Luke 1.31). "For he will save his people from

---

[33]The word ἐπεύγεται may also be translated "belches forth."

[34]Brenton translates the final phrase, "Thou shalt besiege it." For the word περιοχή, see also 1 Kgdms 22.4.

their sins" (Matt 1.21). "He will be great and will be called Son of the Highest, and the Lord God will give to him the throne of his ancestor David, and he will reign over the house of Jacob forever, and of his kingdom there will be no end. And Mariam said to the angel, 'How will this happen to me since I do not know a man?' And the angel said to her, 'The Holy Spirit will come upon you and the power of the Highest will overshadow you; therefore the [child] to be born will be holy; he will be called the Son of God'" (Luke 1.32–35). "And Mariam said, 'My soul magnifies the Lord and my spirit has rejoiced in God my Savior'" (Luke 1.46–47).

3 And who would not admire one who has been raised to such a height as to become Mother of God, something that is truly a most miraculous event and occurrence?[35] If you have trusted me, let us hasten to her as the initiator of the feast, in order that the oration may resume once again from the point where it paused briefly. Come then, let us take up the hymns for the day and, after having short discussions on those things that have been collected together, let us [now] halt the progress of the oration.[36] Human nature, then, having been shattered by the ancestral, original Fall, was in need of the One who fashioned [it] or who renewed [it], and with silent voice cried out a great [plea] to the Creator, "Why, Lord, do you stand far off?" (Ps 9.22). And even more resoundingly through the prophets, it shouted mournfully, saying, "Where, Lord, are your ancient mercies, which you swore to David in your truth?" (Ps 88[89].50). Why then is he "One who delights in mercy"? (Mic 7.19). Did he not overlook and delay; did he not extend his precepts very far? What do these things mean? "Neither shall I forsake you, nor shall I abandon you" (cf. Josh 1.5). And later, when he was returning from

[35]The noun ἄκουσμα in fact means "thing heard," but there does not appear to be an English word equivalent to "spectacle" in relation to what is learned through hearing.

[36]This passage suggests that the sermon may have been interspersed with hymns at this point. To my knowledge, we have no other evidence of this practice in the Byzantine liturgy.

earth to heaven, he said to his disciples from whom he did not separate [himself], [876] "I shall not leave you orphans. I am coming to
you" (John 14.18). And he affirmed this clearly through the prophets
even before his ineffable Incarnation. Since, then, these things were
so, time was already calling [on him] to bring the proclamation to
an end. See what he does, [he] who is bringing about our salvation
from our own dough. He has not imported an instrument from
outside or transformed the vessel from another substance; instead,
having removed the refuse[37] from the same clay and, as one might
say, from the same leaven, he built a temple worthy of himself, of
such a construction that truly surpassed all description. [This was a
temple] in which he himself, the first and only High Priest and King,
performed priestly functions, according to the dispensation, for our
reconciliation with his own Father, and he took up supra-essentially
our[38] entire substance, and [assumed] his substance from human
substance. Then God indeed remembered his own creatures. For all
the nations[39] are his creation. The Lord of the Ages remembered his
compassions that were from the ages;[40] he remembered the covenant
that he had established with humankind. He remembered and, having remembered, he did not set it aside, but at once he conferred his
benevolence. For having remembered David and the things that he
had earlier sworn to him, namely that Christ would arise from his
seed, [Christ] in whom he built up the fallen work of our race like a
tabernacle [and] introduced a paradoxical miracle for a paradoxical
miracle.

4   And indeed, when the prudent Anna was constrained by the
great burden of incomprehension[41] and moreover, her husband was

[37] I have adopted Combefis's suggested emendation of σύρμα for συρμάδα here.

[38] I have emended ὑμῶν ("your") to ἡμῶν here. The two forms are frequently
confused by scribes and the latter makes more sense in the context.

[39] I have elsewhere translated ἔθνη as "gentiles." The sense here, however, requires
a more inclusive term.

[40] See Ps 24[25].6.

[41] I have adopted Combefis's suggested emendation of ἀνοίας for ἀνίας.

bitterly weighed down because of their lack of a child, God undid
the sterility of both. Having been moved also by their supplications,
he gave an offspring to the barren woman whom prayer had already
made fertile.[42] And [he gave] fruit to her husband, which hope had
sprouted, along with an ever-blooming flower for those which had
dried up in the burning heat of childlessness. And [his wife] who had
previously been without issue became productive; a climbing plant[43]
bloomed which had [formerly] not produced a shoot. What will be
more worthy of reverence than that engendering of a child? What
more paradoxical than to see a Mother of God conceived as the fruit
of a pure woman and as a virgin who sprouted from a childless,
barren woman, who was opened but not corrupted in her womb?
Why did this occur? In order that in the surpassing miracle surrounding her [birth], the [miracle] of her own child-bearing might
be believed. For she introduced by nature, yet contrary to nature, a
fatherless child without the travail of birth-pangs, [an event] which
had previously been unknown in human nature, having formed the
Author of nature in her womb by means of a supernatural power;
and she became a mother having escaped the [experiences] of
mothers. The infant did not have anyone he might call father on
earth, since he had been conceived without intermediary seed, nor
did the one who bore him partake of any incipient corruption. But
she, although having many examples of previous people in sterility,
held the all-conquering vote that conquers all [votes].[44] If [877] the
couple had been living together [in the time] of the patriarchs, it
is likely that they would have been deemed worthy of loosing the
bonds of sterility by a similar form of miracle-working, for indeed,
female ancestors of this sacredly born child had anticipated her existence; but whereas they were somewhere very far and very distant

[42]Literally, "prayer gave her seed."

[43]The word κλιματίς does not appear the dictionaries. It is likely that it is borrowed from the Latin *clematis*, a "climbing plant."

[44]The meaning of this sentence is somewhat obscure, but it seems to be concerned with the proof positive of Mary's virginal conception of Christ, even in the
face of doubters.

from the miracle that accords with divine dispensation, they [nevertheless] have a relationship [with it], while she [conceived], later, at this time and even at the utmost limits of all time, when indeed the one [who sought] the royal drachma stood at the doors themselves[45] (and I speak, looking for an image of our times), in order that he might wipe away the dust in which [our nature] had previously been hidden by the cleansing of the divinely perfect Spirit, just as from this point, he would benevolently transform human nature in his own person.[46]

What then is the dust in which our nobility had been hidden? Clearly, it came from that place, even though we may not say [how], since he who created us himself searched out and found what was needed in that dust from which we were originally created, and later recreated. What is this? He who is free of passion in his substance saw the archetype of the image covered up by passions. He sought out the dust which [he used] in Adam. The dust in which that which had been sought was found; it was earth of the same form of body that had been used for us, having the supremely holy virginal womb as its place. Your life-giving ear of corn discovered her as a field in which, without seed or farming, he miraculously germinated and sprouted forth. This is the dust; this is the ear of corn; this is the place on the earth in which we were recreated in a new way and through which our dust was transformed and returned to its ancient dignity.

5 Did you see how many mysteries the birth-giving of Anna encompassed, so that in the miracle that was pre-eminent in her glorious conception of a child, she outdid those previous sterile women? But it was also by reason of such a manner of conception that a virginal girl, the supremely unblemished Mary herself, who was called by God, was considered worthy. And who else among women has ever caused so much amazement among so many and

[45]Cf. Luke 15.8–10; 1 Cor 15.47–49.
[46]This long and complex sentence is typical of Andrew's style. It is difficult to follow the sense since he employs a variety of subjects and images.

such notable [people]? So, since our oration is too weak to be raised
to such a great height from its vantage point and is not able to go
further, let us utter again a few [words] of greeting to the Mother of
joy as we rejoice. For it is good to address an expression of joy to her.
Hail, favored one! Hail, glorified one! Hail, offering bestowing the
joy of universal salvation! Hail, golden censer of truly spiritual fragrances in which Christ, the rational incense, formed from divinity
and humanity, displayed the fragrance of his living and rational flesh,
without confusion and without separation, on fire by his divinity![47]
Hail, tabernacle not made by hands, constructed moreover by God,
into which God, the only and first High Priest, has entered once, at
the culmination of the ages, to carry out worship secretly on behalf
of all in you; [Hail], second curtain [covering] holy things, including
the universal mercy-seat, precious covering of the cherubim [880],
by means of which you covered the Lord of these inaccessible things
himself within your womb [as if] with a veil, while carrying him
inside your belly! Seven-times-lit and seven-burning lampstand of
seven graces which was lit by the seven vessels of oil belonging to
the Spirit! Unquenched wick of the light of the One who illumined
all things, that is mystically fed by the oil of unction! Hail, altar, on
which the living Lamb, Christ, is mystically offered as a whole burnt
offering! The divinely mystical[48] table of holy activity that is beyond
the [human] mind, on which [lies] Christ, the Bread from heaven,
who, as the Lamb above all [others] has been sacrificed as an offering[49] and living, sacrificial victim, giving life to those that partake of
him! The precious vessel of all mystical[50] worship in which God is

---

[47]M. Evangelatou comments on the significance of this passage in her article,
"The Symbolism of the Censer," 121. She notes that Andrew also uses this type in his
kanon on the Nativity of the Virgin in the lines, "You have become a golden thurifer,
because the Word under the inspiration of the Holy Spirit planted the fire in your
womb, and became visible in human form, O pure Mother of God." PG 97, 1324C.

[48]The adjective θεόμυστος is unusual. Trapp (676) refers to this passage. Cf. also
I. Schirò, ed., *Analecta Hymnica Graeca* 3 (Rome 1966–80): 401.28; 5:453, 386, etc.

[49]I have adopted Combefis's suggested emendation of θῦμα for θυμίαμα here.

[50]I have adopted Combefis's emendation of μυστικοῦ for μύστου here.

[51]Note the highly mystical and theological language used to describe the mystery

consumed in the flesh and [in turn] sanctifies all things, and mystically coming to visit human beings, he dwells in them, shares in their being, and allows [himself] to be turned over by the hands of sinners, and to be approached by lips of clay, and to be poured forth into the dust of our flesh, as he is mixed [into us], but not dispersed![51] O inexpressible self-emptying! O what goodness! That God should grant these things through a woman of the same tribe and shared ancestry in a manner above nature and custom! [Through] a woman whose beauty of soul was, times without number, raised without experience up to him in order that the inconceivable Beauty, Christ himself, might arrive at a desire for her beauty and choose the second and fatherless[52] nativity from her. And so, the state of her body was pleasing, and she advanced to such a condition of purity that she was able to contain the bodiless and incomprehensible magnitude of his supra-essential nature, through one of its three hypostases.

6 She is the Theotokos, Mary; the new refuge of all Christians. [She is] the first restoration of the first Fall of [our] forefathers; the return to dispassion of the impassioned race; the vision which was mystically foreshadowed of old in Moses' [burning] bush (cf. Exod 3.3); the fleece of Gideon (cf. Judg 6.38), which he saw symbolically moistened by noiseless drops from heaven, and, having interpreted the act as a miracle and the rain as a sign, confirmed the conjecture by sacrificial victim (cf. Judg 6.19–24); David's divinely embroidered purple robe, which attached the acquisition of flesh, like a purple robe, to the incarnated God of David; cherubic throne, supremely great, fiery and lofty, holding in its womb the Lord King Sabaoth, the hyperthyrum[53] of the inaccessible things in heaven where the seraphim stand covered by their wings; with some [wings] covering their faces, some their feet, while with some they fly; and they cry out

of participation in the Eucharist.

[52] I have substituted ἀπάτορα for ἀπατατορίαν here.

[53] Or a frieze above the lintel.

[54] Literally, "the moist substance of the waters." I have omitted the second reference to the waters to avoid repetition in English.

loudly that fearful hymn since they cannot support the sight of his unbearable glory (cf. Isa 6.1–5). The gate of heaven, through which the Master of the heavens alone passed, having granted the entrance to no one after him or before him (cf. Ezek 44.2).

7 [881] Be glad in her, heaven! For she imitated you, who could not contain the Lord in yourself, when she contained him without constriction. Celebrate her in dance, earth! For her pregnancy raised your condition heavenwards and made those who dwell on earth heavenly. Let even the sea applaud the miracle of the Virgin! For Christ experienced child-birth through her with his body and, having been baptized in the waters, sanctified their moist substance.[54] So then, let all creation rejoice and dance and clap its hands! For today a young girl has been born for us, from whom [will come] salvation and through whom [will emerge] the universal deliverance that is Jesus Christ our God and Word, who is and who was and who is coming, and who endures eternally. With him let us conclude our oration, as if putting into port from the great sea of the virginal oration, by extending one glory and honor and veneration in three expressions of worship[55] to God, the Trinity, worshipped in the Father, the Son himself, along with the Holy Spirit, now and into the unending ages of ages. Amen.

[55]The word ἁγιαστεία may mean "rite" or "office" in a Christian context. Here it appears to mean the offering of praise in three ways to God the Trinity.

KOSMAS VESTITOR

Sermon on the Holy Joachim and Anna, Glorious Parents of the Theotokos Mary[1]

[1005] Father, give a blessing.

1 Yesterday the Nativity festival of the Theotokos glorified the celebration of cosmic joy for us with auspicious hymnody. Today is the day that offers thanksgiving to the progenitors of the Theotokos, through whom the beginning of salvation for everyone has come about. Indeed, the festival of the parents is that of the daughter. For just as a child is glorified too in the glory of its mother, so also is a mother glorified in the blessing of a child. Yesterday thus was a day that was "wonderful in our eyes" (cf. Ps 117[118].23), and today there is happiness in remembering the righteous with speeches of praise.

2 It came to pass in times of old that there was a righteous man from the tribe of Judah named Joachim.[2] He was a man distinguished in holiness and righteousness; a man who was notable in nobility and wealth; a man who was single-minded[3] in his offerings of sacrifices; a man in every way well-pleasing to God; a man of the longings[4] which come from the Spirit. For since he was childless and

---

[1]*CPG* 8151; *BHG* 828; P. Ballerini, ed., PG 106, 1005–1012.

[2]The account that follows is taken from the *Protevangelion* of James. See Elliott, *The Apocryphal New Testament*, 57–67.

[3]The adjective ἁπλοψυχός appears to be a neologism. Trapp refers to this passage (160), translating it "aufrichtig."

[4]I have emended ἐπιθυμείων to ἐπιθυμιῶν here.

139

consumed with desire for a child, he fathered the bride of the Holy Spirit. As a man he truly achieved this, since God hearkened to his prayers and granted him the one who was "beyond all the tabernacles of Jacob" (Ps 86[87].2), or to put it another way, the daughter who is worthily [deemed] higher than all created things in heaven or on earth.

3   And he had a pious wife, whose name was Anna, who also came from the royal tribe of Judah since she was a descendant of David. [She was] a woman who rejected all evil; a woman who lived faithfully before God with her husband; a woman who regularly attended the temple of God along with her own spouse, with prayers, fasts, and pleasing, bountiful gifts; [1008] a woman who in unanimity of soul and bodily chastity always possessed constancy of understanding with her husband. For in accordance with the formation of the one to whom she was married by God, she preserved indestructibly the bone of her husband, thus safeguarding [an attitude of] devout benevolence towards him in their union.

4   For she was not mischievously transformed, like Eve, but was instead joined to her husband as a helper both in the living out of virtues and in daily supplications to God. For the two grew equally weary in their prayer of yearning for a child in the same way that a farmer, together with his wife, when they have worked[5] some barren land, sow the seed and, through prayer, expect to gain a good crop of fruit. [Anna lived] not as Eve lived with Adam, but as one who shared in thanksgiving and worked with [Joachim] on spiritual good deeds; and she was truly a "better half" who completed the union with her husband perfectly. For whereas Eve became the producer of pain for the world by means of the fruit of a tree, Joachim's Anna represented joy for the Creator by means of the fruit of her womb.

---

[5]I have emended καλλιεργήσαντος to καλλιεργήσαντες here in order to agree with Joachim and Anna.

5 It is well known to everyone that Mary the Theotokos was given the good news in the Galilee of the gentiles,[6] in the house of Joseph the carpenter, who had been made the Virgin's husband in order to ward off the devil's deception. And again, it is clear that she gave birth to Christ in Bethlehem and that her native land happened to be the same city as that of her mother, just as the oration will demonstrate below. For [Mary's] ancestral home was situated near the pool by the Sheep Gate in Jerusalem, according to the text,[7] where Christ [who was] also our God raised up and cured the man who had lain as a paralytic for thirty-eight years (cf. John 5.1–9), since he was about to go forth from that house symbolically as the Shepherd of rational sheep. For this reason the grace of baptism is also foreshadowed by the pool of water there, for the illness of chronic deceit that has paralysed the souls of men, just as in the functioning of limbs, has been healed by purification of the Spirit through water, just as the spiritual bread of life was leavened in the figure of Bethlehem. And here Christ was revealed in the form of an angel to Abraham,[8] and he also wrestled with Jacob in angelic shape.[9] For he is the One who came to bring good news to those who are far away and those who are nearby (cf. Acts 2.39); he is the Gospel of righteousness; [1009] he is the One who [carried out] the commandment of the God and Father by means of angels; he is the "Messenger of great counsel" (Isa 9.6), to whom the Father became Counsellor and said, "Let us make man according to our image and likeness" (Gen 1.26). He is also the Bread of true life which was predicted in advance by the name of Bethlehem; for "Bethlehem" means "house of bread," which was baked in the ashes in Abraham's tent, that is to say, bread which was leavened in secret, or the flesh of the Savior that was begotten from the Virgin and Theotokos, Mary.

---

[6]Cf. Matt 4.15 for this epithet; Luke 1.26, ff., for the story of the Annunciation.

[7]The tradition that Mary was born near the "probatic" pool by the Sheep Gate in Jerusalem (John 5.2), where her parents had a house, appeared early although it is not attested in the New Testament or the *Protevangelion* of James. See John of Damascus, *In Nativitem*, Kotter, *Die Schriften* 5, 175; above, 61, n. 36.

[8]See Gen 22.11.

[9]See Gen 32.24.

6   It is therefore fitting, on account of these things, to say that the Lord blessed the house of King David on account of his descendant, life-bearing Mary. He blessed the house of the righteous Joachim and Anna on account of their hallowed daughter. He blessed the house of Joseph on account of the bride, the truly pure and ever-Virgin Mother of Christ and Theotokos Mary, who had been entrusted in civil law to him alone.

Hence, and on account of these things, thrice-blessed are the parents of the Mother of God, to whom the whole world is indebted! [Blessed are] the prophets, who truthfully predicted the Incarnation of Christ through them; the apostles, who were reborn as sons of light through their daughter; the holy martyrs when they received their crowns; the saintly and righteous [Christians], as inheritors of good things to come; [and even] sinners, since they are pitied through the intercessions of the Theotokos.

7   To them let us cry in thanksgiving: Hail, all-pious father of our hope in God, Joachim; may your loins be graced! Hail, all-honored mother of the Mother of our life, Anna; glory be to your womb! Hail, father with a good seed,[10] and farmer of the fruitful offspring! Hail, mother of great fruit, root of our salvation! Hail, father, vine-dresser of the productive bunch of grapes! Hail, mother, field of good earth [which has yielded] a hundredfold![11] Hail, father, gardener of the spiritual paradise! Hail, mother, tree [with] the blameless branch; Hail, father, oyster shell of the spotless pearl! Hail, mother, rock [containing] the pure emerald! Hail, father, source of the life-flowing spring! Hail, mother, water-jug for the thirst of child-bearing!

Our mouths are filled with praise for the special qualities of your holiness, but we are not capable of singing about your duality that is yoked together by God[12] unless we follow the utterance of your

---

[10]The word ἀγαθόσπορος appears to be a neologism. Trapp refers to this passage (4), translating it, "Saër des Guten."

[11]Cf. Matt 19.29; Mark 10.30; Luke 8.8.

[12]Cf. Amphilochius of Iconium, Homily 2.7, PG 39, 53D.

descendant according to flesh, Christ, in blessing you both and say, "Rejoice and [1012] be glad, for the reward of the fruit of your womb is in heaven" (cf. Matt 5.12). For you are the holy ones who were reproached on account of your childlessness and who heard wicked words. But you were made happy after a short time by your child-bearing, and the fact that you have given birth to the Mother of God is sufficient as praise for you!

For the righteous progenitors of the Theotokos were truly perceived in advance as worthy of being related to Christ in flesh and of being honored as belonging to a famous family, by which I mean a kingly and priestly one. For the Theotokos takes her genealogy from both, since the two tribes became intertwined in different ways from the beginning.

8 For this reason [let us] then [expound] the ancestors of the Theotokos as follows: Zacharias, the father of John the Baptist, had a brother who was also a priest, called Aggaei, who had died before him. Joseph, the carpenter, took a daughter of this Aggaei in marriage. From her he begat four sons and two daughters, of whom one was James, who was called the brother of Christ and who became the first bishop of Jerusalem. And the name of [Joseph's] wife was Salome: not [Salome] the midwife, but another [Salome]. After her death, Joseph was engaged to the Theotokos Mary whose maternal line descended from the priest Matthat, who in turn [was descended] from Solomon, the son of David, as the genealogy according to the Gospel of Luke states.[13] This Matthat had three daughters by his wife Mary whose names were Mary, Sobbe, and Anna. Then Mary bore Salome the midwife, Sobbe bore Elizabeth, the mother of John the Baptist, while Anna bore the Theotokos Mary in Bethlehem, who was given the name "Mary" of her grandmother and aunt. As a result, Elizabeth was Anna's niece and the cousin of

---

[13]Luke 3.23–38. Luke actually says that Joseph, not Mary, was descended from Nathan, the son of David (Luke 1.31). Matthew, on the other hand, includes Solomon as an ancestor of Joseph (Matt 1.7).

the Theotokos. The Gospel affirms each of these things, for on the one hand, with regard to the paternal family of Christ, according to the flesh, it states, "Jesus was about thirty years old when he began his work. He was the son (as was thought) of Joseph son of Heli, son of Matthat" (Luke 3.23–24), while on the other hand, with regard to his maternal [line], it states, "Behold, your relative Elizabeth" (Luke 1.36). On account of these things, glory be to the condescension of God, now and ever, and to the ages of ages. Amen.

On the Entrance into the Temple I

On the Entrance [into the Temple] of the Supremely Holy Theotokos[1]

1 [292] Every most divine festival of rejoicing that is accomplished on each occasion fills the worshippers up spiritually from treasures and divinely flowing springs. And [the feast] that is now being celebrated[2] is made more greatly resplendent than all [others], offering refreshment as the source of all perfection,[3] by the fact that its originator, the child of God, takes preeminence. For her most sacred,[4] annual banquet comes around, for which the participants must be inexperienced in sin.[5] And may you, flourishing with most pure understanding and brightly shining fine array,[6] earnestly attend to me, if it seems [good] to you. Let us run together for the plucking of the much desired flowers of the Mother of God's own meadow! Let us anoint well, as if from flower-buds,[7] her rose-colored beauty

---

[1] *CPG* 8007; *BHG* 1103; P. Ballerini, ed., PG 98, 292–309.

[2] The noun ἀρτιύμνητος ("now hymned") appears to be a neologism since it is not used elsewhere, according to texts listed in *TLG*. Lampe cites this passage for the meaning of the word, 231; cf. Sophocles, 254.

[3] For the adjective τελεταρχικός (here used as an adverb), see (ps-) Dionysius the Areopagite, *De caelesti hierarchia* 3.1, PG 3, 164D.

[4] The adjective ἱερουργικός (here in the superlative) means literally, "most priestly," i.e. having to do with divine worship.

[5] Or "innocent."

[6] The noun εὐστολία appears to be a neologism. Lampe cites this passage, 576. It appears that Germanos is using the word in a metaphorical sense, i.e. the mind and disposition are finely attired.

[7] Κάλυξ usually means "cup" or "pod" of a flower (calyx). In Greek poetry it may mean "rosebud."

which comes up full of fragrances, as it has been set beautifully in verse by Solomon in his Songs, when he says, "Who is this that comes up from the wilderness as pillars of smoke, perfumed with myrrh and frankincense, with all the powders of the perfumer?" (Song 3.6). ". . . Come from Libanus, my bride, come from Libanus" (Song 4.8). Let us then eagerly [293] depart together, urging each other on, for the universally beneficial and saving festival of the Mother of God, and let us, having peeped at the sanctuaries, look upon the girl as she advances towards the second veil [of the temple],[8] Mary, the all-pure and Mother of God, who dissolved the sterility of unfruitfulness and who destroyed[9] the shadow of the legal letter by the grace of her birth-giving.[10]

2   For today she enters the temple of the law[11] at the age of three, she who alone will be dedicated and called the spotless and highest temple of the Lord, [who is] High Priest and Author of consecration[12] of all, having dissipated by the innate radiance of her divinely shining splendor the gloom [which resides] in the letter. Today an infant is offered to the priest, [the infant] who will [later] dedicate

---

[8]It is possible that Germanos is referring to the veil of the second temple here, since it is well known that there was only one veil dividing the main part of the temple from the "holy of holies" (2 Chr 3.14). The veil of the temple replicated that of the tabernacle (Exod 26.31) and was woven from blue, purple, and crimson woolen threads and fine linen. Both Jewish and Christian commentators believed that the four colors symbolized the four elements out of which the universe was created, with the red representing fire, the blue, air, the purple, water, and the white linen, the earth. Josephus and other Jewish commentators described the veil as symbolizing the boundary between earth and heaven; in Christian circles it was also interpreted as a figure of Christ's Incarnation. See Josephus, *Life* 1; Heb 10.19–20: "Therefore, brethren, since we have confidence to enter the sanctuary by the blood of Jesus, by the new and living way which he opened for us through the curtain, that is, through his flesh . . ."; M. Barker, *Temple Theology. An Introduction* (London: SPCK, 2004), 27–32; eadem, *The Great High Priest*, 188–228.

[9]Literally, "drove through," from διελαύνω.

[10]Note the play on the words διαλύσασαν and διελάσασαν.

[11]I.e. the Old Testament law of Moses.

[12]For the use of the noun τελετάρχης with reference to God, cf. (ps-) Dionysius the Areopagite, *De ecclesiastica hierarchia* 5.3.2, 5.3.5, 7.3.7, PG 3, 509D, 512C, 564A.

the forty-day-old High-Priest God, who alone was made an infant in flesh on our account, holding in her own arms the Limitless One who is beyond all mortal understanding. Today the newest and most pure, unblemished volume, which will not be written on by hand, but will be gilded in spirit, sanctified by blessings according to the law, is brought as a gift of thanksgiving. Today Joachim, having cleansed himself of the reproach of childlessness, goes openly on the streets to show most boastfully his own child and is shown again to be a spiritual teacher of holiness according to the law. Today also Anna, having exchanged the persistence of childlessness for the blessing of a child and becoming inspired with immense joy, is proclaimed[13] to the ends [of the earth] as having acquired fruit, cradling at her breast the one who is wider than the heavens. Today the gate of the divine temple, opened wide, receives the eastward-facing and sealed gate of the Emmanuel, which is entering into [it] (cf. Ezek 44.1–3). Today the holy table of the temple begins to be made splendid, having assumed the transfer to bloodless sacrifices by participation and the sweetest embrace of the heavenly and life-sustaining bread from a table of divine veneration. Today she alone is dedicated to the place of propitiation[14] for the floods of errors that have overthrown mortals, being called a new, most godlike,[15] cleansing place of propitiation that is not made by hands. Today, she is about to be welcomed by the sanctity of the Spirit into the holy of holies; she, who was raised in a most marvelous way beyond even the glory of the cherubim, is stored up in a most holy way and gloriously in the holy of holies, for a greater sanctity,[16] at an innocent and impressionable[17] age.

[13]The somewhat unusual word διακηρυκεύομαι means, according to L&S, to "negotiate by herald." It is used in Thucydides, *The Peloponnesian War,* 4.38.

[14]The word ἱλαστήριον means the place of propitiation or mercy-seat in the Old Testament temple. See Lampe, 673.2.

[15]The word θεοειδής has firm patristic foundations. It is used to mean the aspects of human beings that are like God, in other words the virtues or the spiritual likeness to divinity. See Lampe, 625.

[16]It is likely that in using the phrase "stored up ... for a greater sanctity," the author refers here to Mary's later role in giving birth to Christ.

[17]Literally, "unknowing" or "ignorant."

3 Today Mary leads the way, whom no one, even having uttered countless [praises], will in any way match; nor yet will he attain his desire, having given up praise, since she was raised by her beauty beyond every tongue and mind![18] For the Heavenly Drop who was born from her revealed the vast sea [that is] her greatness. Indeed, for this reason her wealth became ungraspable in its infinitude[19] and her delight inexhaustible,[20] for she could satisfy everyone in every way.[21] And among the refrains and celebrations in her honor, the banquet [296] is unstinting in its sweetness. Hence even the causes for the hymns are unforced[22] since they have their source [in her], and since the spring is inexhaustible, it is not diminished by heavy use; indeed, even if it is drawn on as much as a hundred times,[23] or if it overflows ten thousand times, it is impossible for those who draw [on it] to exhaust [it]. For in its compassion[24] the mystery overflows and in what it produces, it surpasses [the understanding] even of immaterial minds, not to mention those that are material, O all-blessed and all-pure girl!

4 And her own parents are presenting her to God since she has reached the age of three. But how very great and entirely estimable

[18]The meaning of this sentence is quite difficult to express in English, owing to the unusual choice of words and syntax. I have emended τοῦ αἴνους to τοῦ αἴνου ("praise," in genitive singular). The resulting translation is not completely literal but, I hope, matches the general meaning of the Greek.

[19]See mystical writers for this vocabulary, e.g. Gregory of Nyssa, (ps-) Dionysius, and Maximos. Lampe, 180.

[20]An alternative translation for the word ἀδάπανος would be "without expense."

[21]The use of language that evokes physical and sensual pleasures in this sentence is striking. Germanos transfers such resonances to a purely spiritual context in describing the Mother of God.

[22]Lampe translates ἀνίμαστος as "unscourged," 145. See also Nonnus Panipolitanus, *Paraphrasis in Joannis evangelium* 19:1, PG 43, 897B. The author is referring to the image of the Virgin as a spring or fountain, which is developed in the next clause: praises and hymns flow naturally from her since she produces them unstintingly.

[23]For ἑκατονταπλασίως, see 2 Kgdms 24.3.

[24]The compound κατοίκτρος or –ον appears to be a neologism. Trapp refers to this passage, 811.

is this number three since it [represents] a cause of total certainty
in every [instance]! David strikes the destroyer, Goliath, with three
stones from his slingshot (cf. 1 Kgdms 17.40);[25] Elijah the Thesbite
prepares [the people] to believe by the third circuit [of water], as a
flame from the blaze of heavenly fire comes down in the midst of
[that] water (cf. 3 Kgdms 18.30–38); during the same number of days
Jonah is carried about in the body of a seafaring beast and is recognized as a type of God, who has directed the great monster (cf. Jonah
1.17); of such a number are the children who stand in the furnace
and who, being cheered[26] by a heavenly dew, walk about in a happy
frame of mind (cf. Dan 3.20–27); in three times the cycle of a ten year
period[27] does my Lord Jesus purify me of the defilement of the Fall
(cf. Luke 3.21–23); and equally, while passing through [three] other
years, he cures every illness and every weakness; he ascends with
the same number of disciples that he may fulfill in a most mystical
way the manifestation of his own glory on the mountain (cf. Matt
17.1; Mark 9.2; Luke 9.28);[28] [and] after waiting three days, he raises
up the souls in Hades which have been confined in darkness from
the beginning of time.[29] And why indeed? Observe with me that the
[number] three [characterizes] the greatest things, for the Cause
of everything and Divinity that is the source of all perfection[30] has
chosen to be praised in three divine names,[31] three figures[32] or rather

[25]In fact the text says five stones, yet the Byzantine theological and iconographi-
cal traditions always held that there were three, presumably symbolizing the Trinity.

[26]The verb πιαίνω literally means "to fatten" or "enrich"; a related interpretation,
also allowed by L&S, seems more appropriate here.

[27]This quite recondite way of referring to thirty years cannot be translated exactly
literally.

[28]Jesus took his disciples Peter, James and John with him onto Mt Tabor.

[29]Literally, "from eternity," which is impossible since there is a beginning for
creation and humankind.

[30]See (ps-) Dionysius the Areopagite, *De caelesti hierarchia* 3.1, PG 3, 164D; 8.2,
240C, etc. (Lampe, 1385).

[31]Cf. (ps-) Dionysius the Areopagite, *De divinis nominibus* 1.6, PG 3, 596B. It
is also possible, however, that Germanos is referring to the three sanctifications, or
"holies" in Isa 6:3; cf. Basil of Caesarea, *Adversus Eunomium* 3.3, PG 29, 660D.

[32]In the sense of "persons": see Lampe, 1513.6.

three hypostases, even if one must also speak of the same [beings] as persons, [which] nevertheless are joined wholly consubstantially as by a perfect number in unconfused, or collected,[33] unity; nor is [he] dishonored by the poverty of deficiency [in himself] or imagined fantastically in the numbering beyond himself of many sources, according to Gregory, who is preeminent in divine matters and most accurate in theology.[34]

Thus when he, who is indeed One of the Trinity that is itself all-holy and beyond all beginning, hastened to be contained, by his own will and by the overshadowing of the all-holy Spirit, in the womb of that girl who was a virgin mother,[35] it was necessary for the one who had been distinguished by the same glory of the number to be most splendidly dedicated. [It is] for this reason that she was brought to the temple at the age of three years, since the One who was both her Creator and child clearly and unfailingly arranged for all these things to happen.

5   When, therefore, she had been weaned from the nourishment of our life,[36] her parents[37] [297] carried out the appointment that they had promised. For, it says, having called together all the virgins who were living nearby and in the vicinity, they placed them in front of her, bearing torches, arranging her as a follower behind, so that, pleased by the torch-carrying, she might advance without turning back.[38]

---

[33]The adjective ἀγύρτος is related to the verb ἀγείρω, "to collect" or "gather together." Also cf. the related nouns ἀγύρτης, ἡ (a collector or vagabond) and ἄγυρις, ἡ (a gathering or crowd).

[34]In the prologue of his second theological oration, Gregory discusses the pre-requisites for theologizing, which include purity, detachment from external distractions, and gravity. He ends by invoking the Holy Trinity, praying that "illumination may come upon us from the One God, One in diversity, diverse in Unity, wherein is a marvel." See *NPNF²*, 7:288. Gregory Nazianzen, *Oratio* 2.1.37; J. Bernardi, ed. and trans., *Grégoire de Nazianze. Discours 1–3* (Paris: Éditions du Cerf, 1978), 135, ff.

[35]The term παρθενομήτηρ or παρθενομήτωρ is used quite early by writers such as the Greek Ephrem, Modestos, and Sophronios of Jerusalem. See Lampe, 1037.

[36]I.e. milk from her mother's breast.

[37]The PG text has τοκεῖ here instead of τοκεῖς. I have emended it to the latter.

[38]I have translated a number of present forms in the past tense here for better

And the once sterile and barren Anna went first, giving her hand to God and crying out distinctly in a loud voice, "Come, rejoice with me even more, as many of you as were gathered together at the birth, as I now dedicate to the Lord the one who [emerged] from my womb, as a most divinely beautiful, sanctified gift. Come with me, leaders of the choir, may you begin, with dances and the clashing of timbrels, singing a new, novel[39] song—not with Miriam who journeyed formerly with Moses (cf. Exod 15.20–21)—but with the one who was begotten from me leading [you]."

"Come with me, both neighbors and as many as are strangers, since I have been blessed with a child and offered thanks with very great happiness, cheerfully accompanying me as I deliver the fruitful product of my birth-pangs to the holy places: cry out divinely inspired songs![40] Come with me, company[41] of prophets, which is the chosen gathering: may you prepare the hymn, fashioning it with splendid praises taught to you by the Spirit of God. For where a word of prophetic utterance is blown as through a reed,[42] there every opposing slanderous statement becomes deprived of strength."

6   "But come to me, David, our forefather and divine father, plucking your lyre,[43] make an even more harmonious sound on the strings of the Spirit with your divinely inspired mouth, signifying distinctly

grammatical consistency. It should be noted, however, that the preacher intended to convey a sense of immediacy, as if these events were taking place before his congregation's eyes, and used the present tense for this reason.

[39]It is not clear why Germanos uses the synonyms νέον and καινόν here. The meaning seems redundant and does not gain much from the two words.

[40]I have emended θεοκίχητα, which does not appear in the dictionaries, to θεοκίνητα.

[41]The word θίασος, ὁ has classical origins and may mean "company or band of Bacchic revellers." In a Christian context it was sometimes used to refer to participation in the divine mysteries. See Lampe, 652. It may also mean "company," "religious sect," or "confraternity."

[42]The verb δονακίζω may be a neologism: see Trapp, 404, who refers to this passage. It is derived from δόναξ, ὁ (a reed).

[43]Cf. 1 Kgdms 16.23. The word κιννύρα is the word for a Jewish-stringed instrument (kinnor) which is a lyre. See Andrew of Crete, *In nativitatem* I, PG 97, 817; see above, 81, n. 34.

the procession[44] of young women [in the words], 'Virgins shall be brought to the King behind her; her companions shall be brought [to you]' (Ps 44[45].15). Behold, the multitude of young people is forming a chorus in the streets, while [the daughter] of the King, my child, whom you yourself called daughter, is led through the sanctified dwelling places into the holy temple, in a happy and joyful state, so that she may fulfill your prediction. 'For all the glory of the King's daughter,' you said, is robed from within 'in golden fringed garments' (cf. Ps 44[45].14),[45] [that is] in her undefiled and spotless virginity, and adorned with incomparable comeliness; [and you] are about to say in a similar manner, 'Come here, David's bringer of the dawn' (cf. Ps 109[110].3),[46] 'Who is this that peeps out like the early morning, fair as the moon, choice as the sun? Why were your steps so beautiful in their shoes?' (Song 6.9; 7.1). 'How beautiful you were and how sweet' (Song 7.6), you who would contain the Sun and bring about a new spectacle under the sun."

"Be present, great-voiced Ezekiel, holding onto the divinely-sent book of the life-giving Spirit and shouting praise to the eastward-facing and divinely-entered, sealed gate, along with anyone else from either priestly order, that is to say, the whole remaining group of onlookers: cry aloud, seeing the completion of what was prophesied [actually] coming to pass! And why? Because [you], our forefathers, are about to be released from the curse [300] and are being allotted again to the dwelling-place of the delight from which you were banished! Will you not then praise the cause of your salvation, with suitable[47] panegyrics and very great praises? Or, if it is possible for you to shout, then I should [shout] with you, while the whole of creation should rejoice with both [of us]."[48]

---

[44]The noun ἔφεψις does not appear in the dictionaries and may be a neologism.

[45]Note that our text substitutes ἔσωθεν for Ἐσεβών ("of Esebon").

[46]I have emended ἠωσφῶν to Ἐωσφόρου, "bringer of the dawn" here.

[47]The adjective ἀραρότοις (dative plural) is in fact the perfect participle of the verb ἀραρίσκω, "to be joined closely together," or "suitable," "agreeable," or "pleasing." See L&S, B.IV.

[48]The preceding paragraphs, which are enclosed with quotation marks in this

7   Composing herself in all probability with these thoughts or steps, the prudent Anna, along with her dearest spouse, while sending ahead the one whom they had borne, [accompanied by] virgins bearing torches, reach the temple; and the gates open wide, receiving the spiritual gate of God the Emmanuel, and a starting-point is sanctified by Mary's footstep.[49] Thus, the house [of God] is lit up by torches, but it is even more glitteringly illumined by the brightness of one torch and its acceptable appearance is beautified by her entrance. Cloths for the horns of the altar[50] are made royal[51] by her purple and virginal garment. Zacharias rejoices at having been deemed worthy of receiving the Mother of God; Joachim is happy as he confirms the result of the oracles[52] by the fulfillment of [the child's] restitution.[53] Anna has been made happy at the dedication of her offspring, while forefathers skip as they flee from the confinement of condemnation. The prophets are gladdened and with them, every age [born] in grace leaps joyfully in advance.

8   And so the child of God then enters [and] stands among the horns [of the altar], after both her begetters had given thanks and the priest was about to give a blessing. Again her parents cry to the priest, "Receive the one who will receive the immaterial and incomprehensible fire; receive the one who will be designated as the receptacle of the Son and Word of the Father and only God; take the one who destroyed the reproach of our childlessness and sterility; usher

translation, all represent the imagined speech (or interior monologue) of Anna, as she approaches the temple to present her daughter, the blessed Theotokos, to the priest. The device of inventing dialogues or monologues for Biblical personages is common in Byzantine homiletics. See Cunningham, "Dramatic Device or Didactic Tool," 106.

[49]It is not clear what is meant by this expression, but perhaps it indicates the starting-point of the Incarnation. The author's love of obscure metaphorical language sometimes runs away with him, at the expense of clarity.

[50]See Exod 29.12.

[51]Literally, "made purple."

[52]Although he uses a pagan word here, Germanos of course means "prophesies" or "promises."

[53]Or more literally, the "paying back" of the child in return for God's gift of her to Joachim and Anna.

into the sanctuary the one who will introduce us into our ancient
inheritance of paradise; take charge of the one who, in her own birth-
giving, will take charge of our own cowardice that is bringing in the
power of death and the tyranny of Hades; embrace the one who is
covering up our nature which was made naked in Eden; hold the
hand of the one who will swaddle the One who stops[54] our power-
less and impulsive hand that has been spread out so very stubbornly;
consecrate to God the one who has consecrated us, as a divinely
perfected [being] for the expectation of [our] hopes."

"See, Lord, see! Take the one whom you have given! Usher
in the one whom you have provided! Receive the one whom you
vouchsafed, who releases our childlessness! Condemning natural[55]
sterility through her, you released us, through her, from a most terrible perpetuity [in this state].[56] Accept back this one who passed her
time well with us, whom you chose, and predestined, and sanctified;
draw to yourself the one who is firmly planted, as one who has been
planted firmly and who is enchanted by your fragrance, [the one]
whom you selected as a lily from the thorns of our unworthiness;
hold in your arms [the one] who is offered to you in a most healthy
state! Behold, we are setting her before you and also offering up
ourselves."

9 [301] These were the harmonious [words] of the righteous
[parents]; these were the sounds of the God-loving pair; this was
the well-chosen ascription of the ancestors of God. Then Zacharias
accepted the child, first in all likelihood addressing the parents
[in words such as these]: "O [parents] who are responsible for our
salvation, what am I to say to you? What am I to call [you]? I am
astounded on seeing what sort of fruit you have brought. For [this

---

[54]The word συντελέω has many meanings and it is difficult to choose which to
use here. It could also mean "completes" or perhaps even "fills."

[55]The word νόμου literally means "of law," but it is likely that the author is referring to the law of nature here.

[56]Note the chiastic structure of this sentence.

fruit] is such that it enchants God by its purity to come and dwell in her. Nor has anyone ever become nor will they become illumined by such beauty. You were perceived as two, double rivers who came from paradise, bearing a torch that is above gold and any precious stone, which illumines the whole land by the beauty of its own unblemished virginity and by refreshing flashes [of light]. You were recognized as brilliant stars, as if fixed in the firmament, with each of you both shining brightly on the murky shadow of the gloomy letter and storm-causing law, and prudently guiding the steps, without offence, of those who are faithful to Christ along [the way] towards the new grace of the recent light. You were recognized as the most shining horns of the spiritual temple of the new covenant, holding at your own breasts the sanctified and divinely inaugurated,[57] most rational altar of the holy, sacrificial victim. You, unless it is to speak a little of things that would come later,[58] were also recognized as the cherubim revolving in a most mystical way around the place of propitiation in your nursing of the Priest who guides the universe.[59] You were seen, beyond the burnished gold that in ancient times faced towards the veil of the ark, covering up the spiritual and divine ark of the new covenant, [that is], of the One who guaranteed our redemption on a cross.[60] Cosmic harmony has become yours! Yours is the fame that has been heard as happiness for all! You are blessed, on having become known as parents of such a child! You are praised, on having brought such a well-favored gift to the Lord! Blessed are the breasts by which she was suckled and the womb in which she was borne!"

[57]Θεεγκαίνιστον appears to be a neologism. See Trapp, 667, who cites this passage.

[58]Literally, "have run ahead."

[59]This image is unusual, perhaps even far-fetched. The preacher allegorically compares the cherubim that circle around the holy place of propitiation (i.e. the altar) in the Jewish temple with Joachim's and Anna's care for the Virgin Mary. Thus, the Theotokos represents the altar, or place of propitiation, while her parents are given an angelic status.

[60]This passage expresses the Virgin Mary's symbolic connection with the furniture of the tabernacle, including even the objects in the holiest part of this sanctuary, the holy of holies.

10   "Come then to me, little child, who is more exalted than the heavens! Come, infant that is seen and understood as the divine workshop! Come, sanctify even more the gateway of the sanctuary! For you, in your pure state, are not sanctified by the same thing, so to speak, but instead you utterly sanctify [it]!"

"Come, peep into an inaccessible and awesome inner chamber, you, who will become an immense and unsearchable vessel![61] Enter the front doors of the chancel, you who are breaking up the front doors of death![62] Look upon the curtain,[63] you who are shining in your brilliance on those who have been blinded by their blunted[64] sense of taste! Give me your hands as I used to guide your steps as an infant and hold my hand since I have become weary with old age and am failing, through earthly-minded zeal, in slipping from the commandment,[65] and may you lead me also to life! Behold, I am holding onto you as a staff of old age and restoration of the nature that has become weak because of its fall! Behold, I see you as one who will become a support for those who have descended towards death! Draw near [304] that you may venerate the table, about which it has been expressed in a wealth of symbols that you have been designated as a most rational and unblemished table! Pass through the building of the whole sanctuary, as if breathing out a fragrance of incense, having surpassed myrrh for those who smell [this], and beautifully sounding a censer of the inspired tongue and spirit-bearing prophet!

[61]N. Constas provides many patristic examples to support this translation of the term κειμήλιον, including a number of homiletic references to the Virgin Mary. See Constas, *Proclus of Constantinople*, 149.

[62]The use of the word πρόθυρον twice here is deliberate: it suggests that the Theotokos begins the process of resurrection which Christ will complete.

[63]The word καταπέτασμα, as opposed to κάλυμμα, is used by the Fathers for the veil of the temple, dividing the holy of holies from the outer sanctuary. It may also signify the firmament, which separates the created world from the heavenly one. See Lampe, 714.

[64]The word ἀμβλυοποιός, a neologism, appears to mean "making blunt." See Trapp, 65, which gives the German translation, "abstumpfend."

[65]This is another quite obscure and recondite sentence, using unusual words and concepts. The adjective γεήφρονι, "earthly-minded," may be a neologism. Trapp, 311, cites this passage, along with the ninth-century *Vita Ioannicii*, *AASS*, Nov. II, 1409C.

Go up, go up onto the threshold of the holy dwelling-place, for whose splendor of beauty the happy daughters of Jerusalem weave praise as they rejoice, and earthly kings give blessings; the step that has been recognized as divine and the ladder, established by God, that was revealed very pleasingly to the most patriarchal Jacob. Be seated, O Lady. It is fitting for you, the Queen, who have been glorified above all earthly queens, to sit upon such a threshold. It is fitting that the hallowed place should become a dwelling-place for you, the most cherubic throne. Behold, I have worthily vouchsafed to you, as Queen of all, the preeminent throne;[66] raise up, then, those who have fallen![67] And now therefore I am addressing you, along with David, [with the words], 'Hear, O daughter, and see, and incline your ear, and forget your people and your father's house, and the King will desire your beauty'" (Ps 44[45].10–11).

11   And so the old man thought [these thoughts] within himself, although in fact his mind was filled with even more praises than these. And the parents departed, and the child was left behind, having been consecrated to God. And angels were fearfully[68] ministering by providing nourishment, and the girl was nourished on material food, or immaterial [food], from immaterial beings. And so the most perfect actions of the divine, mystical force[69] came to pass through divine intervention.[70] And so the infant both grew and was strengthened while the whole opposition of the curse that was given to us in Eden became weak.

[66]Προκαθεδρία appears to be a neologism since it does not appear in the dictionaries.

[67]This represents a strong affirmation of the Virgin's power not just to intercede, but to raise up sinners herself. It is true that the statement must be understood in the context of a hyperbolic panegyric, but it does seem that Germanos goes further than most preachers and hymnographers in making this statement. For discussion of Germanos's "pushing of the boundaries" in mariological preaching, see Graef, *Mary. A History of Doctrine and Devotion*, 145–50.

[68]Literally, "with fear."

[69]The word μυσταρχία is unusual, but it does appear in a few other Byzantine texts. See Trapp, 1062, who suggests the German meaning, "mystische Kraft."

[70]There are again echoes of (ps-) Dionysius the Areopagite here.

12   But come indeed, festival that is beloved by God, [and] let us say in one voice, with as much strength as there is in our childish understanding, [the greeting] "Hail!" to the Virgin, not being able to praise her feast completely, but at least consoling our weakness as much as possible, since whatever we are able to do is dear to God. For the one who is recognized as the only Virgin and Mother has transcended all understanding, and the reason for this is clear. For what virgin gave birth, or having given birth, kept her virginity inviolate, except you alone, all-blessed maiden, who have unflinchingly born God for us in the flesh?

13   Hail[71] indeed, therefore, having clothed yourself in a robe with the appearance of purple, that is to say, redemption that is wrapped [around you] by God, by means of the praised and miraculous[72] garment [that you donned] on your entrance today into the holy of holies—you, bride of God, who are the redemption that is given to us from God, [as we lie] in the mire of our errors because of the death-bearing and soul-burning food of Eden that stripped us naked!

Hail, one who today [305] gathers together at the beginning every prophetic celebration[73] of the most splendid presentation that confers sanctification,[74] [including] those who strike up a most divine-sounding noise with euphonious cymbals as musical instruments, while also dancing happily and captivatingly!

14   Hail, one who has trampled underfoot by the rhythm of your steps my terrible guide, the snake who has conducted me towards

---

[71]A more literal translation of χαίροις would be "May you rejoice." For the sake of consistency with other passages of *chairetismoi*, I have chosen the more usual "Hail" here.

[72]Literally, "made without hands."

[73]In Classical Greek, the word θίασος means a Bacchic revel or rout; in Christian contexts it may mean "celebration" or "banquet."

[74]Σεβασμιοφόρου ("conferring sanctification") is not in the dictionaries and is thus probably a neologism.

transgression, [who is] the perverse[75] devil and hater of good; and who grasped the corrupt substance that appeared so hard to catch, which goes along [with him] and [led] it once again towards an immaterial, holy, and ageless habitation.

Hail, one who brilliantly made the day to shine with happiness and rejoicing, by the torch-bearing of your presentation, for those who were caught in the shadow of death and the depths of weakness, and who called to witness a divinely decreed[76] dissolution of gloom that would come about through you, all-supremely wonderful[77] Mary!

Hail, the shining cloud that lets fall drops of spiritual, divine dew on us, having today, at your inconspicuous entrance[78] into the holy of holies, caused a radiant sun to shine on those held in the shadow of death! Divinely flowing[79] spring from which the rivers of divine knowledge disperse the most discerning and brilliant water of right belief, as they destroy the band of heresies!

15　Hail, the most delightful and rational paradise of God, which today is planted towards the eastern parts of his will by the right hand of the All-Ruler, and which blooms for him with the fair-flowering lily and unfading rose for those [facing] towards the west, who quaff the pestilential and soul-destroying bitterness of death; [a paradise] in which the life-giving wood flowers into a knowledge of truth, and which bestows immortality on those who taste of it.

Hail, the palace of the All-Ruler, God, who was sacredly built,[80] undefiled, and most pure, [and] who has encompassed his greatness

[75]Literally "of crooked mind." See also Theodore of Stoudios, *Epistola* 2. 77, PG 99, 1316B.

[76]The adjective θεοβράβευτος ("divinely decreed") is unusual, but appears in the works of George Cedrenos. See Sophocles, 573.

[77]The adjective πανυπερθαύμαστος ("all-supremely wonderful") does not appear in the dictionaries.

[78]The word ὑπεισδύσις, although it does not appear in the dictionaries, appears to mean "entrance by stealth." Perhaps this means that Mary entered the sanctuary inconspicuously.

[79]For the adjective θεόβρυτος, see Sophocles, 574: "made to gush forth by God."

[80]For the adjective ἱερότευκτος, see Trapp, 705, who cites W. Christ and M.

while guiding all your people in mystically directed[81] enjoyment!
One who is now firmly founded in the court of the Lord, that is to
say, in his holy temple in which [is found] the well-adorned bridal-
chamber that was made without hands for the spiritual Bridegroom;
in whom, having wished to restore what had strayed, the Word has
wedded flesh, reconciling those who had become separated[82] [from
him] by their own wish.

16   Hail, the new Sion and divine Jerusalem, holy "city of the
great Ruler God, in whose citadels God himself is known" (cf. Ps
47[48].3–4), making kings to bow down in veneration of your glory
and preparing to lead the whole world in rejoicing at the festival of
your Presentation! The truly golden and shining . . . lampstand with
seven lights[83] that is lit by inaccessible light and enriched by the oil of
purity, guaranteeing a rising of brightness to those who are blinded
by mist in the gloom of transgressions.

[308] Hail, most fat[84] and shaded mountain[85] from God on
which, having been reared, the rational lamb bore our sins and
infirmities! [Mountain] from which was rolled the rock that was cut
without hands (cf. Dan 2.34), which crushed idolatrous altars and
became the head of the corner that was wonderful in our eyes.[86]

17   Hail, the holy throne of God, the divine offering, the house
of glory, the most beautiful ornament and chosen vessel and
universal place of propitiation, and heaven declaring the glory of
God! (Cf. Ps 18[19].2). The East causes a lampstand that is never

Paranikas, *Anthologia graeca carminum Christianorum* (Leipzig: Teubner, 1871), 241;
Andrew of Crete, *In Dormitionem* I, PG 97, 1065A.

[81]For the adjective μυσταρχικός ("mystically directed"), see Trapp, 1062, who
cites various other patristic references along with this one.

[82]For the meaning of the adverb διενηνεγμένως, see Lampe, 366.

[83]For the epithet ἑπτάφωτος used in connection with the Virgin Mary, see also
Epiphanius, *Homilia* 5, PG 43, 497B; George of Pisidia, *Carmina* 11.1. The ellipsis here
seems to indicate a lacuna in the text.

[84]See Ps 67[68].16.

[85]See Hab 3.3.

[86]See Ps 117[118].22.

extinguished[87] to rise, whose "going forth is from the extremity of heaven"; and [whose] heat, that is to say, controlling foreknowledge, no one of those who has ever existed [has been] without (cf. Ps 18 [19].7).[88]

Hail, one who loosed bonds of sterility by your birth, scattered a reproach of childlessness, submerged a legal curse, caused a blessing of grace to flower, and accomplished a fulfillment of parental prayer, a foundation for our redemption, and a completion of joy by your entrance into the holy of holies, since you were initiating a beginning of grace!

18   Hail, favored Mary, holier than the saints, and higher than the heavens, and more glorious than the cherubim, and more honorable than the seraphim, and more venerable than the whole of creation![89] You, as the dove that brings glad tidings, are offering us an olive branch by your glorious and splendid entrance, that is, our deliverer from the spiritual flood and our safe anchorage; [a dove] whose "wings are covered with silver and whose back sparkles with the yellow gold" (cf. Ps 67[68].14) of the all-holy and illuminating Holy Spirit. [You are] the entirely golden jar that holds the most pleasing sweetmeat for our souls, that is, the manna that is Christ!

19   But, O wholly unblemished and all-praised and wholly august one, preeminent offering for God of all created things, untilled earth, unplowed field, luxuriant vine, most cheering chalice, gushing fountain, Virgin who gives birth and Mother with no knowledge of a man, vessel of purity and ornament of piety, by means of your

[87]The adjective ἄδυτος is occasionally used in relation to Christ, the Sun, and is here referred to the Theotokos, using the type of the seven-branched lampstand.

[88]Andrew quotes a slightly different version of the text here or perhaps adapts it. Brenton translates the text, "His going forth is from the extremity of heaven and his circuit to the other end of heaven: and no one shall be hidden from his heat."

[89]This passage echoes the well-known prayer which is used frequently in the divine office and liturgy of the Orthodox Church today: ". . . more honorable than the cherubim, more glorious than the seraphim, you who without defilement bore God the Word . . ."; see *The Orthodox Liturgy*, 78.

acceptable and motherly supplications towards the One who is yours, who came forth from you without a father, both Son and God, the Creator of all things, while guiding the rudders of ecclesiastical good management, steer [us] into a harbor without waves, that is, one that is entirely free of influxes of both heresies and scandals. Clothe the priests splendidly with righteousness and with the joy of famed, unblemished, and simple faith![90] While guiding in peace and stability the scepters of those who have obtained you as a diadem and covering that supercedes every purple-appearing and golden dye, [every] pearl and precious stone, [since you represent] a spotless ornament for orthodox rulers, suppress the barbaric nations that wickedly blaspheme against the God who came from you, by taking the feet from under them![91] Assist the army which is constantly under pressure at the hour of battle by your entreaties and ensure that [the people] which is subject to the rein of good government proceeds in its service in a manner following God's instructions![92] [309] While crowning your city, which possesses you as its tower and foundation, with victorious prizes, keep watch over it, having girded it with strength! Preserve forever the house of God in the comeliness of his church [and] guard those who praise you from every accident and from spiritual sufferings! Be seen as a source of help, awarding rescue to prisoners as well as to homeless people from abroad and those who are solitary! Stretch out your assisting hand to the whole world in order that we may carry out your festivals in happiness and exultation with the most splendid rite that is now being celebrated by us! In Christ Jesus, King of all things and our true God, to whom be glory and power, together with the holy and life-giving Father and the co-eternal and throne-sharing Spirit who is of the same substance, now and always and to the ages of ages. Amen.

[90]See Ps 131 (132). 9.

[91]The meaning of the participle στρωννύουσα is not completely clear. L&S suggests the meaning "to level" or "lay low," 1650.2b. The phrase ποσὶ στρωννύουσα might thus mean "leveling them by their feet."

[92]θεοπαραγγέλτως appears to be a neologism. See Trapp, 676: "im Auftrag Gottes."

On the Entrance into the Temple II

[309] Encomium to the Holy Theotokos, When she was brought into the temple (into the holy of holies), at the age of three, by her parents[1]

1   Behold, yet another festival and splendid feast of the Mother of the Lord! Behold, a procession of the blameless bride! Behold, a first escort of the Queen! Behold a precise sign of the glory that will surround her! Behold, a prologue for the divine grace that is about to overshadow her! Behold, a conspicuous mark of her surpassing purity! For she was brought by her parents for an unbroken sojourn so as to be in the holy, inaccessible [repositories] of grace, where the priest entered not frequently, but only once a year, and carried out the mystical rites. Who ever knew of such a thing? Who had seen or heard, among those living or those long ago, of a female being brought into the innermost holy of holies, which must scarcely be approached even by men, to dwell and be brought up there? Was this not a manifest display of the strange miracle that would befall her later? Was it not a visible sign? Was it not a clear proof?

---

[1]*CPG* 8008; *BHG*ª 1104; F. Combefis, ed., PG 98, 309–20.

2 [312] Let those who are speaking[2] against her reveal to us, as though seeing yet not seeing (cf. Matt 13.13), where they have ever observed such things?[3] [Do they not see] a girl [born] as a result of a promise, and she at the age of three, being taken within the third inner veil as an unblemished gift to live there without interruption, and also being carried in procession[4] by the wealthy among the people? [Do they not see her] preceded by virgins, accompanied by torches, [and] being received by priests and prophets with upturned hands?[5] How then did they not wish to come along? How, on seeing the first things, did they not believe the last ones? How, on previously seeing the strange and different things that happened to her, did they contradict those that occurred afterwards? For the first things that took place with regard to her were not random [events], and they did not happen, as it were, by chance; instead, all were premonitions[6] of the final events.[7] Let those who are wise in their own conceit[8] then tell us vain things: how, even though other sterile [couples] bear children, a little daughter of an insignificant woman is dedicated to the holy of holies and was accepted by prophets? Could they not have spoken, on contemplating such [events] that happened then in such a manner to her, in the same way as those who held the same opinions [said] later about her Son: "What then will this child become?" (Luke 1.66). Yes, indeed.

[2]Literally, "moving their tongues."

[3]It is possible that Germanos is referring here to a group of people, possibly also iconoclasts, who refused to venerate the Mother of God in this period.

[4]The verb λιτανεύω normally means "to supplicate" or "to appeal to"; however, it is possible that the meaning "to process" or "carry in procession" may be meant, as a derivative of the noun λιτανεία, "a religious procession."

[5]According to L&S, 1903, II, the adjective ὕπτιος, when used in connection with χείρ, may mean holding out the hands with the hollow uppermost or, in some sources, the attitude of upturned hands in prayer.

[6]Literally, "prologues."

[7]Germanos is referring here to Mary's miraculous birth from a sterile couple, her careful nurturing in Anna's bedchamber, and all the other events that are recounted about the Virgin's infancy in the first chapters of the *Protevangelion* of James. See Elliott, *The Apocryphal New Testament*, 58–60.

[8]Cf. Prov 28.11.

3 Nevertheless, let those who think abnormally journey the road of destruction, and let them fall into the pit that they have dug. But as for us, the peculiar people of God (cf. Exod 19.5; Titus 2.14, etc.), on the other hand, priests and rulers, lay people and monastics, slaves and freemen, craftsmen and tillers of the ground, gardeners and fishermen, young and old, men and women, come, let us eagerly approach the Theotokos, and let us glimpse the divine mysteries that have, by divine dispensation, been accomplished beforehand in her![9] [Let us see] how the all-holy one is today brought by her parents into the temple of God with the help of his priests, how the living temple of the Lord is taken up to the lifeless one,[10] how the prophet admits her by his own hand and brings her into inaccessible [places], having been in no way displeased and without having said to her parents, "I am not undertaking this most novel practice and leading a girl into the holy of holies to be lodged in these [sanctuaries] and to dwell there without interruption, where I have been instructed to enter [only] one day of the year."[11] The prophet uttered no such

[9]Notice the language of pagan mystery religions being used in connection with Christian mysteries in this sentence. This reflects a long-standing tradition in patristic liturgical writings. It is also interesting to note here Germanos's inclusive call to all Christians, of all classes and genders. This must reflect the fact that the sermon was preached in a large, mixed setting, either in the cathedral of St Sophia in Constantinople, or perhaps in the church of the Chalkoprateia nearby.

[10]The contrast between Mary, the "living temple," and the "lifeless" temple of stone and mortar represents a classic antithesis in hymns and homilies on the Presentation. The Theotokos fulfils in her person, as Virgin and Mother of God, what the Old Testament temples could only symbolically, or immaterially, accomplish: that is, to contain the divine presence within the physical boundaries of a building or human body. The adjectives ἔμψυχος and ἄψυχος are used to express this antithesis.

[11]The Greek rhetorical device of paraleipsis, in which the speaker states what was not in fact said in order to stress the unusual nature of this event. The holy of holies in the Jerusalem temple was in fact the most sacred part of the building, shut off from the rest of the building by the veil, which symbolised the firmament (Gen 1.6–8) and later, the Incarnation itself. In other words, the veil represented the boundary between the created world and the realm of divinity. The high priest was only allowed to enter the holy of holies on one day of the year, the Day of the Atonement. By reminding us of this aspect of Jewish tradition, the preacher emphasises here the extraordinary exception that was made in admitting the Virgin Mary to this sacred space and in allowing her to live there throughout her childhood. On the symbolism

thing; instead he knew in advance what would come to pass, since he was a prophet. [Instead], completely accepting and remaining with her, just as Symeon after him would [receive] her Son, he eagerly received her.[12]

4 Then, perhaps having embraced her and holding the child in his hands, he addressed himself to the mother, saying the following [words], "What is your background, woman? What is your character and what is the aim of such an undertaking? And how is it that, without having any sort of example, you, on your own, have invented this new and unprecedented spectacle, that is, bringing [313] a girl to play a role in the inaccessible places?[13] Tell me, what is your plan and what is your name?" Anna, whose name means "grace,"[14] said to the interpreter,[15] "I was born of a priestly family, of the tribe of Aaron, and of a prophetic and kingly root. For I am a direct descendant of David and Solomon, and so also a kinswoman of Elizabeth, your wife. And I was married to a man, by the law of the Master, and after due time, I was found to be sterile and without a child. Then, having found no medicine that would remedy the misfortune in any way, I fled for refuge to the One who alone is powerful, God who provides for the helpless. And I opened my mouth eagerly to him, with lamentation of the heart, and cried tearfully to him, saying things such as these: 'O Lord, Lord, who hearkens very quickly to afflicted spirits,[16] why did you alter my nature from that of my ancestors? Why

of the Jewish temple and its significance in Christian theology, see Barker, *The Great High Priest*, esp. 146–228.

[12]Germanos employs alliteration in this sentence, using a number of words beginning with προ- or προσ-.

[13]The use of words associated with drama and play-acting is striking here.

[14]This epithet, derived from the Hebrew name, is applied to Anna by John of Damascus, PG 94, 433A and by the patriarch Tarasios in his homily, *In praesentationem*, PG 98, 1488D.

[15]In other words, "priest" or "prophet." The Greek word ὑποφήτης, ὁ means "an interpreter" or "expounder" of Scripture or law.

[16]Cf. 1 Kgdms 1.10, etc. This is a clear reference to the earlier Anna, who prayed to God "afflicted in spirit" (κατώδινος ψυχῇ) because of her sterility before conceiving the prophet Samuel.

did you make me a by-word in my family and a shake of the head[17] in my tribe? Why did you manifest me as sharing in the curse of your prophets, giving me a womb that bears no children and breasts that are dry? Why did you render my gifts unacceptable since [they came] from a barren woman? Why did you abandon me to become an object of scorn among my friends, as one that is mocked by those who serve me, and as a reproach to my neighbors? Look upon me, Lord; hearken to me, Master; be merciful, Holy One.[18] Make me like the birds of the sky, the beasts of the earth, the fishes of the sea! For even these are productive in your presence, Lord. May one who was created by you, according to your likeness and image, (cf. Gen 1.26), not appear worse than these irrational [animals]!"

5   "Saying these [words], and things similar to them, I added,[19] 'I shall of course offer up a thanksgiving gift to you, Master, which will be the child that you would grant me, that it may enter and remain in your sanctuary as a holy offering and all-precious gift, granted to me by you, the most bountiful Giver of perfect gifts.' I remained in the open air in my garden, directing my eyes to heaven, beating my breast with my hands, [and] crying out such things to God who is in heaven. Meanwhile, my husband was all alone on the mountain, fasting for forty days and entreating God with [words] similar to these. And so the Lord, who is disposed to pity and who is a lover of human souls, was indeed moved by the prayers of both of us and sent his angel, who announced to us the conception of my child. All at once, then, nature, having been commanded by God, accepted the fetus,[20] for it did not dare to receive it before the divine grace.

[17]The phrase κίνησις κεφαλῆς must be a colloquial one; it is possible that it means that people shake their heads at her without saying anything—almost more disturbing as a reproach than words.

[18]Anna calls on the whole Trinity to help her here, following the format of the *Trisagion* hymn.

[19]The verb here is in the first person singular, indicating that Anna's direct speech continues through this paragraph and into the next.

[20]The word γονή literally means "offspring."

But when this entered in, the womb, although it had been closed, opened its own gates and, on welcoming in the bequest from God, kept it close until [the time when], with God's good will, that which had been sowed in it came forth into light."[21]

6 [316] "So then, now that the infant has been weaned, 'I am offering prayers to my God, which my lips defined, and my mouth spoke out in my affliction' (Ps 65[66].13–14). For this reason, having gathered together the company of virgins with torches, I called together the priests, [and] I collected my relations, saying these words to all of them, 'Rejoice with me, all of you, since I have been revealed both as a mother and today as one who makes an offering. I am not presenting my child to an earthly king, since this would not be fitting, but I have dedicated her to the heavenly King, as a gift for him.' Accept then, O prophet, my God-given daughter! Accept [her], and leading her in, set her down[22] in a place of sanctification,[23] in a prepared habitation of God.[24] For God has called her here, without interfering, until he should be well pleased that the things concerning her should come to their conclusion."[25]

7 On hearing these words, Zacharias at once answered Anna, [saying], "Blessed is your root,[26] all-honored one! Glorified is your womb, one beloved by your husband! Most glorious is your offer-

---

[21]This description of Mary's conception depends on the late antique idea of the planting of a seed (from the natural father) inside the mother's womb. See John of Damascus's and Andrew of Crete's homilies on the Nativity of the Virgin and accompanying notes.

[22]Literally, "plant."

[23]Cf. Ps 77[78].54.

[24]Cf. Ps 32[33].14. Another interpretation of this clause, which may be intended by the author, would be "*to be* a prepared habitation of God."

[25]Anna's account in her own words comes to an end here. The preacher uses the device of ethopoiia, adding a monologue which reveals Anna's own reactions to the unfolding of events, in order to allow the audience to identify with her emotionally and to understand her point of view. The passage is indirectly based on the *Protevangelion* of James, chaps. 2–7. See James, *The Apocryphal New Testament*, 57–60.

[26]By "root," Zacharias means Anna's ancestry.

ing, lover of God!" Then, holding the child with great joy, he eagerly brought her into the holy of holies, perhaps saying words such as these to her, "Come, fulfilment of my prophecy! Come, completion of the promises of God! Come, seal of his covenant! Come, achievement of his purposes! Come, manifestation of his mysteries! Come, speculum[27] of all prophets! Come, point of agreement for all those who wickedly dissent! Come, conjunction of those who have previously been separated! Come, support of those who have inclined downwards! Come, renewal of those who have become old! Come, the light of those who lie in darkness! Come, most new and divine gift! Come, Mistress of all who dwell on earth! Come into the glory of your Lord, [glory] which for now is here below and treated with contempt, but which will, after a short time, become heavenly and inaccessible to humankind."[28] Having spoken, as is likely, to the child in such a way, the initiate placed her where it was fitting, appropriate, and preordained. And the child, skipping and rejoicing, as if in a bed chamber, walked into the temple of God. She was three years old and supremely perfect with divine grace, since she had been recognized and designated in advance and had been chosen by the God and Steward of all things.

She remained in the innermost holy of holies, nourished with ambrosial food by an angel and given divine nectar to drink, until her second stage of life. Then, with the consent of God and by the will of priests, an allotment regarding her was granted and the righteous Joseph gained her as his share. By divine dispensation, he took this holy Virgin out of the temple of God and from its priests to deceive the snake that caused evil in the beginning, in order that it might not attack the untouched maiden, since she was a virgin, but [instead]

---

[27]The Greek word διόπτρα, ἡ means an optical instrument or speculum, i.e. a lens through which something is seen in better focus.

[28]Germanos appears to be contrasting the old and new dispensations here, implying that God's glory was treated with some contempt before the coming of Christ. The final clause, which suggests that this glory will become inaccessible, perhaps refers to the period before Christ's Ascension and Pentecost, when the Holy Spirit descended to live among human beings.

pass her by since she had become engaged. Therefore the wholly undefiled [girl] was in the house of [317] the carpenter Joseph, kept safe by the Master-builder, God, until the divine mystery which had been hidden from before all ages was accomplished in her, and God was made like mortals out of her. But this belongs to another subject and requires an appropriate occasion. Let our oration be led back to what lies before us and let the day of the Presentation today be praised![29]

8 Depart, therefore, O Mistress, Mother of God, depart towards your inheritance, and walk into the courtyards of the Lord, skipping and rejoicing, nourished and thriving, day after day expecting the coming of the all-holy Spirit upon you and the overshadowing of the power of the Highest and the conception of your Son, when Gabriel will address you! And grant your help and protection and patronage to those who fulfil your feast, delivering them on every occasion by your intercessions from every constraint and from dangers, terrible illnesses, and all sorts of accidents, and from the righteous threat of your Son that is to come![30] Enroll them, as Mother of the Master, in a place of delight, wherein are light and peace, along with the highest gift of desired things. "And let the deceitful lips become dumb, which speak iniquity against you, the righteous one, in pride and scorn" (cf. Ps 30[31].19),[31] and let their image in your city be scorned (cf. Ps 72[73].20); let them be shamed, and let them fail and be destroyed, and let them know that your name is "Mistress."[32] For you alone are

[29]This statement provides clear evidence that this sermon was intended for the feast of the Virgin's Entry into the temple. If, as I believe, Germanos is its author, then we can affirm that the feast was being celebrated in Constantinople in the early eighth century.

[30]This strong statement of the Virgin's compassion in the face of Christ's righteous judgement reflects a well-developed mariological stance on the part of the writer. See Graef, *Mary. A History of Doctrine and Devotion*, 146–7.

[31]It is interesting to note how Germanos adjusts the wording of the psalm slightly in order to fit his reference to the Mother of God here.

[32]Cf. Ps 82 (83).18. It is likely that Germanos is referring to iconoclasts in this passage; indeed, it is likely that he means the emperor himself, along with his supporters,

Theotokos, highest in the whole earth. We praise you in faith, bride of God, and we pay honor to you with longing, and we venerate you with fear, always magnifying and reverently blessing you. For truly blessed is your father among men and blessed is your mother among women! Blessed is your house, blessed are your acquaintances! Blessed are those who have seen you, blessed are those who have conversed, and blessed are those who have served you! Blessed are the places where you have walked, blessed is the temple into which you were brought, blessed is Zacharias, who held you in his arms, blessed is Joseph who was engaged to you, blessed is your bed [and] blessed is your tomb! For you are the honor of honors, and privilege of privileges, and height of heights!

9   But, O Mistress, who are alone my solace from God, divine dew for the burning heat within me, divinely-flowing drop for my withered heart, most far-shining torch for my darkened soul, guide for my journey, strength for my weakness, garment for my nakedness, wealth for my poverty, medicine for incurable wounds, banishment of tears, cessation of groans, alleviation of misfortunes, remission of pains, loosing of bonds, hope of my salvation! Hearken to my prayers! Pity my groans, and accept my lamentations! Having been moved by my tears, have mercy on me; [320] as Mother of the benevolent God, be compassionate towards me. Look upon and assent to my supplication, fulfil my thirsty desire, and join me together with my kinswoman and fellow maid-servant[33] in the land

although the passage referring to "their image" is in fact a reference to Ps 30[31].19. It is thus possible that this homily was delivered after 726, when Leo III may have promulgated his first iconoclast edict. The passage also suggests that along with images, the iconoclasts disapproved of devotional practices surrounding the Theotokos.

   [33]It is unclear to what woman Germanos refers here. Combefis suggests that this may have been a relative, perhaps a sister, who had died. According to him, one manuscript in Paris containing this homily substitutes συγκοίτῳ for συγγόνῳ (line 4). See PG 98, 320, n. 31. It is unlikely that this refers to a wife, unless they were joined in name only, since Germanos had been castrated early in his life. Whatever it may mean, the passage intensifies the deeply personal tone of this sermon and its author's fervent attachment to the Mother of God as intercessor and protector. It also suggests

of the meek, in the tabernacles of the righteous, and in the company of the saints! And, protection and joy and radiant delight of all [human beings], deem me worthy, I beg you, to be happy with her in that truly inexpressible joy of God and the King who was born from you, and [to rejoice] in his incorruptible bridal chamber, and in unceasing and unending delight, as well as in the never-ending[34] and boundless Kingdom! Yes, Mistress! Yes, my refuge, life and succour, weapon and boast, my hope and my strength! Grant that I may enjoy with her the ineffable and incomprehensible gifts of your Son in the heavenly resting-place! For you, as Mother of the Highest, have, I know, the power that accompanies your wish, and it is for this reason that I take courage. May I therefore not be disappointed, wholly undefiled Lady, in my expectation! Instead may I attain this [expectation], Bride of God, who beyond reason bore the expectation of all things, our Lord Jesus Christ, the true God and Master, to whom is due all glory, honor, and veneration, along with the Father without beginning, and the life-giving Spirit, now and always, and to the ages of ages. Amen.

that Germanos may have been approaching the end of his own life at the time that he wrote this homily.

[34]Literally, "unsetting" [of the sun].

JOHN, MONK AND PRESBYTER OF EUBOEA

Homily on the Conception
of the Holy Theotokos[1]

1 [1460] Father, give a blessing. The great apostle Paul, interpreter of the great mysteries, concerning himself with matters relating to our salvation, teaches, rebukes, admonishes and exhorts us to be thankful in all circumstances and to pray without ceasing (cf. 1 Thess 5.17–18). And this is possible for all men. But no one who possesses the unpurified thought [1461] of the inner man is worthy in any way to participate in such matters, being such as I, miserable being, bound fast by the ropes of my mistakes, except that each day "I shall declare my iniquity and be anxious about my sin" (Ps 37[38].19). But when desire draws me on, fear pulls against me, and unworthiness rebukes me to be quiet, and my sins, "like a heavy burden, have weighed heavily upon me" (Ps 37[38].5), I do not know what I am to do. Shall I dare, unworthy though I am, to undertake this? What shall I say? Shall I rebuke myself? Shall I deplore[2] my own misery? Do I hold back from the blessings that are rising up in my heart concerning the all-praised God-receiver,[3] God-bearer, and holy Virgin, Mary?

---

[1]*CPG* 8135; *BHG* 1117; A. Ballerini, ed., PG 96, 1460–1500. It should be noted that the edition printed in Migne's PG is very faulty, with numerous typographical errors. These have been noted below, along with my suggested emendations. It is likely that these errors stem from the transfer of Ballerini's edited text to PG, rather than from the original edition.

[2]Lampe suggests this meaning in the context of this passage, 1371.

[3]The Greek term θεοδόχος literally means "Receiver of God." Nestorius preferred this epithet to "Theotokos," because it does not convey the full magnitude of Mary's role in conceiving and giving birth to God, instead emphasizing her part in containing

173

2 But, O Theotokos, assist me yourself, in order that the will of Christ our God, who was born from you, may be done; in order that my mind, although I am unworthy, may not be darkened; but assist me to write down [my ideas] concerning your praises, as they enter my thoughts even when I am not writing them down.[4] For often, when I have become reflective and tearful on account of my unworthiness, I call to mind the words of the fiery-tongued and grandiloquent Isaiah. For if that divine man who was thought worthy of such a vision considered himself unhappy,[5] what should I do, who am unworthy even of life? For he says, "It came about in the year that the king Uzziah died, that I saw the Lord seated on a high and lofty throne; and the house was full of his glory and seraphim stood round about him" (Isa 6.1–2). And he heard the sound of the *Trisagion*, the "Holy, holy, holy, Lord of Hosts" (Isa 6.3). And Isaiah said, "Woe is me, for I am pricked to the heart; for being a man and having unclean lips, I live in the midst of a people which has unclean lips. And I saw the King, Lord of Hosts, with my eyes. And there was sent to me one of the seraphim, and he had in his hand a coal which he had taken off the altar with tongs. And he touched my mouth and said, 'Behold, this has touched your lips and will take away your iniquities and purge your sins'" (Isa 6.5–7).

But if this great prophet of God thus pronounces himself miserable, what shall I do, who possess[6] a mouth, lips, heart, and senses, [all of which] are unworthy, [1464] unless you yourself, wholly undefiled one, will stretch out your hand to me? But even if I am not ready worthily to present you with praises, I shall offer you supplications

him and making his birth possible. The term nevertheless continued to be used by Orthodox writers in mariological contexts. For references, see Lampe, 625.

[4]This passage provides interesting information about the process of writing and delivering a sermon in this period. John of Euboea suggests clearly here that he writes his sermon, rather than delivering it *ex tempore* and having it recorded by stenographers in the audience.

[5]Read ἐταλάνισεν for ἐταλάκισεν. Cf. Isa 6.5.

[6]I have emended κεκτημένοι to κεκτημένος here, to agree with the subject (ἐγώ).

on behalf of my deficiency towards our God who became flesh from you (for even if everyone [else] is worthy, I am still unworthy), being pulled along and longing that I may become a partaker at the table of the chosen ones, even if [I am a partaker] only of crumbs. For one can reach satiety even from a multitude of crumbs.[7]

3   Behold, it is good to take up the word of the blessed Paul and say, "Behold, now is the acceptable time! Behold, now is the day of salvation!" (2 Cor 6.2). Behold Judah, who having had mercy, Joseph is granted mercy![8] Behold Reuben, the son of Jacob and also his descendant, who caused pain to [Jacob's other] descendant, Judah![9] Behold the unacceptable gift of Cain![10] Behold also righteous Abel who is testified to by God in his gifts![11] And behold, the petition and desire of David has been fulfilled! "Take away from me," he says, "scorn and contempt!" (Ps 118[119].22). Behold, a supplication is borne up from Joachim and Anna, and a favor[12] comes down from the Lord, All-Ruler!

4   Behold, a new ark is being constructed by the Creator, which is countless thousand times stronger [1465] than the one in the time of Noah[13] and in that of Moses![14] For the latter was a receiver of

---

[7]It is common for homilists to profess their unworthiness to preach in the prologues of their sermons, but this section is unusually long and impassioned compared to most. It may reflect John of Euboea's real sense of inadequacy on the basis of his obvious lack of rhetorical and syntactical skill compared to most contemporary preachers whose works survive.

[8]Cf. Gen 37.26; 50.15–21.

[9]It is not clear which part of the story of Jacob's sons the preacher refers to here. It may be Reuben's thwarting of the brothers' scheme to kill Joseph (Gen 37.21–22) or his annoyance with them when they secretly removed Joseph from the pit and sold him to the Midianite traders (Gen 37.29–30). In either case, the verb λυπέω seems somewhat out of place.

[10]Cf. Gen 4.5.

[11]Cf. Gen 4.4.

[12]Lampe cites this passage for evidence for the meaning of the word ἱλασμός.

[13]Cf. Gen 6.14.

[14]Cf. Exod 25.10, etc.

law, whereas this one is a receiver of God. Behold, a boat sails the
sea and seeks[15] expendable fruit from a cargo. Joachim and Anna
were seeking fruit in human form, and behold, they received the
unseeded oyster that bore the heavenly and highly prized pearl,
Christ our God![16] Behold Joachim and Anna! While he was fasting
on the mountain, she was in her garden beseeching God, and they
received a receptacle for the One who set up the mountains and
caused the garden to grow! Behold, the good news of happiness
in a garden, that the garden of old might be returned to humanity! Behold, sorrow changed to joy and lamentation to gladness!
Behold, groaning and timely tears, and unutterable joy for eternity!
Behold, reproach removed and an inalienable gift brought to God,
who contains the uncontainable God in a womb! Behold, Isaiah has
been loosed from the wooden saw,[17] Jeremiah from the mire in the
pit,[18] and Daniel from the lions;[19] even as they remember those great
afflictions, their true prophesy is fulfilled. For Isaiah himself cries
concerning the blessed Anna: "Rejoice, O barren one who does not
bear!" (Isa 54.1).

Behold also the rod of Aaron which has sprouted, even as it
is hidden in the ark covered on all sides with gold![20] And behold
another uncut rod, which is beyond understanding, is sprouting!
And no one of the human race can carry it on a journey, but it bore

---

[15]I have emended ξητοῦσα to ζητοῦσα here.

[16]This epithet for the Virgin Mary is common in Syriac liturgical poetry and also
appears in John of Damascus's homily on the Nativity. See above, 58, n. 21. John of
Euboea's use of metaphor is somewhat clumsy here. Having just called the Theotokos
an "ark," he contrasts an ordinary boat, which carries a profitable load, or fruit, that
may be spent, with Joachim and Anna who bore heavenly fruit. The image is implied
rather than stated, however, and the metaphor is then mixed with that of the oyster
and the pearl, presumably according to the logic that the boat represented by Mary's
holy parents also engaged in pearl fishing! In any case, the maritime imagery is main-
tained throughout these three sentences.

[17]Cf. Isa 10.15.
[18]Cf. Jer 45 [38].6.
[19]Cf. Dan 6.23.
[20]Cf. Exod 37.2; Num 17.8.

the One who bore everything, who stretched out the heavens like a curtain,²¹ and whose hands formed the dry land.²²

5 O, what a marvel! Judah, who of old released Joseph from death and freed his father and his brothers from sharp hunger, is rebuked!²³ The jealousy of the brothers caused Joseph to flourish as a king; the seed of Judah, which was resented and rebuked by the seed of Reuben, has sprouted a virginal queen and an eternal King! [1468] Why are you annoyed, Reuben? You are kicking against goads (cf. Acts 26.14), for did not God speak a word of prophecy to you through the prophet? It was not only to Judah that he said, "Celebrate your feasts, O Judah . . . for one who breathes [life]²⁴ has come into your presence" (cf. Nah 1.15–2.1).²⁵ Who is this one, O prophet? The Creator of all things, who breathed the spirit of life into Adam and who "breathed on his holy disciples and apostles and said [to them], 'Receive the Holy Spirit'" (John 20.22).

6 But let us return to what lies before this. "In the histories of the twelve tribes of Israel, it says that there was one Joachim, a very wealthy man, and he offered his gifts twofold, saying to himself, 'That which is superfluous to me will be for the whole people and that which is intended for my forgiveness will be for the Lord my God as a propitiation for me.' The great day of the Lord approached²⁶ and the sons of Israel offered their gifts. And Reuben stood opposite him and said, 'It is not possible for you to present your gift first since you have

²¹Cf. Ps 103 [104].2.

²²Cf. Ps 94 [95].5.

²³Cf. Gen 42, ff.

²⁴Some translations of the Septuagint suggest "panting" for ἐμφυσῶν. However, the association of the word with ideas of divine indwelling or breathing life into creation seems more persuasive.

²⁵This is a passage in which the Septuagint and Hebrew Bible diverge considerably. The NRSV translates this: "Celebrate your festivals, O Judah . . . A shatterer has come up against you."

²⁶In other words, the Day of Atonement in the Jewish calendar.

not made seed in Israel.' And Joachim was very grieved."²⁷ You have
seen that godly grief procures eternal life, as the blessed Paul has
said (cf. 2 Cor 7.10). O, very great gentleness of David! O, guileless
innocence of a wonderful man! O, godly mind of a righteous root!
He did not defend himself, nor did he insult [Reuben] or run into
the law-court, or curse, or threaten to strike [him], even though he
flourished²⁸ with wealth and good breeding and happened to belong
to a royal family. He did not say, "I am from a blessed lineage whereas
you are from an impious one which defiled the bed of our father
Israel" (cf. Gen 49.4). He could have responded to Reuben with all of
these things, but without attacking him, and walking away with the
swiftest of feet, the righteous man comes to [the record-book of] the
twelve tribes of Israel.²⁹ And not having found what he was seeking
for relief, [1469] he arrives at the mountain. And why is he righteous?
He takes up the song of David entirely and says, "If an enemy had
reproached me, I would have endured it; and if one who hated me
had made a boast at my expense, I would have hidden from him" (Ps
54[55].13). "Lord [and] Master, do not be silent at my tears" (cf. Ps
38[39].13). And he reasoned about these matters entirely as follows:
"If I [alone] in the whole of Israel am childless and a reproach, it
would be better for me to die by wasting away with hunger and thirst,
and not to reproach David harshly like another Shimei."³⁰

7   Why are you annoyed, O firstborn and ungracious Reuben? Why
do you, who are unblessed, take offence at the one who is blessed?

²⁷Cf. *Protevangelion of James*, chaps. 1–2, Elliott, *The Apocryphal New Testament*,
57.

²⁸The literal meaning of the verb κομάω is "to grow one's hair long," from κόμη
("hair").

²⁹According to the *Protevangelion*, chap. 3, Joachim went to look in the register in
order to see whether he was the only one who had produced no offspring in Israel. See
Protevangelion of James, chap. 1.3, Elliott, *The Apocryphal New Testament*, 57.

³⁰Cf. 3 Kgdms 2.8. The Greek name here is Σεμεή, but Shimei seems the most
likely reference. David tells his son Solomon that Shimei, the son of Gera, a Ben-
jaminite from Bahurim, cursed him with a terrible curse on the day when he went to
Mahanaim. He charges Solomon to punish Shimei for this lack of respect, although
he himself spared him.

Why do you, pauper, judge the king? Did not Jacob, the father of both of you, reprove your folly as he died, while blessing Judah?[31] For behold, when he was dying he said, "Judah, your brothers will praise you; your hands will be on the neck[32] of your enemies and your father's sons will venerate you. Judah is a lion's whelp; from the tender plant, my son, you went up.[33] On lying down, you slept like a lion; and as the whelp of a lion, who will rouse him? From Judah a ruler will not fail, nor a leader from his loins, until there comes to him what lies in store, and he is the expectation of the nations. Binding his ass to the vine and the foal of his ass to its branch, he shall wash his clothing in wine and his cloak in the blood of the grape. His eyes are full of joy[34] from wine and his teeth are as white as milk" (cf. Gen 49.8–12). For first he directed a reproach at Reuben. For he said, "Reuben, my first-born and the head of my children, [you are] hard to be endured, hard, [and] self-willed. After taking offence, do not boil over like water. [1472] For you went up into the bed of your father and then you polluted[35] the couch into which you went up" (cf. Gen 49.3–4).

Behold, thus Jacob himself, during the blessing of his sons, prophesies that the eternal kingdom is going to arise from Judah. And do you drive the righteous man from the temple? O, what was accomplished by you, Reuben, with your folly and malice!

8   So then the righteous Joachim comes to [the record-book] of the twelve tribes of Israel and, on not finding another childless man,

[31]Cf. Gen 49.4,8.

[32]I have emended τώτου to νώτου here.

[33]In the Septuagint this reads, "ἐκ βλαστοῦ, υἱέ μου, ἀνέβης." The NRSV has, "From the prey, my son, you have gone up," which reflects a divergence in the Hebrew and Greek versions.

[34]An alternative translation of χαροποιοί would be "productive of joy" or "bringing joy." Note that the Greek Septuagint differs from the Hebrew text here. This whole passage was understood typologically by the Christian Fathers, as we see also in Andrew of Crete's second homily on the Nativity, PG 97, 828; above, 91.

[35]The reading ἐμίας appears to be a misprint. One manuscript suggests ἐμείανας and another ἐμίανας. I have chosen the latter reading.

he goes onto the mountain in a state of affliction, supplicating God with sincerity. Meanwhile Anna was in the house. Both of them were praying by themselves, imitating their forefather David: they cried out that passage of the Psalms which says, "You made room for me in tribulation; pity me and hearken to my prayer" (Ps 4.2).

Then Anna, on contemplating her spouse's[36] delay, began to mourn to herself with a gentle lament and to say, "What is [the meaning of] this withdrawal of my dearest husband?" or "What is the meaning of this delay? As I see it, it is not good. Until now he has been going amongst the Israelites, seeking to find out whether we alone have not produced offspring. When he was present he was happy and had not submerged himself in grief. And God, who gave Isaac to Sarah beyond the season of her age,[37] [and who gave] Jacob to Rebecca,[38] Joseph to Rachel,[39] the prophet Samuel to Anna the wife of Elkanah,[40] and Samson the Nazarite to the wife of Manoah,[41] is powerful. The God who watched over them and hearkened to them is powerful enough to grant us our request. But why shall I mourn, unless I am both a widow and childless? If I did have a shoot, I would not feel such pain concerning the root. If the man whom I desired from my youth were now present, there would be some expectation even with regard to the shoot. Alas, what am I to do? My lord, whom I chose as a result of persuasion,[42] where are you now? Or, how shall I mourn you as a corpse? But I have not seen your tomb! Or, am I to wait as if you departed to a distant land? But no one has reported to me that he has found my lord. Alas, who will report to me where my partner and consort is, where the descendant and follower of Abraham is? Where is the comrade of Isaac? Where

[36]Literally, her "bed-fellow."
[37]Gen 21.2–3.
[38]Gen 25.21.
[39]Gen 30.22–24.
[40]I Sam 1.19–20.
[41]Judg 13.24.
[42]I have emended πεθοῦσα to πειθοῦσα here.

is the oracle of Israel? [1473] Where is the root of Jesse? Where is the offspring[43] of David?"[44]

These events came to pass in the 5483rd year from the beginning of the creation of the universe, in the seventy-fifth generation, even as the true writer Luke bears witness, having begun with Joseph and continued back to God (cf. Luke 3.23–38).

9 And when the Sun of righteousness was about to rise out of Judah, the prophet cries to him from afar, "Celebrate your feasts, O Judah . . . for one who breathes [life] has come up into your presence" (cf. Nah 1.15–2.1). Who is this One, O prophet? Tell us. He who "bowed the heaven and came down" (Ps 17[18].10); he is the One who dwelt in heaven. He is above with the Father and below in a womb, fearful to the cherubim and gentle to human beings; he went down to the gates of Hades and bound one who was once strong (cf. Luke 11.22); he unlocked the kingdom of death, as the Good Shepherd who leads his own sheep out of Hades and walks before them, having called each one of them by name (cf. John 10.2–3). "He who descended," says the apostle, "is the same one who ascended" (Eph 4.10).

10 What feasts do you call on Judah to celebrate, O prophet? Then he who sees says, "Judah will not celebrate the feasts of the law for me, nor those relating to Sabbath observance and new moons and trumpets. For it is time for the Lord to act [and] to scatter your law.

[43]Lampe cites this passage as reference for this meaning of πρόβολος.

[44]The preacher explores Anna's innermost thoughts and feelings in this passage. She speculates that if she had borne a child, her grief for her husband might be somewhat assuaged. If her husband returns, on the other hand, she will again feel the pressure to produce a child. Her feelings, as John presents them, are lifelike and complex: it is just such a mix of thoughts and emotions that people do feel when they are confronted with a life crisis such as the disappearance of a husband. Using the rhetorical device of ethopoiia, according to which interior monologue or dialogue may be invented, the preacher portrays Anna's character dramatically in order to arouse his congregation's sympathy for this holy figure.

I say that he should celebrate the feasts of the grace that has come, namely ten feasts among those which are notable."[45]

First of all the notable feasts is that in which Joachim and Anna received the good news [1476] of the [approaching] birth[46] of the wholly undefiled and God-bearing Mary. And after this, [there comes] her all-sacred Nativity. There was her Conception; here her Nativity. After this, another wholly august and venerable [day] [is celebrated], on which Gabriel walked on earth with rapid[47] feet and addressed the Virgin with "Hail!" Then there is the world-saving[48] Nativity from the Virgin of Christ our God, the Universal Sovereign. Then following that, the Entry into the temple and [Christ's] Reception in the arms of Simeon. And again, the light-bearing Epiphany;[49] and again, the Transfiguration in light on the mountain of Tabor, and the life-bearing Passion, the Pascha of eternal resurrection. And again, [there is the feast of] the Ascension into heaven and the sitting in flesh on the right hand of the Father. And there is the last and great day of the feasts on which the all-holy Spirit came down onto the holy disciples and apostles of our Lord Jesus Christ. "Celebrate your feasts, O Judah!" (Nah 1.15).[50] These then are the feasts that the prophet called on Judah to celebrate.[51]

[45]In other words, the Christian feasts. It is interesting that John of Euboea defines the number of great feasts as ten: he goes on to name a somewhat eccentric list below.

[46]It is possible that γεννήσεως should be emended to συλλήψεως here. This would make more sense in the context, since John is referring to 9th December here.

[47]The adjective οὖλος usually means "wooly," "crisp," or "curly" (as of hair), but L&S also suggests the meaning "rapid" with reference to dancing. This description calls to mind icons of the Annunciation such as the famous example from St Catherine's Monastery, Sinai, in which the archangel seems almost to dance towards the Virgin Mary in his haste to deliver the good news. See K. Weitzmann, *The Icon* (New York: George Braziller, 1978), 92–93, Plate 27.

[48]The word σωσικόσμιος, which is being used here as an adjective, appears to be a neologism. See Lampe, 1368.

[49]It is likely that John is referring to the Theophany, or Baptism of Christ here.

[50]Nah 1.15.

[51]John of Euboea has thus listed ten feasts: the Conception of the Virgin (9

11   As these [events] were already approaching, it was necessary for complete righteousness to be fulfilled. Hence while Joachim was praying on the mountain, Anna lamented in the house.[52] [Then] she went out of her house and entered her own garden in which she would draw refreshment from her extreme affliction.[53] And behold, an angel of the Lord appeared to her, saying, "Anna, Anna, the Lord has hearkened to your supplication, and you will conceive and give birth, and your offspring will be spoken of in the whole inhabited world.[54] Do not feel pain, Anna. Your fruit will stop the pain for those [women] who bear children in pain. For this is the one about whom all the prophets proclaimed in advance, eagerly awaiting salvation through her. You are blessed, Joachim and Anna. Truly one who is more blessed is being born from you," [said] the angel to them.

"Celebrate your feasts, O Judah" (Nah 1.15): not in the old covenant, but in the new! This is the beginning of the new covenant, of the new and God-receiving ark [1477] that was formed in Anna's womb, out of the root of Judah, Jesse, and David. For the prophet says, "And I shall raise up the tabernacle of David which has fallen, and I shall repair its broken parts" (cf. Amos 9.11). Behold, the taber-

December), her Nativity (8 September), the Annunciation (25 March), the Nativity of Christ (25 December), the Entrance into the Temple or Hypapante (2 February), Theophany (6 January), the Transfiguration (6 August), Pascha (movable), the Ascension (movable) and Pentecost (movable). The order in which the preacher lists these feasts is odd and as if recited off the cuff; it is also surprising that he omits Palm Sunday and the Exaltation of the Cross (14 September), both of which are ancient feasts which originated in Jerusalem and were transferred early to Constantinople. We may compare this listing of feasts to that found in Proclus's third homily on the Mother of God. Proclus only cites five feasts, but he uses the same passage from Nahum as justification for celebrating them. See N. Constas, *Proclus of Constantinople,* 198. I–IV.

[52]The verbs in these two sentences are actually in the present tense in order to inject a sense of immediacy; for stylistic reasons I have chosen nevertheless to translate them in the past.

[53]John has got the syntax of this sentence wrong, using a genitive absolute with respect to Anna in the first clause, when she is the subject of the second. This reveals his lack of rhetorical education in comparison with his colleagues, John of Damascus, Germanos of Constantinople, and Andrew of Crete.

[54]Κῇ should read τῇ here.

nacle of David is raised up in the conception and birth of his daughter! For she is the one about whom first of all Jacob was prophesying when he blessed Judah, speaking thus, "Judah, your brothers have praised you" (Gen 49.8).

Truly you are blessed, Joachim and Anna. For you came out of Judah and Jesse and David, as does also the one who comes out of you; and from her [will come] the Giver of the Law and Lord of prophets and Fulfiller of Law in the last times, Christ our Lord.

12 The angel [said] these things to the blessed couple, Joachim and Anna, and he added moreover, "Have courage, rejoice, and exult! For the time which is announced by the prophet has approached [in which] the great Shepherd will come out of Bethlehem and the land of Judah, and he will shepherd not only Israel, but also all the nations."

Blessed and thrice-blessed indeed are Joachim and Anna; infinitely[55] more blessed is the descendant and daughter of David who comes forth from your loins and belly. For you are earth while she is heaven. You are of clay, but through her those who are of clay become heavenly. You are truly blessed since He whom Moses was unable to see, the King of glory, desired the beauty of your daughter (Cf. Ps 44[45].12).

[1480] You are blessed, Joachim and Anna, because you conceived a spiritual paradise. For she is not only blessed by humans, but also by angels and cherubim and seraphim. For she bore from her undefiled womb the Gardener of creation and of paradise.

13 And behold, when Anna heard from the angel of the conception and birth of the wholly unblemished girl, she began to rejoice. But the one who was expected, that is her beloved spouse, was not yet present.

Then, when the righteous Joachim also received the good news of the conception from his loins, he began to prepare doubly and

[55]Lampe suggests this meaning with reference to this passage, 889.

triply the [expressions] of joy, and multiplying these tenfold, he rejoiced and exulted. And indeed, when he had fulfilled everything according to his custom, offering gifts and sacrifices, the sterile woman conceived. And both awaited the fruit of the birth, whatever the outcome might be.[56]

And when the time of the all-sacred nativity of the wholly unblemished girl and Theotokos drew near, the prophetic speech that Isaiah uttered was fulfilled: "Rejoice, O barren one who did not bear!" (Isa 54.1). And the blessed Anna rejoiced and exulted exceedingly, and she said to the midwife, "What have I delivered?" And the midwife said, "A female child." [1481] And Anna said, "I shall bring her as a gift to the Lord God."[57]

14 See then how clearly Mary and Anna and Joachim were serving the Trinity. For when the child was born and was advancing in age (cf. Luke 2.52), they did not bring her forward at two years, nor again at four years; but at the age of three, as a bride of the undivided Trinity and as an undefiled bridal chamber, since she was about to be both [of these].[58] And she was brought to God first as a gift, but then as temple and throne. Thus they brought the Virgin into the temple of the Lord in a prophetic way.

O what a marvel! The living temple and cherubic throne is brought into a temple constructed from stones. For David had cried out about her many generations earlier, saying, "Hear, O daughter of God, and see, and incline your ear, and forget your people and your father's house. And the King will desire your beauty" (Ps 44[45].11–12). And again, "Virgins shall be brought to the King after her" (Ps 44[45].15). How shall they be brought? Clearly "in gladness and exultation" (Ps 44[45].16). What sort of person is she, O prophet? For it was not fitting for the queen to be brought alone into the temple

[56]Cf. *Protevangelion* of James, chap. 4.3–5.1, Elliott, *The Apocryphal New Testament*, 58–9.

[57]Cf. *Protevangelion* of James, chap. 5.2, Elliott, *The Apocryphal New Testament*, 59.

[58]Once again the syntax is very odd here.

of the King; this, being sung [by the prophets], has been told before through the Holy Spirit. And again, "Her fellows shall be brought to you" (Ps 44[45].15). Other virgins too were indeed brought along with the holy virgin; it was made clear in advance that they also had a share of sanctity. For who that follows[59] a King and a queen will not be rewarded with gifts and gratuities from them?

There are also other virgins—but in order that I may not extend the oration, I shall say just a few things about them. These are the ones who guarded their virginity like a royal treasure, who continually pay heed to themselves in order that they may not be compared to those five foolish [ones] (cf. Matt 25.1–13), but are always guarding the royal shrine and pleasing their Bridegroom alone. For he enjoined [them], saying, "No one can serve two masters" (Matt 6.24). And many [virgins] had a blessed end through martyrdom, whereas others were crowned through asceticism and corporeal trials, and [others] are still being crowned.

15 [1484] For this reason it says in another [psalm] that the daughters of Judea should exult (cf. Ps 47[48].12). This, therefore, was spoken concerning the all-holy Mother of our Lord Jesus Christ since she would walk with the daughters of Judea into the holy of holies. For the women had not yet seen a girl being brought up in a holy place, and as paradoxical things were being accomplished according to prophecy, the daughters of Judea exulted to see the all-holy child Mary walking into the holy of holies like a spotless dove, and her parents Joachim and Anna rewarded with unutterable joy, and the high priest paradoxically opening his mouth and blessing her, [and they exulted] as meanwhile the rest of the priests were crying out in a loud voice, along with the council of elders and all the people, and saying, "Let it be, let it be, truly, let it be!" While these things were being accomplished in the manner of which I have spoken, the daughters of Judea exulted according to prophecy, especially in singing triumphant songs: "Skip and exult, not only the daughters of

[59] ἐψιάομαι may be a neologism. See Lampe, 589.

Judea, but also all the families of the nations! For Mary was born and Eve is no longer ashamed! Mary is brought into the temple, and the young girl, as a new temple, is raised up as a God-receiving temple! And the one who sprouted from David will be revealed not only as a temple but also as a cherubic throne, and the temple of the Jews will be destroyed even as the Lord said in the Gospels, "Verily, I say to you, there shall not remain here one stone upon a stone that shall not be thrown down" (Matt 24.2). For everywhere and always, the race of women, whether it should prophesy, whether it should acclaim a king, or again, whether it should denounce and rebuke, must not be called to account in any way since theirs is the weaker part. Look for me, in the [book recounting] the times of Saul, at the virgins who did not fear the wrath of the king, but who shouted at Saul for his thousands and at David for his tens of thousands! (Cf. 1 Kgdms 18.7).

16   Truly the mountain of Sion rejoiced and the daughters of Judea exulted (Ps 47[48].12). When? He tells us.[60] Then, when the temple of God was now brought to God in a temple, when an undefiled girl paradoxically walking into the holy of holies on the fleetest of feet goes to dwell there. Then the virgins, exulting with angels, were fulfilling the spiritual feast. [1485] How, at all events, will they be led "in gladness and exultation" (Ps 44[45].16) into a temple of a King? Where and why and to whom? Clearly [it is] towards the undefiled one, towards the Virgin Mary. For she is the temple of the great King since, as Queen, she was about to lead[61] the virgins as undefiled ones into a King's temple, for her honor and glory. On this account the prophet cried out, saying, "Virgins shall be brought after her" (cf. Ps 44[45].15). Then they were brought. But still other virgins will be brought when the Bridegroom comes forth from her in his glory (cf. Matt 25.10).

See, see, descendents of Reuben and his sons, that whereas Joseph, whom you envied and sold into Egypt, on assuming his

---

[60]The φησί here must refer to ps-James, the author of the *Protevangelion*.

[61]I have emended ἀγατεῖν to ἀγαγεῖν here.

temporal kingdom, did not bear a grudge over the wickedness of your fathers, but rather fed them when they were wasting away with famine (Gen 42–46), the Sun of Righteousness, having arisen as eternal King out of Judah and who is glorified as God in the council of saints, is great and terrible before all those who encircle him. He is the Lord, mighty and powerful, a Lord who is powerful in war. He is the Creator who fashioned a new heaven and throne that was unconsumed with fire[62] out of the earth which had grown old, and who transformed old clay into a heavenly bridal chamber. "Sing to the Lord a new song; sing to the Lord, all the earth. Sing to the Lord, bless his name" (Ps 95[96].1–2), that a virgin girl is offered in a temple, that he who sanctifies the temple may dwell in her; and having dwelt in her womb, may not consume [it]. Rather, just as he watered the bush with fire in the time of Moses, (cf. Exod 3.2), so also God, having dwelt in this [virgin], will save the world.

17   This is the praise and the songs of the exulting daughters of Judea: "Sing and exult and sing psalms!" (Ps 97[98].4). For behold, the devil who usurped our nature has been conquered! Behold, a throne more wonderful than the cherubic one is made ready on earth, about which it has been written: "God is in the midst of her, and she shall not be moved!" (Ps 45[46].6). For she is a throne and a place and [1488] a dwelling-place of the Emmanuel and All-Ruler, Christ.

Behold, a palace of the heavenly King is constructed without human hands, and this palace, which is in Eden, has its gate facing the east; and no one will enter through this gate except the Lord God alone, and the gate will be shut (cf. Ezek 44.1). Truly it is a marvelous palace such that even the powers of heaven are entertained in it. For the affair passes all understanding. This palace, which was prepared without earthly craftsmen, was shown to be higher than the heavens

---

[62]This passage is cited by Lampe as evidence of the meaning "throne unconsumed with fire." More often ἀκατάφλεκτος is used with reference to the burning bush, another Old Testament type of the Virgin Mary.

and wider than the whole of creation, and no one dwelt in it except the Craftsman and Creator and Maker of heavenly and earthly things. And who is this, since he alone created and he alone dwelt [therein]? Never has this been heard, that the gate of that marvelous house will never be opened for anyone else. Who is this King? Does he have no army and military commanders? Does he have no body-guards [1489] carrying out his service in trembling and fear? Does he have no royal officials?[63] Yes, [Scripture] says, all creation is his: "A thousand thousands attend him in heaven and ten thousand ten thousands serve him" (cf. Dan 7.10).

18   And so these [types] contain the manner in which the Theotokos Mary went and dwelt in the holy of holies; and she is revealed as more exalted than all righteousness.

O, the callousness of the Jews! O, their folly! O, the blasphemy of heretics! O, their clouded hearts! For those who clash with strife and jealousy,[64] like an earthen pot against a cauldron, are in no way worse than the presumption of the Jews. For these ones collide and these ones are shattered.[65] Or were the prophets not from their [people]? Now they confess the prophets as of the same race, but they are not persuaded by their speeches. Where, then, in all their generations did they see a girl brought up inside the holy of holies, or again, a virgin after child-birth? Did not some of them, writing with their own hands when the Lord became High Priest, themselves confess the holy Mary to be a virgin? For some considered the Lord to be High Priest out of their [own race], that the word which had been written might be fulfilled: "You are a priest forever according to the rank of Melchisedek" (Ps 109[110].4). They accepted[66] that it was he who advanced in wisdom from God and men (cf. Luke 2.52),

[63]Lampe cites this passage as an example of this meaning for the word βασιλικός.

[64]I have emended ξήλῳ to ζήλῳ here.

[65]The metaphor of a clay pot and a cauldron clashing together represents a good example of John of Euboea's vivid use of imagery in his preaching.

[66]The Greek here literally says, "they made it that . . ."

and that Mary, the holy Theotokos, was from a royal and priestly tribe, according to how they reckoned this customarily among[67] themselves. For when priests came forward, they sought out the father and the mother and wrote their names into the decree of the priesthood. And they asked the holy Virgin, saying, "Is Jesus your son?" And she answered, "Yes." They said, "And who is his father?" The wholly unblemished one answered, "He has no father on earth. I bore him as he alone knows. For God is his Father." But they said, "And should we write him in the script of the roll as Son of God?" She said, "Write [it]." And they wrote on the roll as follows: "Jesus, the Son of God and Son of Mary will be consecrated [as priest] eternally by decree from above." And that which was written was fulfilled, as has been shown above: "You are a priest forever according to the rank of Melchisedek" (Ps 109[110].4). For after the Lord returned from the desert, he went into Nazareth where he had been brought up. And he went according to custom into the synagogue on the day of the Sabbath, and he arose to read and the book of Isaiah the prophet was given to him. And on opening [1492] the book, he found the place where it was written, "The Spirit of the Lord is upon me because he has anointed me" (cf. Luke 4.16–18), and the rest.

This roll is preserved by them until the present day, and the roll will be read at his Second Coming at the examination of the Jews. For prophets did not persuade them, nor did they heed the Lord himself. But they will be examined on the basis of the Scriptures themselves, which were written by the hands of their priests. For while they used to proclaim that the truth was erroneous, always leading [others] astray and being led astray, nevertheless they accept the error with which they will depart into eternal punishment. For the Lord said to them, "I have come in my Father's name, and you do not accept me; if another comes in his own name, you will accept him" (John 5.43).

19   But will you tell me, O Jew, how he is Son of God and Son of man? Listen. Since surely God created man according to his image

[67]I have emended οὖν to ἐν here.

and likeness, the devil, after defeating man by guile, subjected him to death. On this account [God] first sent prophets who proclaimed in advance his coming. And when the fullness of time had come, he sent his only-begotten and beloved Son, and he put on Adam's flesh that he might defeat the one who had dominated man's nature by the will of the flesh and destroy the devil who kills humanity.

For [it is] as when an emperor, who has dispatched [an army] into a country or[68] into a city, but [finds that] those who were dispatched have been unable to subdue the enemy, himself takes up the clothing[69] of that country and goes to destroy the enemy. Meanwhile the enemy, expecting that it will overpower him too, having rushed against the stronger man will be captured; so it was, then, with the one who exalted himself of old and who boasted that he would place his throne in the midst of heaven and also forsake the universe, as he thought. For the shameless one, who fell from heaven like a flash of lightening (cf. Luke 10.18), spoke in the following way: "Having done this, I shall be like the Highest" (Isa 14.14). For he glorified himself, as he thought, as a powerful being. In order then that the Savior might show his destructive artifices to be dead, and in order that he might trap him like a bloodthirsty snake with the divine snare, God's counsel overthrew his artifices as if pulling apart a spider's web.[70]

[1493] David knew of his guile as both by night and by day he did not stop paying reverence, as if on behalf of everyone, offering prayers and supplications to God and saying, "Lord, bow thy heavens and come down" (Ps. 143[144].5), and again, "Lord, stir up your power and come to deliver us" (Ps 79[80].3), and again, "Lord, do not overlook the works of your hands" (Ps 137[138].8).

[68]I have emended ἡ to ἤ here.

[69]The word used here is σχῆμα, which could mean "form," "appearance," or "clothing." The idea that the preacher is attempting to convey is that the ruler takes on the appearance of his army, just as Christ took on human form, in order to defeat the enemy.

[70]The imagery here is interesting, reflecting a popular and lively view of the cosmic battle between God and the devil.

20   Therefore by his counsel which endures forever and by the thoughts of his heart from generation to generation (cf. Ps 32[33].11), he did not forget his poor, but remembered his compassions and his mercy, which is everlasting (cf. Ps 24[25].6). And he chose out[71] the tribe of Judah in order that he might raise up the throne of David, his servant (cf. Ps 77[78].68–70). For before the covenant of law and the prophets' proclamation, Judah delivered Joseph from a cruel death and obtained infinitely more in exchange for the good man, so that from his seed those who had been planted in the house of the Lord, in the courts of God (cf. Ps 91[92].14), Joachim and Anna, would blossom with the Theotokos who is worthy of all praise, the holy Mary. Rejoice, then, Anna and Joachim, in the Lord, and give thanks for a remembrance of his holiness (cf. Ps 96[97].12).

"For Sion heard and rejoiced, and the daughters of Judea exulted" (Ps 96[97].8). For Judah prevailed over the eleven tribes and none of the rest of his brothers was blessed so much as he, who produced our salvation. For the names of the rest changed to that of Judah. They are not called [by the name] of another tribe, as either Reubenites or Benjaminites, or Ischarites or Zoboulonites, or according to [the name of] another tribe, but simply "Jews." O evil nation! O crooked and perverse race! O callousness and hearts wrapped round with a veil! The names of all their tribes changed into that of Judah and they are all called Jews, and they did not believe in the Lord who arose out of [the house of] Judah. And the Savior himself bears witness to this [1496] in a speech, saying, "Salvation is from the Jews" (John 4.22). "I am he, the One who is speaking to you" (John 4.26). The Lord said these words to the Samaritan woman.

21   It is time then to begin the day of rejoicing[72] and to celebrate with all the righteous from Adam as far as Zacharias, whom they [later] murdered between the nave and the altar.[73]

---

[71]Read ἐξελέξατο for ἐξεγέξατο.

[72]Read χαρμοσύνης for χαρμφύνης. L&S cite the LXX as source for the meaning, "day of rejoicing."

[73]Zacharias, the high priest of the Jewish temple and father of John the Baptist,

Rejoice then, Adam, on account of the Mother of God, Mary; since you were deceived through a woman by the snake and since through a woman you will tread on him. For the time has come for the sharpened arrows of the Powerful One to come out of [human] nature itself, since the Enemy sought his weapon from the same source. For just as a tree and a woman became the source of your exile in paradise, now a woman and a tree become your restoration. Whereas a woman who was constructed by the hand of God deceived you, a woman who came from the loins of Joachim and was carried in the womb of Anna, will beget without seed the Conquerer of death and the Destroyer of the one who imprisoned you. And although [one] tree was good for eating, pleasing to the eyes, and beautiful for contemplation, it brought you death; whereas a dry and fruitless tree will destroy the snake and become the agent of eternal life for all those who are born on earth.

You, mother of mothers, Eve, also exult because your children will no longer be [intended] for corruption but will exist in incorruption! Also you, Abel and Seth, sing, since the Highest prepares[74] his tabernacle and comes to bless the earth, which he had cursed! And you, Noah, be thankful that the Lord is coming. Gather together your children who have been scattered abroad that they may venerate the One who preserved [all of] you in the flood! For the Lord is a God of vengeance (cf. Ps 93[94].1) who comes to earth to renew Adam, having put him on, and to lead up from Hades all those who are prisoners. Rejoice also, Abraham and Isaac and Jacob, along with the law-giver Moses and all the prophets, all[75] offering worship after having expounded your books, since your expectation is at hand.

---

was murdered by Herod's soldiers as he stood in the temple between the sanctuary and the altar. See Matt 23.35; Luke 11.51; *Protevangelion of James* 23, Elliott, *The Apocryphal New Testament*, 66.

[74]Read ἑτοιμάζει for ἑτοιλάζει here.

[75]The Greek in fact says "both" here, but the text must be corrupt since it is not clear to which two of the prophets John is referring.

These are the joys[76] of the daughters of Judea: that the righteous Joachim and Anna brought the wholly unblemished Theotokos into the holy of holies. For "Mt Sion rejoiced and [1497] the daughters of Judea exulted because of your judgments, Lord" (Ps 96[97].8). For the virgins who accompanied the holy Virgin Mary, the Theotokos, had nothing to say that was inappropriate or rude, but instead [spoke] only [words] which were spiritual and pleasing to God, which the Holy Spirit bestowed on them at that very hour. For why was there a need in them for other words besides those praising the Queen entirely fittingly, and proclaiming victorious hymns to the eternal King who was about to be born from her without seed, and singing, in the manner in which the holy Spirit allowed them to declaim?

22 Let all of us too celebrate, beloved, the festivals of the Theotokos Mary, rejoicing spiritually and contemplating the saying of the prophet. For he says, "Celebrate your feasts, O Judah . . . for one who breathes [life] has come into your presence and is delivering you from affliction!" (Cf. Nah 1.15–2.1). For she comes out of Judah, and the Lord [will come] out of her according to the flesh.

Therefore among the divine and great feasts, we must celebrate those of our hope, the Theotokos! Thus, besides the fullness of the ten feasts, we are celebrating too her life-bearing Dormition. After the Ascent into heaven of our Lord Jesus Christ and after the descent of the all-holy and life-giving Spirit onto the blessed apostles, which is called both the last and the great one, the completion of the goodness of the dispensation of our Lord and God—[in fact] later than every [other feast], [we celebrate] her all-sacred Dormition.[77]

[76]Lampe offers this as one of the meanings of σκιρτήματα although literally the word means "leaps" or "skips."

[77]This paragraph is very interesting from a liturgical point of view. It is generally accepted by historians that the feast of the Dormition was introduced into the Constantinopolitan calendar at the end of the sixth century, by the emperor Maurice (AD 582–602). Sermons commemorating this feast began to be produced soon after this period, with preachers of the seventh and eighth centuries building on the apocryphal

[We celebrate] the [feasts described] above, which are also declared in advance by the Decalogue of both the Old and New Testaments. For there are three successions[78] of ten statements, just as we have been taught by the all-holy, consubstantial, life-giving, and venerable Trinity. The first is from the Law: "You will love the Lord your God" (Deut 6.5), and the rest. And afterwards, in the New [Testament], [1500] the beatitudes themselves are ten in number. Similarly, the "Our Father" is in ten sentences. Doing honor to these [forerunners], therefore, we celebrate the ten feasts.

23   The first [feast], even if it is not known by everyone, [is that] in which the blessed Joachim and Anna received the good news of the [coming] birth of the ever-Virgin and Theotokos Mary, on the ninth day of the month of December.[79] Take note intelligently, beloved, that what has been passed down among us in writing is neither inefficacious nor unprofitable. For if consecrations of churches are worthily carried out, by infinitely how much more ought we to carry out this festival, with zeal, piety, and fear of God? On [this day] the foundation was placed, not out of stones; the temple of God was built, not by human hands; that is to say, the holy Mary, the Theotokos, was conceived in a womb, but with the Father's good will and the cooperation of the all-holy and life-giving Spirit, Christ, the Son of God, the corner-stone, himself built [her], even as he himself dwelt in her, that he might fulfill the law and the prophets, coming in order to save us. To him be glory and honor and worship, along with the Father who is without beginning, and the all-holy and life-giving Spirit, now and always, and to the ages of ages. Amen.

narratives concerning the Dormition of the Mother of God and reflecting on the theological significance of the event. See above, 23–4; Daley, *On the Dormition*, passim. John of Euboea does not imply in this passage, however, that celebration of the feast could be taken for granted. He does not include it in his list of ten major feasts, but instead suggests that it represents an extra celebration in the festal calendar.

[78]Lampe cites this passage with reference to this use of the noun διαδοχή.

[79]This is a clear indication that, at least in John of Euboea's circles, the feast of the Conception of St Anna was not widely celebrated or even known.

ANDREW OF CRETE

Oration on the Annunciation of the Supremely Holy Lady, Our Theotokos[1]

1 [881] Universal joy has arrived today, releasing the previous curse. He who is everywhere has arrived that he may fill all things with joy. How has he arrived? Not with guards or leading armies of angels or boasting of his advance, but instead in silence and tranquility: he does this so that he may escape the notice of the ruler of darkness, having ensnared the snake by means of crafty wisdom and tricked the mind, the Assyrian, which is also the dragon[2] [884] that has subjugated all human nobility beneath itself, and that he may seize the spoil. His immeasurable mercy towards us refused to lose[3] so great a work, [that is] humanity, on whose behalf he created the vault of the heavens, established the earth, spread out the air, filled the sea, and constructed the whole of the visible creation.[4] For this reason, God is on earth, God is from heaven, God is among human beings, God is carried in the womb of a virgin, he who is contained nowhere. Henceforth human nature receives the prologue of joy and takes the

---

[1]*CPG* 8174; *BHG* 1093g; ed. A. Gallandi, trans. and notes by F. Combefis, PG 97, 881–913.

[2]As Combefis points out in his note 40, the scriptural allusion here is subtle. The "mind" (νοῦν) of the Assyrian may refer to Isa 10.12: " . . . that I will visit upon the proud heart, even upon the ruler of the Assyrians, and upon the boastful haughtiness of his eyes." (Brenton, 845). Andrew appears to identify the Assyrian ruler with the devil, or the "ruler of darkness," here.

[3]For this meaning of ζημιόω, cf. Matt 16.26, Luke 9.25, etc.

[4]Cf. Gen 1.1–31.

beginning of deification. Henceforth, after tonsuring its own wealth of sin with its many delusions, it is escorted in marriage to the Creator. Henceforth our original formation receives a fresh renewal and the world that had grown old casts off its decayed condition[5] of sin. But "let heaven rejoice above and let clouds sprinkle righteousness" (Isa 45.8). "Let mountains drip sweetness and the hills, exultation" (cf. Isa 49.13),[6] since God has shown mercy to his people. For today "the mystery which has been hidden from before the ages" (cf. Col 1.26) is revealed and "everything receives recapitulation in Christ" (cf. Eph 1.10).[7] Today the Source of all authority,[8] who made all things, brings his plan, which he worked out in advance for the creation of everything in existence, to its goal, in order that he may prevent the plan that was devised for us from the beginning by the founder of evil.[9] For this reason angels dance, human beings rejoice, and the whole universe is renewed and restored to itself. What mind, what sort of tongue will encompass these things? Could any word be capable of expressing [them] or any ear able to receive [them]?

2   It is therefore fitting that the current splendid and radiant[10] festival is applauded today as it celebrates the acceptance in all its

[5]Cf. Nah 1.15.

[6]Cf. Gregory of Nazianzus, *Contra Julianum*, PG 35, 545; J. Bernardi, ed. and trans., *Grégoire de Nazianze. Discours 4–5 contre Julien* (SC 309; Paris: Éditions du Cerf, 1983), 108.

[7]The term ἀνακεφαλαίωσις which Paul uses as a verb to express renewal in Christ, was also employed by Irenaeus of Lyons to express the idea that Christ recapitulates the first creation and thereby redeems it. Another possible translation of the word is "renewal."

[8]The word ἐξουσιαρχία is used by (ps-) Dionysius the Areopagite's *De caelesti hierarchia*, PG 3, 240B. This passage, along with others, reveals the influence of (ps-) Dionysius on Andrew of Crete.

[9]A more literal translation would use the pronoun "it," referring back to the "Source of all authority"; since this is clearly God, I have chosen to use a masculine personal pronoun instead.

[10]The verb γάν(ν)υμαι is rather unusual and means "be glad," "rejoice." Lampe also gives the meaning "radiate" (308) and I have chosen "radiant" to express the adjectival use of the participle here. See the example in (ps-) Dionysius the Areopagite, cited by Lampe.

diversity of our dough.[11] What, and of what kind, is [this festival]? It [represents] happiness for all creation [885] and renewal for the race [of human beings]. But there are not only glad tidings of joy today; [there are] indications of God's benevolence and joyful [signs] of universal salvation! Whence, from whom, and to whom have these come? From heaven and from God, and to a virgin who has been betrothed to a man.[12] Who was the virgin? Who was the man? What were their names? Hers was Mary; his was Joseph. Both were from the family of David.[13] Who was attending on these things and whence did he come? The archangel Gabriel was sent from on high to attend on the miracle. It was necessary for the servant of the Highest One, coming down from the highest realms to earth, to arrange a paradoxical mystery in the midst of paradoxical events. What is this [mystery]? It is the descent of the Lord, the ineffable appearance of his dispensation on our behalf, [and] the expression and certainty of the divine plan and foreknowledge which had been hidden since the beginning of time. But where did these things [come about], when and for what reason? In the city of Nazareth of Galilee, in the sixth month, just when John had been conceived, in order that he might proclaim the presence of the One who was coming in [Mary's] womb.[14] Thus, Gabriel, on descending from the ethereal heights to the earthly bridal chamber, arriving in Nazareth and approaching the Virgin, attended noiselessly to the disclosure of the ineffable dispensation. This is the mystery of divine reconciliation with humankind. [It is] this that we celebrate today, the joining of God with humanity, the deification [brought about by] Incarnation, the reshaping of our image and its transformation into something better, the exaltation and ascent to heaven.

[11]The vocabulary and metaphor used here are obscure: Andrew means that the feast is celebrating the Incarnation of Christ and his complete assimilation of human nature in becoming a man.

[12]See Luke 1.26–27.

[13]According to Luke, Joseph was from the family of David (cf. Luke 1.27). Andrew continually tries to prove that Mary was of the same family although the Gospels do not in fact make this explicit. See his *In Nativitatem* III, PG 97, 845C; above, 107–22.

[14]See Luke 1.26, 44.

3 For this reason, everything rejoices today with joy and the whole spiritual order of transcendent powers makes a fresh treaty,[15] with divine [acts of] intercessions towards us. For our correction towards God is dear to them, as is our advance and ascent towards a better state of being. For they are also entirely sympathetic and benevolent towards humankind since they are sent to minister to those who will inherit salvation. Let all things then exult today and let nature skip! For heaven is opened up and earth invisibly receives the King of everyone! Nazareth, imitating Eden, contains the Sower of Eden! The Father of mercies alone secures the lowest human state by the One who alone[16] was brought into being out of him.[17] [888] Gabriel attends on the mystery and says "Hail" quietly to the Virgin in order that the daughter of Adam who arose out of David may restore through herself the joy that the first mother destroyed. Today the Father of glory, having come [in response] to the lamentation of the human race, regards with a forgiving eye the nature that was corrupted in Adam. Today the Giver of mercy reveals the depth of his all-good compassion and creates channels in our nature for his pity so that it is like much water covering the seas. For it was fitting for the One from whom, on account of whom, and in whom all things were established to repay with mercy the condemnation of the ancient curse against us; and by his own glory to discredit the nature which had been disgraced in Adam and with truth to shake off the dangerous counsel of the father of falsehood,[18] the result of which was the first deviation,

[15]The literal meaning of the classical verb ἐπισπένδω is "to make a drink offering." In the middle voice, the verb means "to make a fresh treaty." Cf. L&S 658, II. The implication here is that the transcendent powers, which probably includes the ranks of angels, has been estranged from humanity; with the coming of Christ, there is a reconciliation and a new pact of fellowship. This passage again shows Andrew's admiration for (ps-) Dionysius's mystical theology.

[16]I have emended πόνος in text to μόνος. This is also understood in the Latin translation.

[17]Cf. (ps-) Dionysius the Areopagite, *De divinis nominibus* 1.4, PG 3, 592A; Lampe, 551.

[18]The preacher is referring to the devil here.

the transgression of the man that was fashioned in the form of Adam.[19]

4   Indeed, it is for this reason that the great [king] among kings, David, who was ancestor of God, sang in advance, "Mercy and truth met together; righteousness and peace embraced" (Ps 84[85].11). Why was he saying these things unless perhaps [he meant] the mercy of the Son in accordance with the good will of the Father on our behalf, since the Giver of mercy had mercy on us, becoming like us [in all respects] except for sin in order that [Adam's] transgression might be undone, and that he might raise us from sin who had fallen, and refashion that which had lapsed, [that it might be freed] from destruction? By "truth," [he meant] [Christ's] appearance among men, which was not just a fantasy. For he did not create his assumption [of humanity] out of us in simulation, as one might say, but indeed in truth and with benevolence towards humankind, as the One above substance took on substance from the substance of humanity; and, having deified the Incarnation of our entire nature in himself, he did not feign the dispensation, but he established the truth of the flesh, while [at the same time] his divinity remained untouched by any alienating alteration. Since therefore "mercy and truth met together," according to the prophecy, it is reasonable also that "righteousness and peace kissed [each other]" (Ps 84[85].11). Righteousness, on the one hand, is the sentence that was brought against the one who wronged our first-born [ancestors]. When, and by whom? Today, and by the highest Father. For on [this day] the One who in his nature loves humankind ruled that his own only-begotten Son, who has appeared in a form equal to that of yours [889], should condemn the adversary. Peace, on the other hand, is that which the choir of angels suddenly celebrated in one voice at the birth of the Son in flesh, the Prince of Peace, saying, "Glory

---

[19]Andrew's choice of the phrase τοῦ Ἀδαμιαίου πλάσματος here is somewhat odd. It is a wordy way to refer to Adam, but it also expresses the creaturely state of the first man and his dependence on his Maker.

to God in the highest and on earth peace, good will among human beings!" (Luke 2.14). Glory, which humanity gained from Christ when it become higher than the heavenly vaults and "far above all rule and authority and power," (Eph 1.21), [in the words of] the great apostle.[20] And peace, which he himself mediated when he joined heavenly things with those on earth and provided a different path leading to heaven for those [who dwell] on earth. Good will which the Father himself approved, having sent his beloved Son himself to us who were condemned in order that, as One who is of the same will[21] as the Father, he might bring about in us the salvation which the Father was well pleased [to effect] through him.[22] This is what we are celebrating now: today Gabriel is entrusted with this command, mediates between divinity and humanity, and is the first to bring the good tidings of a pledge of complete reconciliation[23] to the Virgin.

5   For the Father of mercies, on showing mercy to our race which had already been corrupted by the slip into sin, remembered his handiwork and, not being willing to bear the sight of our complete destruction, first of all entrusted to the hands of Moses the law, which had been engraved in writing on stone tablets. But since the written law made nothing perfect (cf. Heb 7.19), he sent out spirit-bearing men, I mean the clear-sighted prophets, who were pointing out all the straight paths of God.[24] But as those to whom they were sent were stopping up their senses,[25] they were similarly disposed;

[20]That is, St Paul.

[21]Lampe cites this passage as evidence for the meaning of the word, ὁμοθελής, 953. It is also used by Procopius of Gaza, PG 87, 1297C.

[22]Andrew plays on the words εὐδοκία and εὐδοκέω, using their various forms repeatedly in this sentence and stressing both the unity between the Father's and the Son's intentions towards humankind and their joint benevolence.

[23]The word καταλλαγή can also mean "change," but I have chosen this more specific meaning for this context.

[24]Cf. Matt 3.3; Mark 1.3; Luke 3.4.

[25]This is a strange expression, but it reflects the idea that truth, as well as evil promptings, are received through the senses. As the ascetic Fathers stress, therefore, it is necessary to recognise the importance of the senses in spiritual development, but to discern the difference between good and evil aesthetic impressions.

yet even so the Creator did not disregard our created form. From his supremely good and wholly unblemished bosom, he sent his Son, who arose as the One who shares his throne, who is equal in power and equally good, to us, the unworthy ones, "on whom the ends of the ages have come" (1 Cor 10.11), having decided rather to bring about salvation for those who had caused offence than to despise such and so great an achievement in his work on our creation. Thus, having given authority to one of his chief angels to attend on the mystery, he commanded the following things, I think, with a sign from his own majesty.

"Come, Gabriel," said [God], "Go to Nazareth, a city in Galilee where a virginal girl who is betrothed to a man named Joseph lives. The virgin's name is Mary." "To Nazareth," replied [the angel], "Why?" "So that the All-Ruler may choose the virginal beauty that is graced by God like a rose from a thorny field, and that, according to the [892] prophecy, 'He will be called a Nazarean.'" (Matt 2.23).²⁶ Who [is this]? The Son of God and King of Israel, who was later proclaimed to Nathanael (cf. John 1.45). And indeed, it is customary for Gabriel to attend on the mysteries surrounding God, as we have learned in the Book of Daniel.²⁷

"Go then into Nazareth, a city in Galilee. And on arriving there, quickly address these glad tidings of joy, which Eve formerly destroyed, to the Virgin. And above all, do not throw her soul into confusion! For the message is one of joy, not of misery; the greeting is one of gladness, not of sadness."²⁸

²⁶The prophecy alluded to here is difficult to identify. It could be a reference to the Branch (Hebrew *neser*) of Isa 11.1 or the Nazirite (Hebrew *nazir*) of Judg 13.7, etc. Matthew may also be alluding to passages that speak of the Messiah as despised, since Jews generally looked down on Nazareth (John 1.46). See *OSB*, 8, note on Matt 2.23.

²⁷See Dan 2.1–45; 4.1–27. (Ps-) Dionysius discusses the archangel's role in the Book of Daniel in his *De caelesti hierarchia* 9.4, PG 3, 261.

²⁸These speeches reveal Andrew's willingness to use the device of ethopoiia, that is, to invent speeches for holy figures in order to amplify the Biblical account and its dialogues. The aim is to understand better the protagonists' motivations and actions leading up to important events, thereby increasing their dramatic and liturgical impact. On the use of dialogue as a rhetorical device in Byzantine homiletics, see Cunningham, "Dramatic device or didactic tool?"

6 For what sort of joy ever was or will be more pleasing than this for the human race, than to become a sharer in the divine nature and by union with him to become one with him in accordance with the definition of unity and therefore of hypostasis?[29] What could be more marvellous than to see the condescension of God reaching as far as pregnancy in the womb of a woman? O paradoxical events! God, "who has heaven as his throne and earth as his footstool" (cf. Isa 66.1), is [contained] in the reproductive parts[30] of a woman! God, who is above the heavens,[31] is in a womb, while at the same time he is sharing power with his Father's eternity. And what could be more paradoxical than this: for God to be seen in human form, having not separated himself from his own divinity, and also to see human nature entirely joined together with the Creator in order that the entire human being, who at first fell under the power of sin, may be deified?

What then did Gabriel [do]? When he heard these things and understood that the command had been confirmed by divine decree and was stronger than his own power, he stood on the brink of joy and fear since he did not possess clear courage from within and did not think it safe to contradict. Nevertheless, having complied with the divine command, he flew down to the Virgin and, on reaching Nazareth, stood before the chamber. Then, entering deep in thought, as if feeling quite at a loss in himself, he was split by various arguments, reasoning within himself, I think, as follows: "How shall I begin to carry out God's purpose? Shall I enter the room at a run? But I will terrify the Virgin's soul. Shall I go in at a more leisurely pace? But then I shall be judged by the girl to have tricked my way

[29]The word ὑπόστασις in Greek is used to indicate the substantive existence of things, and in the course of the fourth and fifth centuries AD it was accepted as a term for the three separate persons of the Trinity who remain one in substance or essence. See Lampe, 1454–61.

[30]According to L&S, μόριον may (in the plural) mean the genitals or reproductive parts of a woman. The literal meaning is simply "parts" or "members."

[31]This may be another word borrowed from (ps-) Dionysius the Areopagite. Cf. *De divinis nominibus*, PG 3, 596C.

in. Shall I knock on the door? But how? For this is not natural for angels [893], nor can any one of those things which restrain or are restrained shut out a bodiless one. Shall I first open the door? But it is possible for me to be inside although the door is closed. Shall I call on her by name? Yet I will disturb the maiden. Therefore I shall do the following. I shall guide my approach in accordance with the purpose of the One who sent [me], for his goal is to save the human [race]. And even if his purpose is in some way paradoxical, it is nevertheless full of compassion and a symbol of reconciliation. How then am I to approach the Virgin? What shall I tell her first? [Shall I tell her] the glad tidings of joy or about the indwelling of my Lord? The arrival of the Holy Spirit or the overshadowing of the Highest?[32] And so, then, I shall salute the Virgin [and] inform her of the miracle; I shall approach, greet [her], and pronounce the [word], 'Hail!' (Luke 1.28). The greeting will be a good introduction to openness. Let 'hail' be a guarantee for me of conversation with her. For the utterance of 'hail' will by itself, in addition to eliminating any fear in the girl, [serve to] steady in advance her soul's composure. Thus I shall begin with joy, proclaiming in advance to her the news which brings joy. It is also fitting that the Queen should be greeted with glad tidings of joy. For the manner in which [these tidings] are brought induces joy; the time is happy, the command [brings] delight, the purpose is for salvation, and [this is] the prologue of immeasurable joy."[33]

The archangel, having then weighed up these things for himself, arrived at the outer court and approached the chamber in which

---

[32]The use of the word ἐπισκίασις evokes the visitation of the divine presence in the Jewish tabernacle and temple. Cf. Exod 40.34–5; Luke 1.35.

[33]This long soliloquy by Gabriel, as he debates within himself how to approach the Virgin Mary without frightening her, is most interesting and, as far as I know, unique in Byzantine homilies and hymns on the Annunciation. Invented interior monologue (ethopoiia) both reveals the character of the protagonist and has a didactic purpose. The preacher teaches us by means of this passage something about the nature of angelic existence (insofar as he is able to discern this mystery), namely that Gabriel is bodiless, but that he may assume corporeal form, that he has feelings and doubts, just like a human being, but at the same time, that he is close enough to God to receive his direct commands and to discern, in some measure, his purpose.

the Virgin lived. He quietly advanced to the door, went inside, and addressed the Virgin in a gentle voice: "Hail, favored one, the Lord is with you" (Luke 1.28). He [existed] before you, he is with you today, and after a short time, he will [emerge] from you; thus he is present both eternally and in historical time. Oh, immeasurable benevolence! Oh, what kindness! He was not satisfied with the message of joy unless he also proclaimed the One who brought about this joy by the Virgin's conception. For the [statement], "The Lord is with you," clearly indicates the presence of the King himself, who was entirely embodied within her and yet was not separated from his own glory.

"Hail, favored one, the Lord is with you." Hail,[34] the instrument of joy, through which the condemnation of the curse was dissolved and the justification of joy was substituted. Hail, truly blessed one! Hail, distinguished one![35] Hail, royal dwelling-place that has been made beautiful [896] for the divine glory! Hail, sacredly-built palace of the King! Hail, bridal chamber in which Christ became the bridegroom of humanity! Hail, one who has been chosen by God before the generations! Hail, the divine reconciler for humankind! Hail, treasure of uncontaminated life! Hail, heaven, celestial house of the Sun's glory! Hail, spacious place for God who is nowhere contained, but who was contained in you alone! Hail, holy, virginal earth from which the new Adam came into existence by means of an ineffable, divine assumption of form,[36] in order that he might rescue the old [Adam]. Hail, holy, divinely perfect leaven out of which the whole dough of the human race has been raised and made into bread from the one body of Christ, coming together into one miraculous compound!

"Hail, favored one, the Lord is with you!" He [is the one] who said, "Let there be light; let there be a firmament" (cf. Gen 1.4, 6), [besides bringing about] all succeeding products of his creative mag-

[34]Literally, "May you rejoice!"

[35]For this meaning of λαμπρύνω in the passive, see Lampe, 792.

[36]The word θεοπλαστία is used by (ps-) Dionysius the Areopagite in his *De divinis nominibus*, PG 3, 648A; cf. also Maximos, *Opuscula*, PG 91, 57C.

nitude. Hail, female parent[37] of incomprehensible joy! Hail, the new ark of glory in which the Spirit of God came down and rested. Ark, in which he who was holy in nature miraculously constructed for himself the sanctuary of new-found glory in the virginal workshop of nature, for the sake of his Incarnation; for he did not change in any way, being immutable, but instead he added that which he was not since he was a lover of humankind. Hail, golden jar containing the one who sweetened the manna and induced honey [to come out] of a rock for the ungrateful Israel (cf. Deut 32.13). Hail, the seraphic tongs for the mystical coal! (Cf. Isa 6.7). Hail, the intellectual mirror of discerning foreknowledge, through which the renowned interpreters of the Spirit mystically contemplated the infinitely powerful condescension of God on our behalf. Hail, foreseeing optical instrument, by means of which those who were overshadowed by the gloomy shadow of sin were mightily illumined and received the Sun of righteousness, rising with glory from on high! Hail, the ornament of all prophets and patriarchs and most true proclamation of the unsearchable[38] foreknowledge of God!

7   [897] "Blessed are you among women and blessed is the fruit of your womb" (Luke 1.42). And it is right that you are blessed. For God blessed you as his tabernacle when you incomprehensibly conceived in your womb a man filled with his Father's ancestral glory, Christ Jesus, who was also God himself [and] who combined in perfection the [two] natures from which and in which he was formed. "Blessed are you among women," who without constriction contained the heavenly treasure, "in which all the treasures of wisdom and of knowledge are hidden" (Col 2.3), in the inviolate treasury of your virginity. You are truly blessed, "whose belly is a heap of wheat" (cf. Song 7.2)[39] since you brought to full growth, without seed and

[37] Another possible translation would be "mother," but I have chosen a different phrase to express the variation in vocabulary employed by Andrew.

[38] I have followed Combefis in emending ἐξιχνιάστων to ἀνεξιχνιάστων.

[39] The word ἅλως actually means "threshing-floor," but I have chosen "wheat" in order to evoke the usual English translation of this biblical passage.

without husbanding, a fruit of blessing, Christ, who is the ear of corn of immortality, [and who in turn reaps] a prolific harvest, ten-thousandfold: thousands of [people] making straight for the Farmer of our salvation. You are truly blessed, who alone of all mothers was made ready to be Mother of your Creator and who nevertheless escaped the [normal experiences] of motherhood. For your special virginity was not destroyed by pangs of childbirth, while your virginal offspring kept safe the seals of your purity. You are truly blessed, who alone conceived without a man the One who stretched out the heavens and, in an extraordinary way, brought the earth of your virginity up to heaven. Blessed are you among women, since you alone were assigned the blessing that God promised to the nations through Abraham. You are truly blessed since you alone were called mother of a blessed Son and our Saviour, Jesus Christ; it is on your account that the nations cry "Blessed is he who comes in the name of the Lord!" (Ps 117[118].26; Matt 21.9) and "Blessed is his glorious name forever and all the earth shall be filled with his glory. So be it, so be it!" (Ps 71[72].19).

8   "Blessed are you among women," whom generations bless (cf. Ps 71[72].17), whom kings glorify, whom rulers venerate; in whose presence the wealthy of the people offer supplications, and virgins, who both follow behind and go before her, hurry in her company into the temple of the king.[40] "Blessed are you among women" (Luke 1.42), whom Isaiah, seeing with prophetic eyes, named "prophetess" (Isa 8.3) and "virgin" (Isa 7.14), and again, "brick,"[41] "garden,"[42] [900]

---

[40]This must be a reference to the *Protevangelion* of James and the story of Mary's entrance into the temple, accompanied by "the undefiled daughters of the Hebrews." Cf. Elliott, *The Apocryphal New Testament*, 60.7.2.

[41]The word used here is πλίνθος. None of the references in Isaiah (Isa 9.10; 24.23; 65.3) seem appropriate as types for the Theotokos, but it is possible that Andrew is thinking here of Ezek 4.1: "And you, O Son of man, take for yourself a brick and you will set it before your place, and you will draw on it a city, which is Jerusalem." Combefis suggests, on the other hand, that he is referring to the "wall" (τεῖχος), as in Isa 16.12 or 4 Kgdms 3.25. See PG 97, 898, n. 64.

[42]Combefis suggests the reading κῆπον here in place of τόπον. This would fit the

"vision" (Isa 1.1; 13.1), and "scroll of a book" (cf. Ps 39[40].8),[43] and clearly called this "sealed" (Isa 29.11). You are truly blessed, whom Ezekiel . . . foretold as "the gate that faces eastward"[44] and which was shut, but it was passed through by God alone, and then again shut (cf. Ezek 44.1). You alone are truly blessed, whom Daniel, the man who was filled with longing, saw as a "great mountain" (cf. Dan 2.34–35), while the marvellous Habakkuk [saw] a "shaded mountain" (cf. Hab 3.3), and your ancestor,[45] who was also a king, prophetically sang of as "both a mountain of God and a rich mountain, a curdled mountain, [and] a mountain in which God was pleased to dwell" (cf. Ps 67[68].16–17). Blessed are you among women, whom the most divine visionary, Zechariah, saw as "a golden lampstand" adorned with seven lamps and seven vessels [for pouring in oil] (Zech 4.2); so then you were illumined with seven gifts of the divine Spirit. You are truly blessed, [since you are] the spiritual paradise of the living wood of salvation (cf. Gen 2.8–10), which contains the Sower of Eden, Christ himself, as he is typologically understood in you. He, like a river, flowing out of your life-bearing womb with ineffable power, irrigates the face of the inhabited world with four sources (cf. Gen 2.10),[46] through the good news: "Blessed are you among women and blessed is the fruit of your womb" (Luke 1.42). Fruit from which

context better since, although the former is found throughout the Septuagint, it does not appear in Isaiah. Garden (ὁ κῆπος), on the other hand, might be taken from Isa 58.11: ". . . and your God shall be with you continually, and you will be satisfied as your soul desires; and your bones will be made fat and will be as a well-watered garden and as a fountain from which the water has not failed," or Isa 61.11: "And like the earth putting forth its flower, and like a garden its seed; so shall the Lord, even the Lord, raise up righteousness and exultation before all nations."

[43]It is interesting that Andrew again mixes up his Old Testament citations here, in suggesting that this verse from the Psalms belongs to Isaiah. The word κεφαλίς probably refers to a "scroll," rather than to a volume of a codex. See L&S, 945.V.

[44]The editor's manuscript contains a lacuna here. Combefis suggests the reading πύλην ἀνατολικὴν or πύλην βλέπουσαν πρὸς ἀνατολὰς for the gap. I have therefore conjectured the first of these readings, which of course refers to the well-known type of the unopened gate that faces to the East (Ezek 44.1).

[45]I have emended προφάτωρ in the text to προπάτωρ.

[46]It is possible that Andrew is also referring symbolically to the four Gospels, the bringers of "good news" to Christians, in his reference to the four rivers of paradise.

Adam, the first-created, ate and [thereby] vomited forth the original ingestion[47] by means of which he had accepted the bait of deceit.[48] Fruit from which sweetness flows freely out of the bitter taste of the tree, purging human nature. He soaked the springs which supplied rivers in the desert to the wandering Israel, sweetened Merrha (cf. Exod 15.23),[49] and rained down bread, a strange and unprepared food. Blessed is the fruit which, with the help of Elisha, revealed the barren and bitter waters as drinkable and fruitful by the sprinkling of salt (cf. 4 Kgdms 2.22). Blessed is the fruit which, having marvellously ripened to a dark hue, bloomed as a bunch of grapes from the undefiled shoot of the virginal womb. Blessed is the fruit from which springs burst with water rushing towards eternal life. [901] Fruit out of which living bread, the body of the Lord, is offered up, and a chalice of immortality is shown forth as a saving drink.[50] Blessed is the fruit which every tongue of those [inhabiting] heaven, the earth, and even the underworld sanctifies with the triple repetition of sanctifying divinity in the Trinity, connecting it in the sameness of substance, but distinguishing it in personal terms by the individuality of the hypostases which exist in unity.[51] "Blessed are you among women and blessed is the fruit of your womb" (Luke 1.42).

[47]The Greek reads literally, "the ancient/original swallowing" (τὴν ἀρχαίαν κατάποσιν).

[48]The meaning of this sentence is not completely clear, but some sort of paradox is implied: Adam ate of the fruit and vomited forth the fruits of corruption. It is possible that Andrew visualises here the gaping mouth of hell which swallows the fallen. However, the imagery is somewhat convoluted since it implies that Adam is both swallowing and "accepting," but also belching forth the disastrous consequences of this ingestion.

[49]This refers to the place in the wilderness to which Moses brought the Israelites and where they were unable to drink the bitter water. Moses cried out to the Lord and was shown a tree. When he cast this into the water, it was sweetened and the people were able to drink.

[50]Note the rhyming final words σῶμα and πόμα in the two balancing phrases.

[51]The adjective ἐναρχικός means "being the principle of unity." See Lampe, 466, who refers to (ps-) Dionysius the Areopagite, De divinis nominibus 2.4, PG 3, 641A; 3.5, 641D, 4.4, 700A.

9 "But she," it says, "was troubled by his speech and pondered within herself, asking what sort of greeting this might be" (Luke 1.29). "She was troubled," it says, not because she was cast into doubt in her mind—away with you!—but instead [she reacted] with piety at the strangeness of the utterance, having considered that what was happening [was] a sign. Zachariah had formerly disbelieved [such a sign] in the inner sanctuaries [of the temple] and did not accept [it]; and it was on account of [this disbelief] that punishment was transferred from his reproductive to his vocal organs and sterility was exchanged for voicelessness (cf. Luke 1.5–20). [Mary], on the other hand, was so purified of every blemish and of any kind of intercourse with a man, and thus free of sexual experience since she had been in the habit of devoting her mind to heavenly contemplation, experienced confusion, which had come over her soul as a result of the greeting. For it was for her, since she was in all likelihood unable to speak freely, a situation of being on the one hand immediately in doubt and on the other, having examined what had been said with an idea which had come to her earlier and not as one might speak in response to what had just happened, so that she did not offer her hearing thoughtlessly to the one who was speaking.[52] Thus the evangelist indicated [this state of affairs] very wisely, [904] saying, "She pondered," testing her reasoning as if by the judgement of [her] pure intelligence, [judgement] that took in what was said not without trial. She was saying [to herself], "What sort of greeting might this be?" (Luke 1.29). It was reasonable for her, as a well-born girl who was also a descendant of David, to have a share in the divine narratives in Scripture and to cast her mind at once to the fall of her ancestress, having remembered the slip [caused by] deceit and all the other sorts of things that have been recounted by the ancients. It is therefore not unreasonable that the evangelist portrayed her as "pondering," but that he might also show how ready of wit she was, he has also set down her firmness and steadfastness in outlook, and, as it were, her

---

[52]The preacher again speculates imaginatively about the inner thoughts and response of the Virgin Mary. See above, n. 28.

freedom from distraction. For since [her] judgement of what was right had not been proven by the scrutiny of reasoned investigation, it was not necessary to set down at once her greeting.[53]

10 Yet because she was eager to repress the confusion in her soul, she did not rush to speak but, having remained in doubt only in appearance for a short time, she demonstrated the condition of her soul by upholding her habitual firmness instead of speaking. [In pondering] "what sort of greeting this might be" (Luke 1.29), she was asking, shall I, alone of all women, renew nature? Is it possible for me alone, as one who has not come together with a man, to conceive fruit? "What sort of greeting might this be?" Who is it who [brings] the glad tidings, and whence did he enter and convey them [to me]? Shall I consider that it is a human being who is speaking to me? But he seems to be bodiless. Should I deem him to be an angel? But he speaks like a man. Why do I not recognise what I am seeing and why am I at a loss at what is being said? What then [did] Gabriel [do]? As soon as he sensed the confusion of the girl, which he had not at all intended, he at once resumed speech and said, "Do not be afraid, Mariam, for you have found grace with God" (Luke 1.30).[54] First he dispelled her fear and then he raised her courage, saying, "Do not be afraid, for you have found grace with God," [grace] which Eve destroyed. In saying "grace," he dissolved the doubt in her mind and what had seemed for a while [to her] to be an attack.[55] By means of the statement that followed,[56] "You have found grace with God," he

[53]This paragraph represents a good example of Andrew's prolixity when he veers off into a periodic high style. It is interesting that this rhetorical style should accompany a passage devoted to a psychological style of exegesis concerning Mary's motivations and actions in this one verse (Luke 1.29).

[54]The normal translation (KJV and NRSV) of χάρις is "favor," but I have chosen "grace" since this English term conveys better the significance of the Greek word in Scripture and patristic exegesis. See Lampe, 1514–19.

[55]I have used Combefis's suggested reading, ἐπίβουλον, instead of ἀμφίβολον here.

[56]One meaning of ἐπαγωγή, which is usually translated as "introduction," is an inductive argument. Andrew seems to be implying that the archangel followed up his greeting to the Virgin, with this further statement.

persuasively banished the Virgin's fear. "Do not be afraid, Mariam." My manner is not wily nor have I come to lead you astray; nor again does a snake speak to you, hissing, nor am I addressing you from the ground. For I have come to you from the highest places, conveying the glad tidings—not just glad tidings, but glad tidings of joy. "Do not be afraid, Mariam." The greeting is not in jest and the message does not bring grief.

11   "The Lord is with you" (Luke 1.28), the Giver of all joy and the Savior of the whole world. He who has not been separated from his father's bosom[57] has been conceived in your womb. I called you "favored one" so that [905] I might disclose the joy of the mystery [which is taking place] in you. I called you "favored one" since you have received the entirety of joy itself in your womb, [and because you have received] a robe which has truly been graced with the brightness of divine gifts. I addressed you with, "The Lord is with you," in order that I might make known the power of the one who came earlier in you.[58] For he is "the Lord and God supremely powerful, Prince of Peace" (cf. Isa 9.6), and he [will be] Father of the age to come, Son of you, the Virgin, and Savior of all. "The Lord is with you." Grace and truth are with you. For he is both Lord of the law and Father of grace, and Spring of truth. "Do not be afraid, Mariam. The Lord is with you." He is a powerful Ruler[59] of all dominion, the Son of the Father of lights, who was begotten without beginning from him and who in time was made flesh out of you. In heaven he is entirely in [God's] bosom,[60] while here below he is entirely borne in your womb. He is with you and in you. For having hastened to leap in,[61]

[57] Cf. Ps 73(74).11; Luke 16.22; John 1.18, etc.

[58] Gabriel must be referring to Isaiah, not John the Baptist, here as he goes on in the next sentence to quote the prophecy of the former.

[59] The word ἐξουσιάρχης may be a neologism. Cf. Isa 9.6 (ἐξουσιαστής).

[60] Ὁ ἄνω ὅλος σὺν αὐτῷ ἐγκόλπιος. On the image of the Son being enfolded in the Father's breast, see Anastasios of Sinai, *Hodegon* 17, PG 89, 264B.

[61] This vivid imagery and unusual vocabulary is typical of Andrew's rhetorical style.

he slipped into your belly, and thus, he who is contained nowhere in nature became contained in you. "Do not be afraid, Mariam. For you have found grace with God" (Luke 1.30). Grace which Sarah did not accept, which Rebecca did not understand, and Rachel did not recognise. "You have found grace," of which the renowned Anna was not deemed worthy, nor was Peninnah who was her rival.[62] Whereas these [women] appeared as mothers after being childless, casting away their sterility along with virginity, you will keep your virginity intact along with being a mother. Indeed, "Do not be afraid, for you have found grace with God" (Luke 1.30). Grace which no one has found from the beginning of time, apart from you. And what sort of grace might there be from God that has such a special quality?

12   "You have found grace with God, and behold, you will conceive in your womb and bear a Son and you will name him Jesus" (Luke 1.29–30). Oh, the marvel! First he solved the obstacle of perplexity, then he introduced the statement of explanation. See how much he does in a short time! He banishes fear, explains [the meaning of] grace, interprets the conception, predicts the birth, and records[63] the name of the One who is being born. His speech did not stop with these [words], but in order that the greatness of the power of the One who has been conceived might be revealed, he added at once, "He will be great and he will be called the Son of the Most High, and the Lord God will give to him the throne of his ancestor David, and he will reign [908] over the house of Jacob forever, and there will be no end to his kingdom" (Luke 1.32). Have you seen how he did away with[64] the Virgin's fear? Have you seen how much he

[62]See 1 Kgdms 1.2. Peninnah, or Phennana was the second wife of Elkanah. She had children, whereas Anna initially had none. Cf. Andrew of Crete, *In Nativitatem* II, PG 97, 841; above, 103, n. 48.

[63]It is not clear why Andrew chooses the verb ὀνοματογραφέω here in what is clearly an oral dialogue. According to Lampe, the name is used in early Christian writings to mean "enroll" or "enter into a list," of the newly baptized, for example. Lampe, 965.

[64]The compound verb παρυφαιρέω is not in the dictionaries and thus may represent a neologism; judging from the meaning of the noun, ὑφαίρεσις, it may mean

emboldened her soul? For by speaking of the Son of the Most High and naming David as the ancestor of the One who was soon to be born, he at once inspired[65] her entire mind as he showed what would follow. And notice the Virgin's intelligence. For as she learned these things and recognised the unchanging authority of the divine will in accordance with [God's] pre-eminence, "She said to the angel, 'How will this be, since I have no knowledge of a man?'" (Luke 1.34). You are promising strange things to me, she was saying, and announcing things which transcend nature. I happen to be inexperienced in marriage, for I have been betrothed, but not wedded. I know Joseph only as my fiancé, but not as a husband. I live with my fiancé, but I do not sleep with him. My belly is without seed and thus not fruitful.[66] "How will this be, since I have no knowledge of a man?" (Luke 1.34). For, she was saying, surely, nature will not reveal me alone as a mother without having married. Surely, I alone will not bring about a strange but natural nativity that transcends nature. Marriage has not preceded this, nor have I had any experience of a man. For I have not come to know Joseph—he was introduced to me as a guardian and not as a husband—"and how will this be for me?"

13 Gabriel quickly answers and refines the earthly nature[67] of the question by the loftiness of his response, saying, "What sort of things are you saying, all-blessed one? Why do you put forth such words? I have come from heaven, bringing you [news of] the strangeness of your conception. I am not addressing you from earth when I say, 'The Lord is with you.' And are you at a loss [when you answer], 'How will this be?' I am bringing glad tidings to you of One who came into

literally "stole away." It is worth noting how consistently Andrew varies his vocabulary. He has stated this idea several times already, each time using a different verb to express how the angel Gabriel eliminated the Virgin Mary's fear.

[65]Literally, "put into flight" or "furnished with wings."

[66]Literally this reads, "My belly is seedless, but not fruitful," which does not make sense in English.

[67]It is difficult to translate this idiom literally into English. The adjective παχύς means "gross," "thick," or "stout." The author is thus depicting the earthly, literal nature of the Virgin's response at this time.

your womb before my arrival,[68] while you speak to me about a man and about birth here below, and you are saying, 'How will this be?' Understand how the rod has blossomed, how the rock has produced water, [and] whence you have become pregnant. [Understand also] how fire stole into the thicket of the bramble without burning it. For if you do not disbelieve these events, do not disbelieve me either. He who is accomplishing these, [and accomplished] those things, is the One who is carried in your belly. You will indeed become nurse of the One who has been conceived in you by a strange ordinance that transcends nature. [It is not the way] in which Elizabeth [conceived], or Anna who gave birth to you. For they became mothers after being inseminated, but you will produce as a child the One who has dwelt within you,[69] begotten without seed or any man. And if you should seek to find out the manner [in which this is done], I will tell it to you clearly."

14 "The Holy Spirit will come upon you and the power of the Highest will overshadow you" (Luke 1.35). For he who is born will not be out of the will of the flesh. Pleasure of the flesh will not play a part in the birth-giving of the Mother of God, for she has risen above the boundaries of nature. [909] And if she has been completely deprived of [childbirth] in accordance with nature, she in any case contains the transcendent Word who is Master of any [law] of nature.[70] Therefore no suffering accompanied the conception, as always occurs here below, nor the heavenly birth. "The Holy Spirit

---

[68]Andrew seems to suggest here that Christ entered the Virgin Mary's womb even before the arrival of the angel Gabriel. This cannot be intended, since Mary's assent to the Incarnation represents a vital aspect of Christian doctrine. It is likely that it reflects instead the preacher's dramatic intent and that it does not reflect a systematic theological approach to the question. It is interesting to note that Germanos also conveys this impression in his homily on the Annunciation. See Germanos, *In Annuntiationem*, Fecioru, ed., 83; below, 231, n. 33–232, n. 34.

[69]Again, Gabriel implies that the conception has already taken place. See above, n. 68.

[70]The text is somewhat corrupt. I agree with Combefis that an active verb rather than a participle is needed here and have therefore accepted his emendation of ἔχει for σχόντα.

will come upon you and the power of the Highest will overshadow you" (Luke 1.35). See where the mystery of the Trinity is revealed. For when [Gabriel] said "Holy Spirit," he meant none other than the Paraclete. [In saying] "the power of the Highest," he clearly describes the Son. And with the word "Highest," he introduces the person of the Father. Meanwhile, in [the words], "will overshadow you," it seems to me that he is referring to Habakkuk who earlier, glimpsing with discerning eyes, called the Virgin "a shady mountain" (Hab 3.3), all but suggesting that the power of the Spirit had overshadowed her, creating an ineffable tabernacle[71] within her by the word of Incarnation, according to which [it created] the temple of [his] body not cut by hands in the womb of the Virgin, like a place deserted by the passions, she being free from all material inclination[72] and attachment, as is clear from what follows.

15   For [Gabriel] says, "Therefore the [child] to be born will be holy; he will be called the Son of God" (Luke 1.35). For the infant [conceived] from the Holy Spirit and formed incomprehensibly before eternity through the Holy Father will rightly be holy and will be called Son of the Highest, having appeared as co-eternal Word of the Highest. [The angel] has thus clearly shown the Virgin why, whence, and in what manner [the infant] was conceived in her and from her, and that he would be born as Son of God. In order then that he might explain to her the power of the word even more distinctly and explicitly, he introduced the conception of Elizabeth. It is as if he were saying, "He who was able to show an old woman's womb to be fertile [in a manner] beyond expectation, will manifestly reveal a virgin miraculously bearing a child." For this reason, he proceeded [as follows]: "For nothing will be impossible for God" (Luke 1.37).[73]

---

[71]The word σκηνοπηγία actually means "an encampment" or "pitching of tents." The word evokes biblical dwelling-places and implies the transient nature of Christ's life on earth. Cf. John 1.14, etc.

[72]I have emended μετασίας (Combefis) to μετουσίας here.

[73]Both the KJV and the NRSV versions translate the sentence in this way, although literally it means, "No saying at all will be impossible for God."

When the Virgin heard these [words], or rather, as her mind was illumined by the Light of the one who dwelt within her, and she was gladly set right by the joyful nature of the announcement, she became entirely overjoyed. [912] And in just such a way as Scripture describes David, [Mary] proved to be graceful in soul with a beauty of eyes, since she was delighted by the miracle and gladly accepted the greeting.[74] For what was being said was full of unutterable joy. Gabriel, very easily and with great clarity, persuaded the virgin to receive the miracle gladly, by introducing it with [the words], "For nothing will be impossible for God" (Luke 1.37).[75] What does the Gospel say next? "Mariam said, 'Behold the handmaid of the Lord; may it be with me according to your word'" (Luke 1.38). Did you see her intelligence? Did you see the great degree of her modest reserve? When, on learning of the conception of the child, she understood the origin of her child-bearing, who and of whom her Son would be and what he would be called, as well as whose throne he would receive and whom he would rule, and finally, that the One who would be born would not be without a kingdom,[76] she raised her voice, returning joy for joy, [saying], "Behold the handmaid of the Lord; may it be with me according to your word." Clearly, she was saying the following: behold, I stand ready; so do not prevent anything. My soul is eager and my belly is ready, for it is preserved untouched for the Creator alone. "Behold the handmaid of the Lord," ready for obedience, urgent[77] for service, and prepared for reception. "May it be with me according to your word." For, she was saying, since you have reported everything well, as far as is possible, up to now, the entire completion of joy and of glory from the highest has

---

[74]Note the highflown language and Andrew's decision to dwell on that momentous moment when Mary accepted the greeting of the angel; in other words, the moment of the beginning of the Incarnation of Christ.

[75]See n. 73.

[76]Cf. Luke 1.33. On this use of ἔξω see L&S, III.

[77]The adjective εὐτρυνής does not appear in the dictionaries. Combefis suggests the alternative reading, ὀτρυνής, meaning "eager," "stirred up," etc. Εὐτρυνής may be a neologism, meaning roughly the same thing.

been fulfilled. "Behold the handmaid of the Lord; may it be with me according to your word." Well done for the unutterable dispensation! Well done for grace! Supremely well done for the divine will and foreknowledge without beginning! Truly the Holy Spirit dwelt in the Virgin and the power of the Highest overshadowed her in accordance with the preordained will and foreknowledge of God.

16 "And the angel departed from her" (Luke 1.38), it says. He had clearly fulfilled the service that had been commanded of him. The angel departed from her, but the Lord did not depart. For whereas the former is circumscribed, although bodiless, the latter is uncircumscribed, even though he was contained in a virgin's body and womb. And whereas the former announced in advance the One who was coming, conceived from a Virgin for the salvation of humankind, the latter took on our very being, formed it into himself, having given back to [human] nature what was in [God's] image as well as the original dignity, which had been [913] lost because of the carelessness of our ancestors. And having taken him up, "he seated him in the heavenly places, far above all rule and authority and power, and above every name that is named, not only in this age but also in the age to come" (cf. Eph 1.21).[78] To him be glory and might and honor and veneration, with the Father who is without beginning and with the all-holy and life-giving Spirit, now and forever, and to the ages of ages. Amen.

[78]Andrew is either using a slightly different version of the text here or has remembered it inaccurately.

Oration on the Annunciation of the Supremely Holy Theotokos[1]

1 [65] Let us, [all] peoples, tribes, and tongues, and every rank, as well as this feast-loving, loquacious[2] assembly and the people who are gathered around, now celebrate spiritually and with joyful souls the radiant and supremely glorious commemoration of the present honorable and royal office,[3] and let us with all zeal weave divine hymns for the queen who [was born of the race] of David. And let us establish a springtime feast of feasts and festival of festivals for our hope, "on the famous day of our feast" (Ps 80[81].4).

2 For today truly the spiritual powers of heaven have bent down from heaven and celebrate invisibly along with you, who are born on earth![4]

Today the prophecy of David has been fulfilled which says, "Let the heavens rejoice and let the earth exult!" (Ps 95[96].11). For behold, now both have been filled with joy!

[1] *CPG* 8009; *BHG* 1145n–q; *BHG*[a] 1145n–r; D. Fecioru, ed., "Un nou gen de predica in omiletica ortodoxa," *Biserica Ortodoxa Romana* 64 (1946): 65–91; 180–92; 386–96. The homily is also edited by F. Combefis in PG 98, 320–40, but with lacunae at the beginning and end of the homily. This translation is based on the Fecioru edition, but I am currently preparing a new edition of the text.

[2] The adjective πολύρρευστος does not appear in the dictionaries and may thus be a neologism. According to Lampe, ῥευστός may mean "fluent" or "eloquent."

[3] The word σύναξις has many meanings, including a eucharistic gathering. Here it probably refers to the church service currently taking place, which may be a vigil rather than a Divine Liturgy.

[4] It is at this point (τῶν γηγενῶν) that a long lacuna begins. Combefis, using Codex Parisinus Graecus 773 (fifteenth century), picks up the text again with the words ἐν ᾗ ἡ ἔμψυχο . . . (see below, 226, n. 17).

Today the crowded assembly of holy feast-lovers is clad in white garments!

Today, as if out of a chilly winter, a warm spring has shone upon us, and the gold-beaming sun, even more delightful and gracious, has arisen for us!

Today the divinely planted Eden is opened, and the divinely molded Adam, who is again enrolled in it by the goodness of [God's] benevolence, dwells there!

Today the ancestral sentence of pain has been released, and the invidious humiliation of our ancestress Eve has ceased, along with her wearisome penalty![5]

Today the ranks [of angels] above dance with those on earth by means of this present office that is bounded by four walls, and the whole universe is illumined by a shining light!

Today the spotless Church of Christ is magnified in a way that befits its unified form,[6] and is made splendid as if in golden tassels (cf. Ps 44[45].14) by the beauty of the present, much desired day!

Today the spectacular[7] Jerusalem of holy name,[8] which is below, rejoices fully with the one above; and the new Sion, to speak prophetically, is making merry!

Today Bethlehem, the city of David and of the beautiful, child-like maiden, is revealed [67] as an earthly heaven and is adorned like a beautiful bridegroom!

Today the notable city and land and whole race of human beings sing of this all-bright, universal festival!

[5]The emphasis on Eve in this passage reflects the fact that the Theotokos especially undid Eve's disobedience and punishment, because she, as a woman, agreed to do God's will at the Annunciation. The "wearisome penalty" (ἐπίμοχθον ἐπιτίμιον) probably refers to Gen 3.16, when God says to Eve, "I will greatly increase your pangs in childbearing; in pain you shall bring forth children, yet your desire/submission shall be for your husband, and he shall rule over you."

[6]The adverb συμμορφοπρεπῶς may be a neologism. It does not appear in Lampe or in L&S.

[7]Meaning literally "much seen," the compound adjective πολύβλεπτος does not appear in Lampe or L&S and may be a neologism.

[8]The adjective ἀγιώνυμος is unusual. It also appears in Andrew of Crete's second homily on the Dormition of the Virgin, PG 97, 1073A.

Today kings of the earth and all peoples royally celebrate the blessed memory of our blameless queen and Mother of God!

Today daughters of kings and queens, extolling [this festival], rush in close array from the eastern as far as the western [regions] of the sun, towards the honoring of the royal bridal chamber!

Today young maidens and brides, mothers and virgins, noblewomen and every rank, bless the Mother and Virgin and nourisher of our life!

Today the holy of holies is praised by everyone, heaven and earth are pell-mell,[9] and all created things keep festival together!

Today the sacredly written book of the prophets is brought into our midst, and each of them proclaims in advance the grace of the present feast!

Today the patriarch Jacob prophetically and rightfully exults—also providing an account [of this] in that mystical and blessed ladder, which has been set up from earth to heaven (cf. Gen 28.12–17).

Today Moses, that prophet of old and leader of Israel, tells us clearly about that bush on the mountain of Horeb (cf. Exod 3.2–3).

Today Zachariah, the notable elder, cries thus, through his own prophecy, saying, "I saw, and behold, a lampstand all of gold and the bowl on top of it!" (Zech 4.2).

Today Isaiah, the great and marvellous herald even among prophets prophesies, crying out, "A rod will arise out of the root of Jesse and a flower will come forth from it!" (Isa 11.1).

Today the wonderful Ezekiel cries, "Behold, the gate has been closed and no one will enter except the Lord God alone, and the gate will be closed!" (Ezek 44.1–2).

Today the wonderful Daniel, who from long ago now has been shouting about future things as if they were present, [cries], "A rock was cut from a mountain without a hand," that is to say, without a man (cf. Dan 2.45).

[9]The adverb ἀναμίξ is classical and may also mean "promiscuously." It is used only rarely in Byzantine liturgical texts.

Today David, the escort of the bride, singing about the Virgin as if of another fair city, cries thus, "Glorious things were spoken about you, the city of the great King!" (Ps 86[87].3).

Today Gabriel, the commander,[10] hastening down from the vaults of heaven, greets the Virgin and Theotokos, speaking in the following way: "Hail, favored one. The Lord is with you!" (Luke 1.28).

3   Today let all angels as well as we ourselves take up the angelic speech, and let us offer his praises, along with him, to the agent of grace, saying:

Hail indeed, daughter of David, the king, and true Mother of the heavenly King, who above all strengthens the sceptres of the faithful!

Hail indeed, daughter of Joachim and Anna, who blamelessly [69] bore you [as a result] of a prayer at the appropriate time of their cohabitation!

Hail indeed, daughter of David and Virgin Theotokos; the divine praise truly [says], "Blessed is the fruit of your womb" (Luke 1.42).

Hail, favored one, who sprouted beyond hope from the royal tribe of David and from Anna, who bore a divine child!

Hail, favored one, who was nourished from infancy, who grew, was recorded in the genealogy, and received food from the hand of an angel; and who secured ineffable and truly indescribable joy for the whole world!

Hail, favored one, the royal robe, purple in appearance, that clothed the King of heaven and of earth who was made flesh!

Hail, favored one, the spice-bearing earth and life-bearing container and new vase of unguent for the Spirit, that filled the whole universe with a perfumed scent![11]

---

[10]The term ταξιάρχης is used to describe the archangels because they are the commanders of the heavenly host. See (ps-) Dionysius, *De caelesti hierarchia* 8–9, PG 3, 237–72.

[11]On the importance of smell in early Christian and Byzantine spirituality, see S. Ashbrook Harvey, *Scenting Salvation. Ancient Christianity and the Olfactory Imagination* (Berkeley, Los Angeles and London: University of California Press, 2006).

Hail, favored one, truly the golden censer and the pure and all-holy and spotless treasury of purity!

Hail, favored one, all-golden and wholly unblemished beauty, and transcendent and truly most marvellous dwelling-place of the Word!

Hail, favored one, who caused the Sun that is eternal to arise for the world in flesh, [a Sun] who dazzled the whole of creation with his goodness!

Hail, favored one, the all-bright cloud of the life-giving Spirit, which carries the rain of compassion and sprinkles all creation!

Hail, favored one, salvation of those born on earth, who transformed grief into joy, and joined the things on earth with those in heaven, and who loosed the dividing wall of enmity!

Hail, favored one, the divinely sealed and divinely entered[12] gate of our life, through whom the Co-eternal Word of the God and Father passed! (Cf. Ezek 44.1–2).

Hail, favored one, untouchable plant of purity and shady tree of compassion and gold-purple[13] lily of true virginity!

Hail, favored one, the heifer unused to the yoke, who fed the fatted calf and carried in her womb that heavenly greatness![14]

Hail, favored one, the spotless ewe-lamb,[15] who cherished in her undefiled hands that purple-dyed sheep which was willingly sacrificed on behalf of everyone!

Hail, favored one, blameless and unwedded maiden who showed her relatives a strange conception and inexplicable birth-giving that was without travail!

---

[12]Θεόδευτος is an unusual word which I would suggest is a compound made up of θεο- ("divine") and -ὀδεύω ("to go" or "to travel"). Lampe, 625, on the other hand, suggests "God-drenched" in connection with a reference to the burning bush in Theodore of Studios's homily on the Nativity of the Virgin, PG 96, 689D.

[13]χρυσοπόρφυρον may be a neologism. It does not appear in the dictionaries.

[14]This refers to the type of the three-year-old heifer (Gen 15.9).

[15]The type of the ewe-lamb appears in Num 6.14: "And he shall bring his gift to the Lord . . . one ewe-lamb of a year old without blemish . . ."; cf. Lev 14.10, 22.

Hail, favored one, ark of the sanctuary and divinely-planted rod of righteousness, which flowered with the genuine flower.[16]

Hail, favored one, [71] the golden lamp-stand bearing a bowl (cf. Zech 4.2), and shining tabernacle, and table which contained in itself the life-giving bread!

Hail, favored one, the cherubic and most strange seat for the King of Glory, and truly an imperial palace for the flesh of the Word!

Hail, favored one,[17] in whom the living and honored and divinely ruled city, being fortified, is always honored!

Hail, favored one, the all-gold jar of manna and the tabernacle truly made of purple, which the new Bezaleel adorned in golden style![18]

Hail, favored one, forever purple, God-bearing[19] cloud and spring eternally pouring out grace for everyone!

Hail, favored one, the high and exalted throne of the Creator and Redeemer of all things, who holds all things in his hand whether in heaven or on earth!

Hail, favored one, the living temple of magnificent glory, for the One who became human on our behalf and took on flesh for the sake of our salvation!

Hail, favored one, who brings Life and nourishes the Nourisher; who provides milk for the One who formerly caused honey to spring forth from a rock![20]

---

[16]It is difficult to convey in English the alliteration of this sentence, which plays with the letter *theta* in Greek: ". . . καὶ ῥάβδος ἡ θεοφύτευτος τῆς εὐθύτητος, ἡ τὸ ἀνόθευτον ἄνθος ἀνθήσασα."

[17]Combefis's text and Paris. Gr. 773 rejoin the text here, after a lacuna. See above, n. 4.

[18]The words πορφυροποίητος and χρυσοπρεπῶς do not appear in the dictionaries. For Bezaleel, the constructor of the tabernacle, see Exod 31.2; 35.30; 36, 38.

[19]Lampe cites only Germanos for the adjective θεοβάστακτος. It is used again in this homily at col. 324D.

[20]Cf. Deut 32.13.

Hail, favored one, mountain of God, rich mountain,[21] shaded mountain,[22] uncut mountain,[23] visible mountain of God.[24]

Hail, favored one, exultation[25] of the soul, universal object of worship for the whole world, and truly good mediator for all sinners!

Hail, favored one, joy of the afflicted and formidable protectress of those who with sincere hearts confess you as Theotokos!

Hail, favored one, who carried in your womb the benevolent Master for the general salvation of the human race!

Hail, favored one, marvellous and compassionate refuge for all Christians and spectacle loftier than all magnificent beauty!

4 Even so, we who are of least account, having learned these things from the divinely inspired Scriptures, addressed these things with unworthy lips to the heavenly bride and queen and Theotokos! Let us, full of desire, then come to the divine Annunciation of the archangel Gabriel and hear what he, on reaching the blameless one herself, proclaimed as glad tidings.

The Angel: "Hear, glorified one; hear the secret words of the Highest One: 'Behold, you will conceive in your womb and bear a son, and you will name him [73] Jesus.' (Luke 1.31). Prepare yourself, then, for the coming of Christ, for I have come to bring you glad tidings of things that were foretold, before the foundation of the universe."

The Theotokos: "Depart from my city and native land, sir! Depart and quickly leave my chamber! Flee far from my threshold, O speaker, and do not offer such glad tidings to my humility."

The Angel: "Wishing to fulfil an ancient plan and to have mercy on humanity which was led astray, the Benevolent One was well pleased

[21] Cf. Ps 67(68).16.

[22] Cf. Hab 3.3; echoed in Luke 1.35.

[23] Cf. Dan 2.45. This well-known type also appears in homilies by Proclus, Or. 4.1; John of Damascus, Hom. 10.2, and many others.

[24] On the "mountain" types for Mary, see Arch. Ephrem, "Mary in Eastern Church Literature," 67–71.

[25] Cf. Ps 31(32).7, etc.

to come into being and to become a man, in the goodness of his benevolence. Why then do you not accept my greeting, favored one?"

The Theotokos: "Young man, I see the striking[26] beauty of your elegant form and the splendid sight of your figure;[27] and I am listening to your words [the like of which] I have never heard before, and I am rapidly beginning to suspect that you have come to lead me astray."

The Angel: "Clearly understand and be persuaded that it is rather I who, on perceiving such divinely etched[28] beauty in you, have fallen into amazement; and seeing you now, I think that I am becoming aware of the glory of my Lord."

[75] The Theotokos: "I heard a voice which I did not recognise and have looked on a countenance which I never saw [before]. How shall I not be amazed? I have started to tremble all over inasmuch as my betrothed is a righteous man and I have not been at all accustomed to converse with a stranger."

The Angel: "Accept from my news a joy that is worthy of note and praise that entirely befits you. For he who is born from you 'will be called Son of the Highest,' (Luke 1.32), and he will be borne by you in an abundance of sanctified goodness."

The Theotokos: "I am afraid and tremble at such words. And I suppose that you have come to lead me astray, like another Eve. But I am not like her, so you may not entrap me like her. How can you [thus] greet a girl whom you have never seen before?"

The Angel: "I am bringing you good tidings of joy; I am bringing you good tidings of your unknowable birth-giving; I am bringing you good tidings of the inexplicable arrival in you of a high King. Perhaps, indeed, the purple robe which you are wearing foretells the royal rank."

---

[26]The word ἀξιογράφιστον is unusual and difficult to translate in this context. It actually means "worth recording," according to Lampe, 167.

[27]On Byzantines' beliefs about the appearance of angels, see G. Peers, *Subtle Bodies. Representing Angels in Byzantium* (Berkeley, Los Angeles and London: University of California Press, 2001).

[28]The adjective used here is θεογράφιστον.

The Theotokos: "Since you report these things to me and keep on reporting them, I shall say to you now that I do not believe such good tidings from you, inasmuch as you have come to undermine my virginal reputation and to cause pain to my betrothed [husband]."

[77] The Angel: "The prophet Zachariah, who is also beloved by your kinswoman Elizabeth, will give you assurances, [thereby leading you] out of disbelief. Go then to her that you may learn from her what has happened to him."

The Theotokos: "Joachim and Anna, my parents, are a most noble and blameless pair. How could I, their offspring, become blemished? Who would see and give assurances to them, saying, 'Mary has not transgressed?'"

The Angel: "At the time when my words are fulfilled at their appropriate time, then you will understand the power of the incomprehensible mystery. Then you will know the outcome of my words."

The Theotokos: "You have heard that I am descended from the house and family of David; how then shall I assist in such terrible and heavenly mysteries? And how shall I receive the holy Jesus, who is seated on the cherubim?"

The Angel: "You will be called a God-bearing[29] throne and royal seat of the heavenly King inasmuch as you are Queen, Lady, daughter of an earthly King, and possess a royal form."

[79] The Theotokos: "Explain to me, O speaker, how I shall become a throne for the Highest One and how flesh of clay will touch that untouchable light which transcends the sun. You are proclaiming tidings which are impossible, young man."

The Angel: "For what reason, why, and on what account[30] have you so much disbelieved my glad tidings, glorified one? And for

---

[29]Lampe cites this passage as evidence for the meaning of the adjective θεοβάστακτος. It may be a neologism.

[30]Such repetition would be regarded as tautological in English prose. In Greek rhetoric, on the other hand, the repetition of the same idea, using different words, is accepted: this is the device known as "synonymia."

how long will you not obey the angel who has been sent to you from heaven? For I am not the one who led Eve astray."

The Theotokos: "I saw your multi-faceted countenance[31] and heard your most amazing statements which no one has ever heard before. And it is on this account that I am unable to accept such glad tidings."

The Angel: "Even if my appearance terrifies you, I know that the words of my mouth will produce great glory for you; and later, heaven and earth will bless you" (cf. Luke 1.48).

The Theotokos: "On what basis shall I understand this—that what has been said by you will be fulfilled—since I am an unwedded virgin and there is no reproach of self-indulgence in me? For I am a servant of the Lord who made me."

[81] The Angel: "I shall tell you clearly that Elizabeth, your kins-woman, will also bear a son in her old age at this time, and many will rejoice and marvel at his birth. And his name will be John."

The Theotokos: "Take gifts from me and depart from me, O speaker. For whether you are an angel or a man, I do not truly understand this. I recognize an angel by your form and I perceive a man with my sight."[32]

The Angel: "When you were in the holy of holies, did you not see me, blessed one? You saw me then and received nourishment from my fiery hand. For I am Gabriel, and have always stood before the glory of the Lord."

The Theotokos: "I possess a sober, holy, and righteous betrothed husband, who is fully conversant with the craft of carpentry. And I am concerned lest he should happen to find me speaking with you, a stranger, especially since we are alone."

---

[31]The multi-faceted appearance of the archangel reflects his various states of being, depending on the requirements of his mission.

[32]The meaning of this sentence is not altogether clear. The Virgin Mary seems to be saying that she recognises two aspects of Gabriel's appearance: one, she begins to recognise, is his true nature as an archangel; the other is his resemblance in form to a human being. This passage reveals the beginning of a change in Mary's response to her interlocutor. Slowly, she is starting to accept that he may indeed be an angelic messenger.

The Angel: "Now I have begun to speak. I am filled with heavenly words. I shall tell you then, that the Lord, King of Kings, is about to be born with your help, 'and he will reign eternally in the house of Jacob, and there shall be no end to his reign'" (cf. Luke 1.32–33).

[83] The Theotokos: "Now my soul is troubled and I do not know what to think of this terrible vision. For I consider that your words are true; and Joseph will give me up into the hands of those who judge these matters."

The Angel: "I am shocked, glorified one, that you still doubt me when I have come to you from such heights. For it is possible that I instead should be reverencing you, as the one who will be Mother of my Lord, and I tremble at your royal rank."

The Theotokos: "Then your glad tidings are a surprise, and your authority is displayed both in your words and your manner. For you came to my chamber and approached me unannounced, perhaps viewing me more as a little girl than as a Lady."

The Angel: "I am amazed at the extent to which you have disbelieved my words, favored one, when you are so entirely pure and blameless. For behold, the King of Glory has come to dwell in you the queen, I think, even as I speak."[33]

The Theotokos: "As one who greets a virgin with no experience of men and who utters such words to an unwedded maiden, you know the truth; [85] but I do not understand when, whence, and 'how then this shall be since I know no man'" (Luke 1.34).

The Angel: "'The Holy Spirit will come upon you and the power of the Highest will overshadow you. Therefore the One being born will be holy; he will be called Son of God. Do not be afraid, Mariam, for you have found favor with God'" (cf. Luke 1.35, 30).

---

[33]This statement is remarkable from a theological point of view. The archangel Gabriel appears to be saying that the conception has taken place, even before the Virgin Mary has given her consent. Andrew of Crete conveys the same impression in his sermon on the Annunciation, having the archangel Gabriel say that Christ had entered the womb of the Theotokos even before his arrival. See his *In Annuntiationem*, PG 97, 905; above, 216, n. 68.

The Theotokos: "You came from heaven bringing an eagerly sought mystery and announcing to me the coming of the Holy Spirit. Tell me, O speaker, how I may no longer distrust this miraculous good news that you bring?"

The Angel: "Cast off your mistrustful opinion, virgin. For behold, it seems to me that my words have been fulfilled and your womb is beginning to swell. And even if you do not wish for this, 'with God every word shall not be impossible'" (Luke 1.37).[34]

The Theotokos: "I am a shoot from the Davidic root and I am afraid lest unexpected contempt from another union should attach itself to me and then that the holy tablet of the priest will expose me."

The Angel: "You will give birth to the Lord who is Savior, One of the life-giving Trinity, and you will secure unutterable joy for the world, [87] [joy] which no one, either angel or human being, has ever secured; and your name will be blessed."

The Theotokos: "Do you say that I shall give birth to a Savior? Tell me, young man! For your glad tidings truly astonish the intellectual powers of angels and archangels, and the fiery orders of those [beings] with many eyes."

The Angel: "Your words are entirely delightful and sweet, glorified one, and for this reason I will tell you that your pregnancy will come about not by the will of the flesh, but by the will of God and by the visitation of the Holy Spirit."

The Theotokos: "Who will give assurance to Joseph that I shall conceive not by the will of the flesh, but by the will of God and by the visitation of the Holy Spirit? For it is unheard of, even from all ages, for a virgin to bear an infant without having experience of men."

The Angel: "The whole race of human beings will take refuge under your compassion and every tongue of clay will bless you;[35] and your name will be spoken of in every generation and genera-

---

[34]It is striking that again in this passage Germanos seems to give the Theotokos little power of choice.

[35]This passage strongly suggests the important role that the Virgin Mary played in this period, as mediator and compassionate intercessor.

tion, because the Lord, the Light of the world, is about to be born from you."

The Theotokos: "Being made of matter and as one who has had an earthly birth, how shall I contain Christ, the Light of the world?[36] Or how will that Sun which never sets[37] [89] be carried beneath the moon? Or how will the race of humankind flee for refuge to me?"

The Angel: "Assume a bright gaze, glorified one. For you are about to become heaven, a temple containing God, and a living tabernacle of God, wider, higher and more marvellous than the seven firmaments."

The Theotokos: "I shudder at the consecration of the miraculous [event], my strange childbirth! But I also reverence Joseph and I do not know what will then happen to me. It is appropriate therefore for me to go to Zachariah's house, to my kinswoman."

The Angel: "You will become a universal source of propitiation[38] for all Christians. For this reason I am addressing you again with a fitting salutation, [saying], 'Hail, favored one, the Lord is with you. You are blessed among women and blessed is the fruit of your womb'" (Luke 1.28).

The Theotokos: "I bear a royal appearance and grew up in the palace of my [native town] of Bethlehem;[39] I was blamelessly set apart in the holy places from my childhood and I happen to be a virgin; how then shall I hear myself called the mother of my child?"

[91] The Angel: "The Highest One, having searched through the whole universe just as he intended, wished, and was well pleased [to

[36]This passage emphasizes Mary's natural origins and ties with the rest of humanity. Her query also represents an interesting insight into her own feelings about the exalted role that she is about to play.

[37]Cf. (ps-) Sophronios of Jerusalem, *Oratio,* PG 87, 4004A.

[38]Cf. Rom 3.25. The same word is used for the "mercy-seat" of the ark in the tabernacle. Cf. Exod 25.16, etc.

[39]According to Matthew and Luke, Joseph came from Bethlehem because he was descended from the house and family of David (Matt 1.2–17; Luke 2.4). Mary's ancestry is not elaborated in the Gospels, but most patristic writers assumed that she came from the same family and thus would have regarded Bethlehem as her ancestral home.

do], and discovered no other mother like you, will become incarnate from you, holy one, because of his love for humankind."[40]

The Theotokos: "I shall sing psalms and praise the Lord 'for he has looked upon the humility of his servant; for behold, from now on all generations will call me blessed' (Luke 1.48). And the people of the nations will praise me without ceasing."

The Angel: "O Virgin, agent of heavenly joy, delightful and marvellous dwelling-place and place of propitiation for the whole world, you who alone are truly blessed among women: prepare then for the mystical coming of Christ!"

The Theotokos: "O young man, agent of heavenly joy, who have appeared from the ranks of the bodiless ones and are conversing with one who is made of clay, how long shall I withhold my consent from you, and when will you cease speaking? 'Behold, the servant of the Lord; let it be with me according to your word'" (Luke 1.38).

5   And so the all-praised and blessed Virgin spoke in a suitable way, or perhaps even used more mystical and fitting words than these. But let us now hear, if you are willing, beloved ones, what the righteous Joseph also said to her:

[180] Joseph: "I took you, an undefiled [girl], from the house of the Lord and I left you, a pure virgin, in my house. What is this that I now see—one who is an expectant mother and not a virgin? Speak to me, Mary. Tell me the truth quickly."

The Theotokos: "You left me undefiled, as you said, in your house, and you have encountered me again, I think, in an unblemished state. For from my childhood I have hated the soiled garment of flesh and there is no trace of licentiousness in me."[41]

---

[40] Apart from the future "he will become," the active verbs in this sentence are in the aorist. I have translated them in the present tense to fit the sense better in English.

[41] This passage reflects the widespread belief that Mary followed an ascetic way of life. See Graef, *Mary. A History of Doctrine and Devotion*, 50–53. The sentence could also be understood to affirm the Virgin's freedom from sin from the time of her conception and infancy, a concept which was later codified in the West in the Papal Bull of 1854. It is likely, however, Germanos is just expressing a widely held view

Joseph: "Have reverence for the judge's tribunal, Mary, the strict council-chamber of the Jewish synagogue and the unerring law-court. Speak to me clearly; do not conceal from me what has happened to you."

The Theotokos: "Have reverence for the awesome tribunal and the immutable judgment-seat of the age to come, Joseph, where even angels and those who have never sinned tremble; do not concern yourself at all with the earthly king and law-court!"

Joseph: "It has been written in the book of Moses, as follows: 'And if anyone should come upon a virgin and, having forced her, should lie with her, that man will give the father of the young girl fifty didrachmas' (Deut 22.28).[42] What then will you do in answer to that?"

[182] The Theotokos: "It has been written in [books of] the prophets that 'the sealed book will be given to a man who knows his letters and he will say, "I am not able to read it"'" (cf. Isa 29.11). It seems to me that this prophecy was perhaps referring to you."

Joseph: "Reveal the one who plotted against my house, Mary. Bring into our midst the miscreant so that I may cut off his head with my carpenter's knife, since he has dishonored my grey hairs and now the twelve tribes of Israel will pour scorn on me."

The Theotokos: "You are righteous and you are also blameless. And my God will reveal to you in a fitting way what will happen to me, and he will show you in a dream the One whom you call 'a plotter.' For I was not accustomed to being led into his exalted [presence]."

Joseph: "Leave my house quickly and hurry to your young lover. For from now on I shall not feed you: you may not eat bread from my table since you have dishonored my grey hairs with grief and contempt instead of joy."

on this matter without attempting to be systematic with regard to the dogma of the Immaculate Conception.

[42]Byzantine Orthodox tradition holds that Moses authored the first five books of the Old Testament (the Pentateuch). The "didrachma" is a coin with the value of two drachmas.

The Theotokos: "Wait a short time, Joseph, and do not banish me secretly [184] from your house. For I have not been accustomed to living away from home and I do not yet know my right hand from my left.[43] And I do not know where I will go in any case, nor do I know with whom I shall take refuge."

Joseph: "Since you are poised between life and death, Mary, tell me the truth: who has despoiled you? Reveal to me who it was that conversed with you. Explain his rank to me. Tell me from what city he came in order that I may go there and ruin him."[44]

The Theotokos: "May the Lord my God live,[45] for I am pure and I do not know a man.[46] For the one who appeared to me is, I think, an angel of the Lord, who took the form of a man: he discretely removed himself some distance away, and thus he stood and conversed gently with my humble self."

Joseph: "A charge of adultery will affect not only you, but also myself, [although I am] an old man; and it will be accompanied by unlooked for contempt from those who judge these affairs. And the water of the conviction will then convict us both, even if we do not wish for this."[47]

[43]In other words, the Virgin is saying that she does not know how to cope with everyday living or how to look after herself on her own. The language used in this section of the dialogue is quite colloquial, probably reflecting idiomatic usage of the eighth century.

[44]It is likely that Joseph means here that he will destroy the man's reputation, not that he will physically eliminate him.

[45]This phrase probably represents a pious oath used by Byzantine Christians. The Theotokos of course means to say, "May he live forever!"

[46]In other words, "I am a virgin."

[47]The seriousness of the sin of adultery is set out in Numbers 5.2–28. The water referred to here is "the water of conviction that brings the curse" (Num 5.18). It represents both a punishment and a test: if the woman who drinks this water is guilty, it will cause her to miscarry. Thereafter "the woman shall become an execration among her people." If she is innocent, on the other hand, she will be immune and able to conceive children even after drinking the water. Joseph's statement that he will be convicted along with Mary is not supported by this biblical passage; Numbers 5.31 states, "The man shall be free from iniquity, but the woman shall bear her iniquity." The *Protevangelion* of James, chap. 16, is the source for this version of the story: it also states that both Mary and Joseph drank the water of conviction and were exonerated because they felt no ill effects. See Elliott, *The Apocryphal New Testament*, 63.

The Theotokos: "You have heard that Elizabeth, the wife of Zachariah who is also my kinswoman, has conceived beyond expectation a prophet and forerunner at this time. For if he were not a prophet, he would not have venerated the Lord who is hidden in me by leaping [in her womb]" (cf. Luke 1.41).

[186] Joseph: "I marvel at you and I am completely astounded. I know that you have become a subject of gossip[48] for the sons of Israel, and the Lord my Master[49] will condemn me because I took you from the Holy Spirit, from a holy dwelling-place into safe-keeping, and I have not kept your virginity safe."

The Theotokos: "A day of affliction has overtaken me and the censure of suspicion has come upon me. In addition, my betrothed one's scrutiny is pressing upon me while pregnancy with my child condemns me. And the angel who said 'Hail' to me swiftly disappeared. I do not know what to think now."

Joseph: "I saw the swelling of your womb which earlier was pure, and I have come to be wholly and constantly tremulous. For tell me, where shall I hide you or where shall I make you visible? And how shall I be able to escape the notice of the Jewish council? Depart then from my house! Depart quickly!"

The Theotokos: "Behold, you are chasing me from your house, Joseph, and I do not have any idea where I shall now go. Shall I return to the house of the holy sanctuary or shall I rejoin my parents? But with what sort of countenance shall I look upon them?"

Joseph: "Even if I keep quiet about your transgression, your womb will cry out[50] and the holy of holies will shout loudly, inasmuch as I took [188] you into safe-keeping from that enrolled priest and did not guard your virginity."

The Theotokos: "Then I shall hide myself in one of the caves of my [native city] Bethlehem and I shall await the appointed time of

---

[48]The word διαλάλημα is not in L&S or Lampe. It may represent a neologism.

[49]The word used here is Ἀδωναί, which represents a Greek transliteration of the Hebrew word for "Lord" or "Master."

[50]Cf. Luke 19.40.

my pregnancy; and I may learn who is to be born from me. For I think that God will perhaps watch over my humility."

Joseph: "Tell me clearly, who was that stranger and traitor who came unannounced into my room like some spy—and especially when I was absent and was not within the walls of the city of Nazareth?"

The Theotokos: "When I took the urn to go to the well and draw water in order that I might drink, a voice quietly entered my ears, saying the following [words]: 'Hail, favored one, the Lord is with you'" (Luke 1.28).

Joseph: "Surely you did not conceive [at the sound] of the voice? It has never been heard of, in all eternity, for a virgin with no experience of men to become pregnant by the sound of words. Nor have our ancestors reported to us that such a thing [has ever] happened in the past."

[190] The Theotokos: "But has it not been written in the [books of the] prophets that 'a Virgin will conceive in her womb and will bear a child for us?' (Isa 7.14). Surely you can't say that the prophets are lying? You are making a mistake now, Joseph, in being so angry."

Joseph: "Now I see, Mary, that you have followed in the footsteps of your mother Eve. But whereas she was evicted from paradise because she listened[51] to the one who whispered to her, you, as a guilty one, will be thrown out of my house."

The Theotokos: "Now you have assailed me as if you belonged to another family and another tribe, and as an accuser; not as someone who is addressing a queen. And I shall be chased secretly from city to city—how, then, shall I defend myself?"

Joseph: "The birth-giving, it seems to me—and not only to me— will astonish both angels and humanity, and they may not believe [in it]. Who has ever heard of a virgin giving birth to an infant, especially when she is without experience of men?"

The Theotokos: "I know that what is being said will astonish you, and that the paradoxical mystery of the sacred pregnancy fills your

---

[51]The literal meaning of the Greek here is: "she spread out her hearing."

mind with terror. [192] But I am not the cause of the circumstance that has affected me, since from my childhood [onwards] I have been accustomed to worship my Lord who created me."

Joseph: "Did I not say to you, 'Show me the one who plotted against my house and I will release you from such an accusation?' Did I not say to you, 'Go with haste to your lover?' What else do you hope for from this man?"

The Theotokos: "I do not clearly understand [the meaning of] the statement, 'In what sort of places does he reside?' For at that time I too truly wished to meet him [and] I wished to gaze on his beauty, which is worthy of depiction,⁵² and to cross-question him since he said 'Hail' to me—and now I feel grief."

Joseph: "How shall I not cower and strike my face, since I took you as a virgin from the house of my Lord and did not guard you? How shall I approach the Lord my God from now on and fulfill the regulation of the law according to my usual custom?"

The Theotokos: "Believe in God's prophets and do not mortify yourself so much with excessive grief. For you will find written in their [books the lines], 'Behold the virgin will conceive in her womb and will bear a son and they will call his name Emmanuel'" (cf. Isa 7.14).

[386] Joseph: "A high-priestly staff persuaded me to take you from the house of prayer into my protection;⁵³ and I then left you, with all propriety, in my house. Why then, Mary, did you not wait for me to complete my sojourn [elsewhere] and my affairs?"

The Theotokos: "As the Lord lives, I have no knowledge of the wrinkle⁵⁴ of another bed or stain of carnal desire; but I am pure in that I was holding the purple [thread] in my hands⁵⁵ when I heard

⁵²The Greek word used here is ἀξιοζωγράφιστον; this is an interesting allusion to the possibility of portraying in an icon the unusual beauty of angels.

⁵³See the *Protevangelion* of James, 9, in Elliott, *The Apocryphal New Testament,* 60–1.

⁵⁴The noun ῥυτίς literally means a "wrinkle" or "fold," as in a textile. This translation is quite literal and it means that the Virgin had never slept in another man's bed.

⁵⁵*Protevangelion* of James, 10–11; Elliott, *The Apocryphal New Testament*, 61.

an angelic voice crying to me, 'Do not be afraid, Mary, for you have found favor with God'" (Luke 1.30).

Joseph: "Be content in my house for a short time longer, just this once, since the time of registration has arrived now while Caesar Augustus rules as emperor. I am taking care to register you as my wife, especially on account of [your] Davidic kinship."

The Theotokos: "I shall then guard your words in my heart and I shall be content in your house a short time longer. And I shall wait for the time of registration and for the day of my delivery, until you shall fulfil your dues to Caesar Augustus, who now rules over the Romans."

Joseph: "Perhaps it was an angel who appeared to me in sleep, and said to me, [388] 'Joseph, son of David, do not be afraid to accept Mary as your wife; for that which has been born in her is from the Holy Spirit. She will bear a son and you will call his name 'Jesus'" (Matt 1.20).

The Theotokos: "Perhaps, my lord, that was the one who addressed me with the [greeting], 'Hail!' But meanwhile prepare a place and a cave, and seek out a Hebrew midwife from our family. She will keep the secret and serve me in the accustomed way."

Joseph: "Since he has appeared to me, he will surely show me both the place and the cave. But you, Mary, prepare the swaddling clothes. We do not know whether the one who will be born may be a prophet or a king, [but only] that 'he will be called a Nazorean'" (Matt 2.25).

The Theotokos: "I suspect[56] that the one who is to be born will be called King, for it has been written in the [books of the] prophets, 'Rejoice greatly, O daughter of Sion! Proclaim it aloud, O daughter of Jerusalem! For behold, your King is coming to you, righteous and a Savior'" (Zech 9.9).

Joseph: "The one who called on me in my sleep will then also reveal the things that will befall us after that. I am anxious about

---

[56]I have emended Ὑπολαμβάων in the Fecioru text to Ὑπολαμβάνω. The latter reading is also found in PG 98, 388, and in the manuscripts.

Herod; that one day, when someone has made this known to him, he will conduct a search for the child who is being born to us."

[390] The Theotokos: "The sign will appear in heaven. For it has been written in the prophets, 'A star will arise out of Jacob and a man will rise up from Israel, and he will crush the leaders of Moab'" (Num 24.17).

Joseph: "Mistaken in my suspicion yesterday, I heaped blame on your beauty and on your comeliness. Now, having received assurance from on high, I shall defend [you] and I shall eternally venerate your magnitude with reverence, since the Lord has taken pity on his people."[57]

The Theotokos: "It seems to me that gold, frankincense, and myrrh will be brought (cf. Matt 2.11), as if to a King and to God and to a Man, in order that David's statement, [which says], 'The whole earth will be filled with his glory; so be it, so be it!' (Ps 71[72].19), will be fulfilled."

Joseph: "Let us seek out, if you wish, an untouched place,[58] since the time for the birth is approaching. But we also need a mule for the journey. For I see you looking worried, and I think that you want to give birth."

The Theotokos: "Examine[59] once again the prophet Micah and you will find a place. For he says, 'And you, Bethlehem, house of Ephratha, are you not few in numbers to be [reckoned] among the thousands of Judah? For there will come forth to me, out of you, a Leader to be Ruler in Israel'" (cf. Mic 5.2).[60]

[57]The text which appears in PG 98 (edited by Combefis and following Paris.gr. 773) ends here, following a lacuna in the manuscript. Most other manuscripts contain the end of the dialogue between the Virgin and Joseph, along with a short epilogue. Fecioru's edition, which I am using for this translation, also contains the full text.

[58]Literally, "let us touch an untouchable place . . ."

[59]The same verb, ψηλαφίζω, is used here as in Joseph's preceding speech ("feel out"), but with a different connotation. The word play in these two speeches, also involving the adjective ἀψηλάφητον ("untouched"), is very interesting since each use of the root conveys a sense of mystery which may be sensed or touched (or the reverse).

[60]The wording here differs somewhat from the Septuagint version. See Rahlfs, 2:516.

[392] Joseph: "As I see it, that angel who appeared to me in a dream will not depart at all until everything that has been written about us is fulfilled at the appropriate time, but he will accompany us on the way."

The Theotokos: "How great and blessed is this day, 'for the Mighty One has done great things for me! And holy is his name and his mercy is for those who fear him, from generation to generation!'" (Luke 1.49–50).

6   But whereas the angel graciously spoke these [words] with so much reverence in dialogue with the Theotokos, Joseph responded in a similar way to the favored one, while remaining confused about the power of the mystery.

And so, with what colors of eulogy may we, who are of clay, delineate the virginal icon?[61] With what words of praise may we brighten the spotless image[62] of purity?

This one, the inaccessible sanctuary of incorruption!

This one, the hallowed temple of God!

This one, the golden altar for the burnt offerings!

This one, the divine incense of the union!

This one, the holy oil of unction!

This one, the most precious alabaster jar of the mystical ointment of nard![63]

This one, the priestly ephod![64]

This one, the seven-branched lamp-stand which always carries golden lamps![65]

---

[61] Although he uses the Greek word εἰκών here, the author intends a metaphorical understanding of the term "image" or "icon." He is of course referring to the written "icon," his own oration.

[62] The word χαρακτήρ means "image" or "stamp." Here it probably represents a near synonym of εἰκών in the previous sentence.

[63] Cf. Mark 14.3; Exod 30.34-38. For a similar use of this type, see Andrew of Crete, *On the Nativity IV*, above, 127, n. 23.

[64] That is, the priestly garment containing the oracular Urim and Thummim in a pouch attached to the front. Cf. Exod 24.9–12; Judg 17.5, 18.14, etc.; 1 Kgdms 2.18, 14.3, etc.

[65] Cf. Exod 25.31–40.

This one, the sanctified bodily and spiritual ark which has been gilded both inside and out, in which the golden censer [was placed], along with the golden jar which contains the manna, and the rest of the things about which [Scripture] has spoken!

This one, the first-born heifer, unused to the yoke, whose ashes, that is, the body of the Lord which was taken from her, purifies those who have been profaned by the defilement of sin!

This one, the gate facing east, which is closed eternally by means of the entrance and departure of the Master!

This one, the new volume of the New Testament, through whom the sovereignty of the demons was swiftly despoiled and the captivity of humankind was quickly alleviated![66]

This one, the three dimensions of humanity, [namely] of Greeks, barbarians, and Jews, in whom the inexpressible Wisdom of God concealed the leaven of its own goodness!

This one, the treasury of spiritual blessing!

This one, who carries the royal, undecaying wealth from Tharsis,[67] [394] bringing conversion to the heavenly Jerusalem from the worldly land of the gentiles!

This one, the lovely bride of the [Book] of Songs, who took off the old tunic and washed her worldly feet, and is reverently receiving the incorruptible Bridegroom in the inner chamber of her soul!

This one, a new wagon for the faithful, which carries the living ark[68] of the dispensation and, by means of two first-born heifers, makes straight the unerring way of salvation!

This one, the tabernacle of the testimony,[69] from which the true Jesus has come forth as a young child in accordance with the nine-month period of gestation!

---

[66] The verb here is προνέμω, in the aorist passive. The usual meaning of the word is "to assign beforehand," but this does not fit the context.

[67] Cf. 3 Kgdms 10.22. This refers to the ship with which Solomon brought materials to Jerusalem for the building of the temple. The Theotokos, according to this type, is the ship and brings precious substances for the conversion of God's people.

[68] Cf. 1 Kgdms 6.7–10.

[69] Cf. Exod 27.21.

This one, who is the casket that was sealed on the outside and within, adorned with understanding and piety, in which the spiritual Moses is kept safe from the legal Pharaoh; [that spiritual Moses whom] [Pharaoh's] daughter, that is, the Church of the gentiles, nourishes in her virginal arms, whilst he promises to give to her the reward of eternal life![70]

This one, the fifth well of the oath of the covenant, in which the water of immortality bubbled up on account of the incarnate dispensation and presence of the Lord, in the fulfilment of the fifth covenant! For the first was written down in the time of Adam, the second in that of Noah, the third in that of Abraham, the fourth in that of Moses, and the fifth at the time of the Lord. So at that time he went out five times, hiring pious laborers for the vineyard of righteousness; [he went out] at the first hour, and the third, and the sixth and ninth, and at the eleventh.[71]

This one, a spotless fleece placed on the worldly threshing-floor, on which dew from heaven came down and filled the whole earth with the bountiful gift of good things—[earth] which had been dried out by the immeasurable load of evil, and in addition dried itself out by the moist secretions of the passions in the flesh!

This one, the fruitful olive tree planted in the house of God (cf. Ps 51[52].8), from whom the Holy Spirit took the corporeal piece of wood and transferred the peace which is proclaimed from above into the wintry[72] nature of humankind!

---

[70]Cf. Exod 2.3. This somewhat elaborate type is based on the story of the concealment of Moses in a papyrus basket and his discovery by the pharaoh's daughter. Germanos carefully identifies the basket (called θίβις rather than θήκη as here) with the Mother of God, "the spiritual Moses" as Christ, the pharaoh's daughter as the church, and the pharaoh as the legalistic, Hebrew interpretation of the Law. Christ, with the help of the church who nurtures him, will offer eternal salvation to the faithful. The syntax of the sentence, however, is faulty, since "the daughter" is the subject of the final clause but the verb ὑπισχνεῖται ("promises") demands a different subject. I have adjusted the translation to fit this sense.

[71]Cf. Matt 20.1–16; 1 Tim 5.18.

[72]Literally, "distressed by winter storms."

This one, the ever flourishing and incorruptible paradise, in which the Tree of life was planted and produced without hindrance the fruit of immortality for everyone!

This one, a bringing forth of the new creation in which the water of life gushes!

This one, the exultation of virgins, the support of the faithful, the diadem of the Church, the mark of Orthodoxy, the currency of truth, the garment of chastity, the variegated robe of virtue, the stronghold of righteousness, the boast of the holy Trinity in accordance with the evangelical pronouncement: "The Holy Spirit will come upon you and the power of the Highest will overshadow you; therefore the holy one to be born will be called Son of God" (Luke 1.35).[73]

7   But we, O Mother of God, confess [you] in faith, we pay honor to you with longing, and we venerate you with fear, always magnifying and reverently blessing you![74]

Blessed is your father among men and blessed is your mother among women! Blessed is your house, blessed are your ancestors, and blessed are your relatives! Blessed are those who saw you, blessed are those who talked with you, and blessed are those who served you! Blessed is Joseph, your betrothed [and] blessed is your tomb, for you are the honor of those honoring, privilege of privileges, and height of heights!

But, O Mistress, who are alone my solace from God, divine dew for the burning heat within me, divinely-flowing drop for my with-

---

[73]This whole section, beginning on 242 near the beginning of section 6, ". . . And so, with what colors of eulogy . . . ," is identical to the passage in Proclus's Homily 6, which also includes long sections of dialogue between Gabriel and Mary, and Mary and Joseph. See Leroy, *L'Homilétique de Proclus*, 321–4; Introduction above, 40, n. 101.

[74]The whole of section 7, beginning with the words, "But we, O Mother of God," is almost identical (although there are a few variants) with the final section of Germanos's second homily on the Presentation (see above, 171–2). Striking in this section, as noted above, is the reference to a "kinswoman and fellow maid-servant," who may be a sister or other close relative who has died. This homily only refers to her once, however, whereas the one on the Presentation contains several further references in the paragraph in which she is mentioned. See above, 171–2, n. 33.

ered heart,[75] most far-shining torch for my darkened soul, guide for my inexperience, strength for my weakness, garment for nakedness, wealth for poverty, medicine for incurable wounds, banishment of tears, cessation of groans, alleviation of misfortunes, remission of pains, loosing of bonds, hope of salvation! Hearken to my prayers, have pity on my groans, and accept my lamentations! Having been moved by my tears, have mercy upon me! As Mother of your benevolent God and our God, be compassionate towards me! Look upon and assent to our supplication, fulfil my thirsty desire,[76] and join me together with my kinswoman and fellow maid-servant[77] in the land of the meek, in the tabernacles of the righteous, and in the choirs of the saints! And, protection and radiant delight of all [human beings], deem me worthy to rejoice with you in joy! I beg to be with you in that truly inexpressible joy of the God and King who was born from you, in his incorruptible bridal chamber, and in unceasing and unending delight, as well as in the never-ending[78] and boundless Kingdom!

Yes, Mistress, my refuge, life and succour, weapon and boast, my hope and my strength! Grant that I may enjoy the indescribable and incomprehensible gifts of your Son and God, and our God, in the heavenly resting-place! For you, as Mother of the Highest, have, I know, the power that accompanies your will. On this account, I request that I may not be disappointed, wholly undefiled Lady, of my expectation! Instead may I attain this [expectation], bride of God, who bore the expectation of all things, our Lord Jesus Christ, the true God and your Son and Master of all things visible and invisible, to whom is due all glory, honor, and worship, along with the Father without beginning, and the all-holy Spirit, now and always, and to the ages of ages. Amen.

[75]I have emended the punctuation to put these two clauses together; this seems to balance the passage better.

[76]I have emended the reading καταύμιον to καταθύμιον, which appears in Cod. Bodl. Clarke 44 (twelfth century).

[77]It is unclear to what woman Germanos refers here. See above, n. 74.

[78]Literally, "unsetting" [of the sun].

[372] Oration on the Consecration of the Venerable Church[1] of Our Supremely Holy Lady, the Theotokos, and on the Holy Swaddling Clothes of our Lord Jesus Christ[2]

1   "Glorious things have been spoken of you, O city [373] of God" (Ps 86[87].3), sang the divine David to us in spirit. Again it is indeed most evident concerning whom such "glorious things" have been spoken. In calling this [Virgin] most clearly and incontrovertibly a city of the great King, I think that he means the one who has truly been elected and who surpasses all others, not in pre-eminence of buildings or in height of swelling hills, but who instead has been exalted by the nobility of godly virtues and who transcends all others in purity: Mary, the supremely chaste and surpassingly unblemished Theotokos. He who is truly King of Kings and Lord of those who rule took up his abode in her; or in other words, the whole fullness of divinity dwelt bodily in her.

2   She indeed is a glorified city; she is a Sion that is apprehended by the mind. She it was, I believe, whom David, divinely inspired,

---

[1]The word ναός that is used here literally means "temple"; however, it was often used in Byzantine texts to mean a Christian church. Elsewhere the title of this homily (as in *CPG* 8013) is simply, "In s. Mariae zonam" or "On Holy Mary's Belt."

[2]*CPG* 8013; *BHG* 1086; F. Combefis, ed., PG 98, 372–84.

also foretold (cf. Ps 2.6, etc.). But if someone should also call her house a glorified city, he would not speak beyond what is true and appropriate. For if names are assigned to earthly things, then they preserve the memory of the appellation for a long time. But if in the case of others, whose names it is not right even to take into [one's] mouth, statues and sacred precincts and idols exist even to this day, even if only by repute, but therefore they have been extended beyond measure and have reverberated on the ears of the simple-minded as if they were themselves present—what would one then say about the divinely glorified and all-praised girl who is wholly undefiled and wholly unblemished? For if she was designated the living City of Christ the King, then her all-holy church, whose consecration we celebrate today, rightly is, and is called, a glorified city. She is a city which does not enroll its citizens into the power of an earthly and mortal emperor, but which [dedicates them] to the heavenly One, who delivers them to eternal life and offers his own Kingdom to those who follow him.

3   On hearing of a consecration, O honored and worshipful audience, do not associate the name of "consecration" with newly constructed buildings and freshly made fixtures, but rather with renewal in spirit through which our inner man, taking off the old and ragged garment of sin and putting on the new one of piety, embarks on a new way of life. These are the ones in whom the wholly unblemished one also rejoices. And along with them, renewed in virtues and in the pious way of life according to God, let us chastely take delight in the chaste consecration of the chaste one, and, as if preparing to approach [her] in person, [376] [and] going to her venerable church, let us put everything into order and change everything for the better, in deed and in word and in thought. Let nothing of ours be unworthy of the day! Let not a step of the foot, a laugh with the teeth,[3] anything said, or a garment of clothing, transgress what is proper! What then

[3]This is a strange Greek expression, but is literally what is stated. It presumably means a laugh with the teeth showing.

am I saying? Let us put our ideas themselves in order! And before all these things, let mercy, by which God is served, take precedence, so that renewed both in soul and body we may celebrate the day of the consecration of the wholly undefiled Mother, according to flesh, of God in a new way!

4 Together with this [festival], the deposition and veneration of her honored and revered belt shine forth, along with those of the most honored and wholly undefiled[4] swaddling clothes of her Son. Of that belt, which encircled that all-holy body and covered God who was hidden in her womb. Of that belt, which adorned the ark of God in a beautiful and sacred fashion. Of that belt, which was often enriched by undefiled drops of milk from the one who was wholly undefiled. And none of those grumblers regard it as inappropriate when we address [these relics] as if they were living and when we offer them praise.[5]

5 For if a vessel which has been in contact with myrrh even for a short time knows how to preserve its sweet smell for a long time after it has been emptied, what might one say about the belt that was wound about and attached for a long time to that truly inexhaustible and divine myrrh—I mean the most pure and wholly unblemished

---

[4] I have emended πανακράντων (PG 98, 376B) to παναχράντων.

[5] It is not clear to whom Germanos is referring here, but it is possible that some contemporary Christians objected to the style of veneration that he describes. There is no clear evidence concerning iconoclasts' attitudes towards holy relics in the early eighth century, although later Constantine V was accused of dishonoring them. See de Boor, *Theophanis Chronographia* 1, 439; Mango and Scott, trans., *The Chronicle of Theophanes Confessor*, 607: "[Constantine V] suppressed and obliterated their relics whenever it was said that those of some famous saint were reposing for the good of spiritual and bodily health and, as usual, were venerated by the faithful." G. Dagron suggests that at the beginning of the eighth century, discussion of these issues, and some opposition to methods of veneration and the concept of intercession, may have existed without open condemnation of relics or icons yet having made themselves felt. See G. Dagron, "L'ombre d'un doute: L'hagiographie en question, Vie–XIe siècle," *DOP* 46 (1992): 59–68. The adjective μεμψίμοιρος means "faultfinding," "criticizing," or "querulous." See L&S, 1101.

body of the Theotokos? Would it not preserve eternally the sweet smell of healing and fill those who approach it with faith and desire? [It is] a sweet smell which is not in any way effeminate or worthless, but which is divine and wholly venerable, a most fervent opponent[6] of sufferings of both soul and body.[7] And if the lifeless vessel of which we spoke, which has had contact with lifeless myrrh, knows how to partake of its quality, what should we say about the [belt] that has come close to the living dwelling-place of God the Word? Shall we not run to it? Shall we not fall down before it? Shall we not beg always to receive purification for both soul and body from it? What else? Shall we not converse with it as if it were living and offer up hymns of praise? Indeed, let us do this!

6   O belt, which girded the source of life and which gives eternal life to those who honour you![8] O belt, which grants to the loins of those who run towards you on the one hand, death to the passions, and on the other, courage for the practice of virtues and for activity! O belt, which restrains and binds up the weakness of our nature, while entangling both our invisible and visible enemies! But what has happened to me? Pierced by desire for the all-pure one and caught up in the flow of my speech, I have forgotten the swaddling clothes! And this is not surprising, for when the Mother is glorified, this mother-loving Son rejoices. Furthermore, we are giving way to a law of nature, even if these matters are above nature, [377] when we first make an expiatory offering to the Mother. The Lord, who is supremely good, will in no way push us away. For just as he was well

---

[6]The word ἐλάτειρα comes from the root ἐλαύνω which is associated with driving (especially horses, as in a chariot) or striking. This is the feminine noun, associated in Classical Greek with Artemis. In the late antique period, the noun could be used for "exorcisers"; see Lampe, 445. In this context, there may be a deliberate juxtaposition with classical or late antique meanings, but Germanos is in fact describing the healing power of the scent that is preserved in the Virgin's and Christ's articles of clothing.

[7]On the importance of smell in association with holy people or relics in early Christianity, see Ashbrook Harvey, *Scenting Salvation*.

[8]It is impossible to convey in English the word play using the words ζώνη ("belt") and ζωῆς ("life") here.

pleased to come forth from her truly as a man and thought fit to be called her Son, so will he who is most compassionate accept the daring which has come about in accordance with our human nature. But having recalled the swaddling clothes, I will return again to the one who bore him. For she prepared these with her own pure hands. She wrapped the great Lord in them as befits an infant with her motherly hands. She carried him with them at her bosom and suckled the One who gives breath and food to all nature.

7   Yet, O swaddling clothes, which wrapped the Lord who is Liberator and who released the chains of our transgressions![9] O swaddling clothes, which encircled the mighty Lord and strengthened the weakness of our race! O swaddling clothes, which both guard and protect the faithful but which bind and throw down our adversaries! O swaddling clothes and sacred belt! May you grant sanctification, strength, propitiation, and health both to me and to those who approach and venerate with longing your sacred church. O sacred belt, which surrounds and encompasses your city and keeps it unassailable from barbaric attack! O honored belt, which enveloped God the Word when he was in the womb and which became enriched with the blessing of healings from there and [now] passes them on to us! O bright belt, which in a sacred manner came into contact with the surpassingly holy body of the Mother of the incorruptible God and from there assumed incorruptibility [and] which now remains unshakable and incorruptible, according to a truthful tradition that has come down to us![10]

---

[9]The Greek conjunction ἀλλά ("but" or "yet") is employed here in order to justify the praise for the swaddling clothes that follows, after Germanos has just finished excusing himself for having left this until after his praise of the belt. It is difficult to render this sensibly in English, but one might substitute "on the other hand" or "however."

[10]This phrase suggests that Germanos feels the need to justify the authenticity of this relic. Perhaps this "tradition" (λόγος) was oral or perhaps he is referring to a written text.

8 But why do we undertake the impossible and hurry to leap too far[11] in our attempt to honor these things with the honor of speeches that they deserve, even though this is impossible for angels? Nevertheless, O honored belt of the Mother of God who is supremely honorable, gird our loins with truth, righteousness, and meekness![12] Make us heirs of the eternal and blessed life and keep this transient life of ours unassailable from both invisible and visible enemies! Preserve the faith inviolate in peace! Save your inheritance, your people, O wholly undefiled belt of the wholly undefiled [Virgin], [keep them] in faith with right belief, safe in the way of life according to God, and unharmed from all kinds of abuse. May we have you as our strength and help, wall and rampart, harbor and safe refuge!

9 But what are you with regard to me? O all-pure, all-good, and most merciful Lady, consolation of Christians, warmest remedy for the afflicted, and most ready refuge for those who sin; do not abandon us as orphans, bereft of your succor! For if we should be abandoned by you, where would we now run? What will become of us now, O all-holy Theotokos, the breath and life of Christians?[13] [380] For just as our body possesses breathing as a sure sign of vital activity, so is your all-holy name offered up continuously in the mouths of your servants, in every time and place and manner, not [only] as a sign of life and delight and help, but also becoming the producer [of these]. Shelter us with the wings of your goodness! Watch over us with your intercessions! May you offer us eternal life, hope of Christians, who cannot be put to shame! For let us, as paupers of divine works and ways, on seeing the wealth of goodness

---

[11]See L&S, 1604: perfect passive participle of σκάπτω, in a metaphorical sense.

[12]Germanos uses various forms of the root τιμ- ("honor") here, employing the device of metaclisis, or the repetition of the same word with different inflections. In English, the choice of different words in a sentence, or in successive sentences, is generally viewed as better style, whereas in Greek writers frequently repeated the same word for rhetorical effect.

[13]The punctuation should be emended in this sentence, putting the question mark at the end and replacing it with a comma.

which has been given to us through you, say, "The earth is full of the Lord's mercy" (Ps 32[33].5). We, who were driven from God in the multitude of our sins, have sought God through you and we have found [him]. And on finding [him], we have been saved. Therefore your help is powerful with regard to salvation, Theotokos, and it has no need of any other mediator before God. We understand this, but indeed [we] also learned it by experience, since at those frequent times that we implore you as our warmest [source of] succor, we receive the answers to our requests in abundance. And now we, your people, your inheritance, your flock that is adorned by the calling of your Son, take refuge in you. Indeed there is no limit to your greatness; there is no end to your succor; there is no numbering of your benefits. For no one is saved except through you, all-holy one.[14] No one is released from terrible things except through you, wholly unblemished one. No one is granted the gift of forgiveness except through you, all-pure one. No one receives the grace of mercy except through you, all-sacred one. In return for these things, who will not bless you, who will not magnify you—even if not in a manner worthy of you, nevertheless with the greatest eagerness—you who have been glorified, you who have been blessed, you who have been granted great things, huge and marvelous, from your Son and God himself, for which reason all generations give honor to you.

10   Who, after your Son, cares for the human race as you do?[15] Who so helpfully supports us in our afflictions? Who, so quickly anticipating [these], delivers us from the afflictions that overwhelm us? Who fights on behalf of sinners [in response to their] supplications? Who

---

[14]This passage is very striking in the emphasis that it places on the Theotokos as the source of all mediation before God. Germanos seems to go further in this homily than do other preachers in extolling Mary's central role in obtaining God's mercy for humankind. See Graef, *Mary. A History of Doctrine and Devotion*, 145–50.

[15]The verb προνοέω has the meaning "to foresee" (in advance), but Lampe also suggests "provide for" or "care for" (4), taking a genitive. See Lampe, 1156. Nevertheless, the succession of verbs with the prefix προ- in this passage suggests that Germanos intends to convey the idea of advance knowledge on the part of the Virgin Mary.

defends to such an extent the unrepentant, speaking on both sides? Since you [381] have maternal freedom of speech and strength in the presence of your Son, and are saving us, who have been condemned by our sins and who do not dare to gaze on the heavenly heights, by means of your petitions and intercessions, ransom us also from eternal punishment! It is for this reason that anyone who is afflicted takes refuge in you, that one who is wronged runs to you, that one who is experiencing terrible things calls on your help. Everything about you, Theotokos, is miraculous; everything surpasses nature; everything is beyond speech and power. It is on this account that even your patronage is beyond understanding. For those who have been pushed out, pursued, and embattled, you have reconciled and made your friend by giving birth and further, you have made them sons and heirs. Stretching out helping hands to those who are daily drowning in their sins, you drag them out from the waves. You drive away the insurrections of the evil one against your servants merely by the invocation of your all-holy name, thereby saving them. Come and redeem, wholly unblemished one, those who call on you from every necessity and from all sorts of trials. It is for this reason that we eagerly run to your church and, standing in it, think that we stand in heaven. Glorifying you in it, we think that we dance with angels. What race of men other than Christians has possessed a share in such glory, has met with such succor, or has been enriched with such patronage? Who, having gazed earnestly and with faith on your honored belt, Theotokos, is not filled at once with delight? Who, on fervently falling down before it, has left without his petition being granted? Who, on contemplating your token,[16] does not immediately forget every affliction? Words cannot express the nature of joy, well-being, and happiness that have been enjoyed by those [people] who come and stand in your sacred church, in which you have

---

[16]It is not clear whether Germanos is referring here to an image of the Virgin or to the belt, which is a token or a figure of her presence. The Greek word χαρακτήρ is ambivalent, and one would expect a word like εἰκών if the preacher were referring to an icon.

been well pleased for your honored belt to be placed, along with the swaddling clothes of your Son and our God, whose deposition we celebrate today.

11   Yet, O jar, from which we who have been burnt by terrible things have drunk the manna of refreshment! O table, through which we who were starved of the bread of life have been filled beyond measure! O lampstand, by which we who sat in darkness have been illumined by a great light! You have from God the praise that is worthy and fitting for you: do not reject our unworthy [praise], which is nevertheless offered to you out of longing! Do not reject a hymn from filthy lips, all-praised one, which is offered to you out of affection! Do not feel loathing at a speech of supplication from an unworthy tongue. Instead, measure out our desire, one who is glorified by God, and grant us remission from our sins, the enjoyment of eternal life, and deliverance from all harm. Look down from this holy dwelling-place of yours at your most faithful assembly, gathered here, which [384] has been enriched by having you as mistress, [384] patroness, and lady, and which has come together to sing of you from the heart, Theotokos! And after tending to them by your divine visitation, remove them from every misfortune and affliction; snatch them from all sorts of illness, harm, and abuse; fill them with complete joy, every cure, and all grace; and at the coming of your Son, our God who loves humankind, when we all shall be standing there to be judged, lead us away from eternal fire with your mighty hand since you have maternal freedom of speech and strength, and deem us worthy to attain eternal blessings by the grace and benevolence of our Lord Jesus Christ who was born from you, to whom belong glory and power, now and forever. Amen.

Glossary of Rhetorical Terms

ALLITERATION: A figure of speech in which consonants, especially at the beginnings of words, are repeated for poetic effect.

ANAPHORA: Frequently used in speeches, this is the device which involves the repetition of the same word, or group of words, at the beginning of successive sentences or clauses.

ANTITHESIS: The juxtaposition of contrasting or antithetical words in a sentence or clause. This device is frequently used in patristic literature in order to express the paradox of the incarnation, e.g. "a mixture of both divinity and humanity, of suffering and impassibility, of life and death . . ." (John of Damascus, *On the Nativity*, above, 60).

APOSTROPHE: A figure of speech in which a thing, place, abstract quality, or absent person is addressed as if present, e.g. "O holy couple, Joachim and Anna, accept from me this birthday oration!" (John of Damascus, *On the Nativity*, above, 69).

ARGUMENT: The main body of an oration in which ideas introduced in the prologue are expounded and, if appropriate, an argument is developed.

"ASIANIC" STYLE: A form of oratorical delivery in which short, rhythmic phrases are preferred to longer, periodic sentences. This style of homiletic delivery, which Gregory of Nazianzus used in some of his festal orations, became popular especially in the early fifth century AD. Preachers such as Proclus of Constantinople, Hesychius of Jerusalem, Basil of Seleucia, and others developed it fully, with rhythmic, sometimes rhyming sermons which are almost hymnic in style.

CHAIRETISMOS: A greeting, such as 'Hail', which may be used, by means of the rhetorical device of anaphora, to introduce a series of epithets or praises addressed to the Mother of God.

CHIASM/CHIASTIC: From the Greek letter 'chi', or the concept of placing ideas 'cross-wise', this device expresses ideas symmetrically in order to express their close relationship one to another. See, for example, '. . . how much that which is being revealed, is hidden, and that which is being hidden, is revealed.' (Andrew of Crete, *On the Nativity I,* above, 72).

EKPHRASIS: A rhetorical exercise, which may be used in a section of a sermon, which provides a vivid description of a person, place, or thing.

ENCOMIUM: An oration in praise of a person, usually delivered after his/her death. This Christian literary genre was adapted from the pagan form of the "basilikos logos," or praise of an emperor; it normally follows a structure which includes a prologue, argument (including a discussion of the ancestry and birth of the person being praised, an account of his/her life), and epilogue. The fact that festal sermons honouring the Mother of God, which may be fairly loose in their structure and content, are called "encomia" in manuscripts, shows that the literary form was interpreted loosely by later Byzantine writers and scribes.

EPILOGUE: The conclusion of an oration. This may include moral injunctions in exegetical and festal homilies, although other topics such as recapitulation of the argument or a series of "chairetismoi" may also be introduced in this section.

ETHOPOIIA (Latin: *sermocinatio*): From the Greek for "character description," this rhetorical device allows the preacher to invent interior monologue and dialogue for biblical characters and even for Christ. It is an affective figure which serves to introduce dramatic feeling into narrative or exegetical passages of an oration.

HOMOIOTELEUTON: Rhyming or similar-sounding endings to successive phrases. This device adds a poetic quality to some passages in festal sermons.

METACLISIS: the repeated use of the same root or word in different forms or inflections.

METAPHOR: From the Greek "to transfer" or "carry across," the metaphor is a rhetorical, figurative expression of similarity in which a direct, but non-literal, connection is made between two things. This device is so commonly used in modern speech and thought that we are often no longer aware that we are using it: for example, "to wade through a pile of papers." In Greek festal homilies, metaphors are used to express cataphatically the signs by which we recognise God in creation and in his incarnation, for example, "For an oyster is born in her, the one who will conceive in her womb from the heavenly lightning-flash of divinity and will bear the pearl of great price, Christ" (John of Damascus, *On the Nativity*, above, 58). There is a connection between metaphor and typology (e.g. the burning bush, the fleece of Gideon, etc.), but the two categories are not exactly the same in that types are signs discerned by prophets and by the Fathers, rather than merely being metaphors.

PARALEIPSIS: The preacher, or a character through whom the preacher speaks, states what was *not* said in a given dialogue in order to stress the unusual nature of the event. See, for example, "[Let us see] how the all-holy one is today brought by her parents into the temple of God with the help of his priests . . . how the prophet admits her by his own hand and brings her into inaccessible [places], having been in no way displeased and *without* having said to her parents, 'I am not undertaking this most novel practice and leading a girl into the holy of holies to be lodged in these [sanctuaries] and to dwell there without interruption, where I have been instructed to enter [only] one day of the year.' The prophet uttered no such thing; instead he knew in advance what would come to pass, since he was a prophet. [Instead], completely accepting and remaining with her, just as Symeon after him would [receive] her Son, he eagerly received her . . ." (Germanos, *On the Entrance into the Temple II*, above, 165–6).

PROLOGUE: The opening section of an oration in which the preacher expresses his reasons for delivering the sermon and sometimes his feelings of inadequacy, calling on the saint or holy figure who is being commemorated to help him in his task.

Bibliography

Allen, P. "The Greek Homiletical Tradition of the Feast of the Hypapante: The Place of Sophronius of Jerusalem." Pages 1–12 in *Mediterranea Byzantina. Festschrift für Johannes Koder zum 65, Geburtstag.* Edited by K. Bleke, H. Kislinger, A. Külzer, and M.A. Stassinopoulou. Vienna, Cologne, and Wimar: Böhlau, 2007.

_____. "The role of Mary in the Early Byzantine Feast of the Hypapante." Pages 1–22 in *Patristica.* Supplementary Vol. 2 of *Festschrift in Honour of Shinro Kato on His 80th Birthday.* Edited by K. Demura and N. Kamimura. Nagoya: Shinseisha, 2006.

Antonopoulou, T. *The Homilies of the Emperor Leo VI.* Leiden: Brill, 1997.

Ashbrook Harvey, S. *Scenting Salvation. Ancient Christianity and the Olfactory Imagination.* Berkeley, Los Angeles and New York: University of California Press, 2006.

Aubineau, M. *Les homélies festales d'Hésychius de Jérusalem.* 2 vols. Brussels: Société des Bollandistes, 1978.

Auzépy, M.F. "La carrière de S. André de Crète." *Byzantinische Zeitschrift* 88.1 (1995): 1–12.

Baldovin, J.F. *The Urban Character of Christian Worship: The Origins, Development and Meaning of Stational Liturgy.* Orientalia christiana analecta 228. Rome: Pontificium institutum orientalium studiorum, 1987.

Barker, M. "Justinian's 'New Church' and the Entry of the Mother of God into the Temple." *Sourozh* 103 (February 2006): 15–33.

_____. *The Great High Priest.* London and New York: T&T Clark, 2003.

Baynes, N. "The Finding of the Virgin's Robe." Pages 240–7 in *Byzantine Studies and Other Essays.* Edited by idem. London: Athlone Press, 1955.

Boss, S.J. *Mary. The Complete Resource.* London and New York: Continuum, 2007.

Brock, S. *Bride of Light, Moran 'Eth'o.* 6 vols. Kottayam, India: St Ephrem Ecumenical Research Institute, 1994.

————. *The Luminous Eye. The Spiritual World Vision of St Ephrem the Syrian*. Rome: Corso Vittorio Emmanuele, 1985. Rev. ed., Kalamazoo, MI: Cistercian Publications, 1992.

Burghardt, W.J. "Mary in Eastern Patristic Thought." Pages 88–153 in vol. 2 of *Mariology*. Edited by J.B. Carol. Milwaukee: Bruce Publishing Company, 1957.

Cameron, A. "The Theotokos in Sixth-Century Constantinople: A City Finds its Symbol." *Journal of Theological Studies* n.s. 29 (1978): 79–108.

————. "The Virgin's Robe: An Episode in the History of Early Seventh-Century Constantinople." *Byzantion* 49 (1979): 42–56.

Capelle, B. "La fête de la Vierge à Jérusalem au Ve siècle." *Le Muséon* 56 (1943): 1–33.

Chevalier, C. *La Mariologie de S.Jean Damascène*. Orientalia christiana analecta 109. Rome: Pontificium institutum orientalium studiorum, 1936.

————. "Les trilogies homilétiques dans l'élaboration des fêtes mariales, 650–850." *Gregorianum* 18 (1937): 361–78.

Chirat, H. "Les origins de la fête du 21 novembre: St Jean Chrysostome et St André de Crète: ont-ils célébré la Présentation de la Théotokos?" Pages 121–33 in *Psomia Diaphora. Mélanges E. Podechard: Études de sciences religieuses offertes pour son émériat au doyen honoraire de la Faculté de Théologie de Lyon.* Lyons: Facultés Catholiques, 1945.

Constas, N. *Proclus of Constantinople and the Cult of the Virgin in Late Antiquity. Homilies 1–5, Texts and Translations.* Leiden: Brill, 2003.

————. "Weaving the Body of God: Proclus of Constantinople, the Theotokos and the Loom of the Flesh." *Journal of Early Christian Studies* 3 (1995): 169–94.

Cooper, K. "Contesting the Nativity: Wives, Virgins, and Pulcheria's *Imitatio Mariae*." *Scottish Journal of Religious Studies* 19 (1998): 31–43.

Cunningham, M. "Dramatic Device or Didactic Tool? The Function of Dialogue in Byzantine Preaching." Pages 101–13 in *Rhetoric in Byzantium* Edited by E. Jeffreys. Aldershot: Ashgate, 2003.

————. "The Meeting of Old and New: The Typology of Mary the Theotokos in Byzantine Homilies and Hymns." Pages 52–62 in *The Church and Mary*. Edited by R. N. Swanson. Woodbridge, Suffolk and Rochester, NY: Boydell & Brewer, 2004.

————. "Polemic and Exegesis: Anti-Judaic Invective in Byzantine Homiletics." *Sobornost* 21:2 (1999): 46–68.

Daley, S.J., Brian E. *On the Dormition of Mary. Early Patristic Homilies.* Crestwood, NY: SVS Press, 1998.

De Boor, C., ed. *Theophanis Chronographia.* 2 vols. Leipzig: B.G. Teubner, 1883. Repr., Hildesheim: Georg Olms, 1963.

Dölger, F. "Iohannes von Euboia." *Analecta Bollandiana* 68 (1950): 5–26.

Ehrhard, A. *Überlieferung und Bestand der hagiographischen und homiletischen Literatur der griechischen Kirche.* 3 vols. Leipzig: J.C. Hinrichs Verlag, 1936–39.

Elliott, J.K., ed. *The Apocryphal New Testament. A Collection of Apocryphal Christian Literature in an English Translation based on M.R. James.* Rev. ed. Oxford: Clarendon Press, 2004.

Evangelatou, M. "The Symbolism of the Censer in Byzantine Representations of the Dormition of the Virgin." Pages 117–31 in *Images of the Mother of God.* Edited by Vassilaki. Cf. Vassilaki.

Fecioru, D., ed. "Un nou de predica in omiletica ortodoxa." *Biserica Ortodoxa Romana* 64 (1946): 65–91, 180–92, 386–96.

Fletcher, R. "Three Early Byzantine Hymns and Their Place in the Church of Constantinople." *Byzantinische Zeitschrift* 51 (1958): 53–65.

Garitte, G., ed. *Le Calendrier palestino-géorgien du Sinaiticus 34 (Xe siècle).* Brussels: Société des Bollandistes, 1958.

Graef, H. *Mary: A History of Doctrine and Devotion.* London: Sheed & Ward, 1963. Repr., 1987.

Haldon, J.F. *Byzantium in the Seventh Century. The Transformation of a Culture.* Cambridge: Cambridge University Press, 1990.

Halkin, F. "La passion de Ste Parascève par Jean d'Eubée." Pages 231–7 in *Polychronion. Festschrift für Franz Dölger.* Edited by P. Wirth. Heidelberg: C. Winter, 1966.

Holum, K. *Theodosian Empresses: Women and Imperial Domination in Late Antiquity.* Berkeley and London: University of California Press, 1982.

Jouassard, G. "Le problème de la sainteté de Marie chez les Pères depuis les origines de la patristique jusqu'au concile d'Ephèse." *Études Mariales. Sainteté de Marie. Bulletin de la Société Française d'Études Mariales* 5 (1947): 15–31.

_____. "Marie à travers la patristique. Maternité divine, virginité, sainteté." Pages 69–157 in *Maria. Études sur la Sainte Vierge.* Edited by H. du Manoir. Paris: Beauchesne, 1949.

Jugie, M. "L' Église de Chalcopratia et le culte de la ceinture de la Sainte

Vierge à Constantinople." *Échos d'Orient* 16 (1913): 308–12.

————. *Homélies mariales byzantines* I. Patrologia orientalis 16. Fasc. 3. No. 79. Paris: R. Graffin, 1921. Repr., Turnhout: Brepols, 2003.•

————. *Homélies mariales byzantines* II. Patrologia orientalis 19. Fasc. 3. No. 93. Paris: R. Graffin, 1925. Repr., Turnhout: Brepols, 1990.

————. *La Mort et l'Assomption de la sainte Vierge*. Studi e Testi 114. Vatican City: Bibliotheca Apostolica Vaticana, 1944.

————. "La première fête mariale en Orient et en Occident: l'Avent primitif." *Échos d'Orient* 22 (1922): 153–81.

Kalavrezou, I. "When the Virgin Mary Became *Meter Theou*." *Dumbarton Oaks Papers* 44 (1990): 165–72.

Kazhdan, A., L.F. Sherry, and C. Angelidi. *A History of Byzantine Literature (650–850)*. Athens: The National Hellenic Research Foundation, 1999.

Kennedy, G. *Classical Rhetoric and Its Christian and Secular Tradition from Ancient to Modern Times*. London: Croom Helm, 1980.

————. *Greek Rhetoric under Christian Emperors*. Princeton: Princeton University Press, 1983.

Kishpaugh, M.J. *The Feast of the Presentation of the Virgin Mary in the Temple: An Historical and Literary Study*. Washington, DC: The Catholic University of America Press, 1941.

Kotter, B., ed. *Die Schriften des Johannes von Damaskos*. 5 vols. Berlin and New York: Walter de Gruyter, 1969–88.

Ladouceur, P. "Old Testament Prefigurations of the Mother of God." *St Vladimir's Theological Quarterly* 50, no. 1–2 (2006): 5–57.

Lamza, L. *Patriarch Germanos I. von Konstantinopel*. Würzburg: Augustinus-Verlag, 1975.

La Piana, G. *La Rappresentazioni sacre nella letteratura bizantina dale origini al secolo IX*. Grottaferrata, 1912. Repr., London: Variorum Reprints, 1971.

Lash, Arch. E. *Kontakia on the Life of Christ. St Romanos the Melodist*. San Francisco, London, and Pymble: HarperCollins, 1995.

————. "Mary in Eastern Church Literature." Pages 58–80 in A. *Mary in Doctrine and Devotion*. Edited by Stackpoole, OSB. Dublin: Columba Press, 1990.

Leroy, F.J., ed. *L'Homilétique de Proclus de Constantinople. Tradition manuscrite, inédits, études connexes*. Studi e Testi 247. Vatican City: Bibliotheca Apostolica Vaticana, 1967.

Lewis, A.S., ed. *A Palestinian Syriac Lectionary: Containing Lessons From the Pentateuch, Job, Proverbs, Prophets, Acts, and Epistles.* London: C.J. Clay and Sons, 1897.

Limberis, V. *Divine Heiress: The Virgin Mary and the Creation of Christian Constantinople.* London: Routledge, 1994.

Linardou, K. "The Couch of Solomon, a Monk, a Byzantine Lady, and the Song of Songs." Pages 73–85 in *The Church and Mary.* Edited by R.N. Swanson. Cf. Swanson.

List, J. *Studien zur Homiletik Germanos I. von Konstantinopel und seiner Zeit.* Athens: Byzantinisch-neugriechischen Jahrbücher, 1939.

Louth, A. *St John Damascene. Tradition and Originality in Byzantine Theology.* Oxford: Oxford University Press, 2002.

Maas, P. and Trypanis, C.A., eds. *Sancti Romani Melodi Cantica: Cantica Genuina.* Oxford: Clarendon Press, 1963. Repr., 1997.

McGuckin, J. "The Paradox of the Virgin-*Theotokos*: Evangelism and Imperial Politics in the Fifth-Century Byzantine World." *Maria* 2 (2001): 8–25.

Mango, C. "Constantinople as Theotokoupolis." Pages 17–25 in *Mother of God.* Edited by Vassilaki. Cf. Vassilaki.

————. and R. Scott, eds. and trans. *The Chronicle of Theophanes Confessor. Byzantine and Near Eastern History, AD 284–813.* Oxford: Clarendon Press, 1997.

Mansi, J.D., ed. *Sacrorum Conciliorum Nova et Amplissima Collectio.* 53 vols. in 58 pts. Florence and Venice: A. Zatta Veneti, 1759, ff. Repr., Graz: Akademische Druk, 1961.

Mary, Mother and Arch. K. Ware, trans. *The Festal Menaion.* London: Faber & Faber, 1969. Repr., S. Canaan, PA: St Tikhon's Seminary Press, 1998.

Mateos, J., ed. and trans. *Le Typicon de la Grande Église: Ms. Sainte-Croix no. 40, Xe siècle.* 2 vols. Rome: Pont. Institutum Orientalium, 1962.

Mimouni, S.C. *Dormition et assomption de Marie: Histoire des traditions anciennes.* Théologie historique 98. Paris: Beauchesne, 1995.

The Orthodox Liturgy. Oxford: Oxford University Press, 1982.

Peers, G. *Subtle Bodies. Representing Angels in Byzantium.* Berkeley, Los Angeles and London: University of California Press, 2001.

Peltomaa, L.-M. *The Image of the Virgin Mary in the Akathistos Hymn.* Leiden: Brill, 2001.

Pentcheva, B.V. *Icons and Power. The Mother of God in Byzantium.* University Park, PA: Penn State University Press, 2006.

———. "The supernatural protector of Constantinople: the Virgin and her icons in the tradition of the Avar siege." *BMGS* 26 (2002): 15–16.

Porter, S.E., ed. *Handbook of Classical Rhetoric in the Hellenistic Period, 330 BC–AD 400.* Leiden: Brill, 1997.

Price, R.M. "Marian Piety and the Nestorian Controversy." Pages 31–8 in *The Church and Mary.* Edited by R.N. Swanson. Cf. Swanson.

———. "Theotokos: The Title and Its Significance in Doctrine and Devotion." Pages in 56–73 in *Mary. The Complete Resource.* Edited by S.J. Boss. Cf. Boss.

Rahlfs, A. *Septuaginta. Id est Vetus Testamentum graece iuxta LXX interpretes.* 2 vols. Stuttgart: Privilegierte Württembergische Bibelanstalt, 1935. Repr., 1982.

Renoux, A. *Le codex arménien Jérusalem 121.* 2 vols. Patrologia orientalis 35–36. Turnhout: Brepols, 1969–71.

Rousseau, A. and L. Doutreleau, eds. and trans. *Irénée de Lyon: Contre les heresies.* Sources chrétiennes 211. Paris: Éditions du Cerf, 1974.

Shoemaker, S. *Ancient Traditions of the Virgin Mary's Dormition and Assumption.* Oxford: Oxford University Press, 2002.

———. "The Earliest *Life of the Virgin* and Constantinople's Marian Relics." *Dumbarton Oaks Papers* 62 (2008): forthcoming.

———. "Marian Liturgies and Devotion in Early Christianity." Pages 130–45 in *Mary. The Complete Resource.* Edited by S.J. Boss. Cf. Boss.

———. "The Virgin Mary in the Ministry of Jesus and the Early Church according to the Earliest *Life of the Virgin*." *Harvard Theological Review* 98, no. 4 (2005): 441–67.

Strycker, E. de. *La Forme la plus ancienne du Protévangile de Jacques.* Subsidia hagiographica 33. Brussels: Société des Bollandistes, 1961.

Swanson, R.N., ed. *The Church and Mary.* Studies in Church History 39. Woodbridge, Suffolk and Rochester, NY: Boydell & Brewer, 2004.

Szweykowski, Z.M. "Jewish Music." Page 620 in vol. 9 of *The New Grove Dictionary of Music and Musicians.* Edited by S. Sadie. 20 vols. London: Macmillan, 1980.

Tsironis, N. "From Poetry to Liturgy: The Cult of the Virgin in the Middle Byzantine Era." Pages 91–99 in *Images of the Mother of God.* Edited by Vassilaki. Cf. Vassilaki.

———. "The Mother of God in the Iconoclastic Controversy." Pages 27–39 in *Mother of God.* Edited by Vassilaki. Cf. Vassilaki.

Vailhé, S. "La fête de la présentation de Marie au temple." *Échos d'Orient* 5 (1901–1902): 221–24.

—————. "S. André de Crète." *Échos d'Orient* 5 (1902): 278–87.

Van Esbroeck, M. "Le culte de la Vierge de Jérusalem à Constantinople aux 6e–7e siècles." *Revue des études byzantines* 46 (1988): 181–90. = idem. *Aux origins de la Dormition de la Vierge.* Aldershot: Ashgate Publishing, 1995.

—————. "La lettre de l'empereur Justinien sur l'annonciation et la noël en 561." *Analecta Bollandiana* 86 (1968): 355–62; 87 (1969): 442–44.

Vassilaki, M., ed. *Images of the Mother of God. Perceptions of the Theotokos in Byzantium.* Aldershot: Ashgate Publishing, 2005.

—————., ed. *Mother of God. Representations of the Virgin in Byzantine Art.* Milan and Athens: Skira, 2000.

Vincent, H. and F.-M Abel. *Jérusalem: recherches de topographie, d'archéologie et d'histoire.* 2 vols. Paris: J. Gabalda, 1912–26.

Voulet, P., ed. and trans. *S. Jean Damascène, Homélies sur la nativité et la dormition.* Sources chrétiennes 80. Paris: Éditions du Cerf, 1961.

Wenger, A. *L'Assomption de la t.s. Vierge dans la tradition Byzantine du VIe au Xe siècle.* Archives de l'Orient Chrétien 5. Paris: Institut Français d'Études Byzantines, 1955.

—————. "Les homélies inédites de Cosmas Vestitor sur la Dormition," in *Mélanges M. Jugie. Revue des études byzantines* 11. (1953): 284–300.

Weyl Carr, A. "Threads of Authority: The Virgin Mary's Veil in the Middle Ages," in *Robes and Honor. The Medieval World of Investiture.* Edited by S. Gordon. New York and Basingstoke: Palgrave, 2001.

Wilkinson, J. *Egeria's Travels.* Warminster: Aris & Phillips, Ltd., 1999.

Young, F. *Biblical Exegesis and the Formation of Christian Culture.* Cambridge: Cambridge University Press, 1997. Repr., Peabody, MA: Hendrickson Publishers, 2002.

POPULAR PATRISTICS SERIES

ST VLADIMIR'S SEMINARY PRESS
1-800-204-2665 • www.svspress.com

We hope this book has been enjoyable and edifying for your spiritual journey toward our Lord and Savior Jesus Christ.

One hundred percent of the net proceeds of all SVS Press sales directly support the mission of St Vladimir's Orthodox Theological Seminary to train priests, lay leaders, and scholars to be active apologists of the Orthodox Christian Faith. However, the proceeds only partially cover the operational costs of St Vladimir's Seminary. To meet our annual budget, we rely on the generosity of donors who are passionate about providing theological education and spiritual formation to the next generation of ordained and lay servant leaders in the Orthodox Church.

Donations are tax-deductible and can be made at
www.svots.edu/give.
We greatly appreciate your generosity.

To engage more with St Vladimir's Orthodox
Theological Seminary, please visit:

www.svots.edu
online.svots.edu
www.svspress.com
www.instituteofsacredarts.com